böhlau

Alexander Drost · Olga Sasunkevich
Joachim Schiedermair · Barbara Törnquist-Plewa (Ed.)

COLLAPSE OF MEMORY – MEMORY OF COLLAPSE

NARRATING PAST, PRESENCE AND FUTURE ABOUT PERIODS OF CRISIS

BÖHLAU VERLAG WIEN KÖLN WEIMAR

Gedruckt mit Unterstützung der Deutschen Forschungsgemeinschaft aus Mitteln des Internationalen Graduiertenkollegs 1540 „Baltic Borderlands: Shifting Boundaries of Mind and Culture in the Borderlands of the Baltic Sea Region“

Published with assistance of the Deutsche Forschungsgemeinschaft by funding of the International Research Training Group “Baltic Borderlands: Shifting Boundaries of Mind and Culture in the Borderlands of the Baltic Sea Region”

Bibliografische Information der Deutschen Nationalbibliothek:
Die Deutsche Nationalbibliothek verzeichnet diese Publikation in der Deutschen Nationalbibliografie; detaillierte bibliografische Daten sind im Internet über http://dnb.d-nb.de abrufbar.

Umschlagabbildung:
The Course of Empire. Destruction, 1836. Found in the collection of New York Historical Society. © Heritage Images / Fine Art Images / akg-images

Einbandgestaltung: Satz + Layout Werkstatt Kluth
Satz: büro mn, Bielefeld
Druck und Bindung: Hubert & Co., Göttingen
Gedruckt auf chlor- und säurefreiem Papier
Printed in the EU

Vandenhoeck & Ruprecht Verlage | www.vandenhoeck-ruprecht-verlage.com

ISBN 978-3-412-22537-7

Content

Foreword

This book emerged from the conference "The Collapse of Memory – Memory of Collapse: Remembering the Past, Re-Constructing the Future in Periods of Crisis" in Lund 2016. The conference aimed to explore, how the management of crises is affected by previous experiences and memories and how crisis, disaster or collapse affect cultural memory and political agency. The topic, moreover, represents yet another turn in the research agenda and methodology of the interdisciplinary International Research Training Group (IRTG) "Baltic Borderlands: Shifting Boundaries of Mind and Culture in the Borderlands of the Baltic Sea Region".

The starting point of investigation and theorization laid out in 2010 had been the application of "borderland" as an analytical category to various strata of spatial organization. As a result, the core question focused on the cultural implications of border change within the entire Baltic Sea Region from the 15th century until today. In "Die Neuerfindung des Raumes. Grenzüberschreitungen und Neuordnungen" (The Rediscovery of Space. Crossing borders and new orderings, 2013) researchers of the IRTG challenged conventional understandings of region and space, and instead proposed alternative (disciplinary) perspectives on social, cultural, cognitive, etc. spatial orders. Many of these orders had been located along established border lines defined by political orders like monarchy or nation and, as earlier studies argued, the topography. In the following volume "Beyond the Sea. Reviewing the Manifold Dimensions of Water as a Barrier and Bridge" (2015) international experts both from within and outside the IRTG challenged the peripheral treatment of the sea that characterized conventional accounts and instead discussed the cultural impact of agents, their practices and narratives in crossing the seas and also living along their shores. The sea hereby emerged as "a borderland of communication, a space to govern and to invest with symbolic meaning". Comparative approaches nurtured another paradigmatic shift in researching borderlands. In "Globalizing Borderlands Studies in Europe and North America" (2016) doctoral students and professors of the IRTG and of the Ancient Borderlands Research Focus Group at the University of California, Santa Barbara, juxtaposed for the first time the roots and developments of border and borderlands concepts. This was achieved by introducing individual case studies and approaches to borderlands research that featured a twin focus on the Baltic Sea region and also the contested US-Mexican border. The interdisciplinary discussion associated with the global perspective on borders opened up new directions and topics for the researchers at the IRTG. Trauma, crisis, memory, media, narration, institutions are just a few terms and categories that condition the appearance, conceptualization and changes within borderlands. Two of them, crisis and memory, showed considerable promise and appeal for scholars within and outside the IRTG. Combined with a narratological perspective, crisis and memory introduced yet another turn in our research field of Baltic Sea region and borderlands studies. "The Collapse of Memory – Memory of Collapse. Narrating Past, Presence and Future about Periods of Crisis" presents the first results of this emerging field and challenges both disciplinary boundaries as well as research approaches by assuming a narratological perspective and introducing a flexible concept that takes into consideration not only agents, but also those affected.

The conference and book represent a collective undertaking, which could not have been realised without the active assistance of a number of people. For all organizational efforts, I like to thank especially Niklas Bernsand and Barbara Törnquist-Plewa at Lund University. Also, each chapter of this volume has been peer reviewed. I sincerely thank all referees for their valuable comments, which greatly enhanced both the readability and academic quality of the contributions.

A special word of gratitude is also extended to Böhlau, and particularly to Dorothee Rheker-Wunsch, for their interest in this topic. Our greatest debts are to Charlotte Haugg, Jan Richard Reinicke, Gero von Roedern, Jörn Sander, Friederike Schmidt and Sarah Thiele who took on most of the heavy lifting in preparing the manuscript for publication, and to Doreen Wollbrecht and Hielke van Nieuwenhuize for seeing the book through the final stages of production.

Michael North, Greifswald, summer 2018

Alexander Drost

Collapse Makes Memory: An Introduction

The fascination of failure and destruction sustains an entire sector of the media industry, for compelling stories can be drawn from catastrophes, crises and collapse. The decline of empires and kingdoms as much as earthquakes and infectious diseases have fired the imagination of authors, film makers and painters. They become motivated to present their vision of catastrophes as a key turning point for individuals, nay, even for entire societies. Taken this way, catastrophe emerges as a multi-faceted construct of experience, interpretation and emotion. The resulting narrative combines analyses of facts about the collapse with a retrospect evaluation, update and confirmation of these facts in the cultural memory of a given society. When the incisive event enters into the collective consciousness, the narrative frames the event in time and also permits a view into the future. The objective is not only to overcome collapse but also to prevent similar catastrophes from (re-)occurring in future. In this process, the narrative is key in understanding collapse and its impact on society as well as societies' interpretation of collapse through cultural memory.

For these reasons, the contributors of this volume have taken a narratological approach in examining collapse, disaster, catastrophe and how these in turn manifest themselves across different types of media. In this way narrating collapse is understood as an active process of forging meaning by selecting certain occurrences to construct a story. This process transforms the random occurrence into a memorable event. Considering how such events are constructed from a narratological perspective, the contributors have broadened their approach to include: mechanisms of construction, such as the use of particular media, narration strategies as well as the impact of cultural memory in narrating and thereby coping with collapse.

Two observations guide their analyses of how past experiences and knowledge are re-interpreted and employed in order to overcome situations of crisis and collapse. First, the narrative of collapse is the key element of how and why we perceive certain events and developments as collapse or crisis. Second: The diversities of collapse narratives derive from the selection of facts, their combination and interpretations. Therefore, we introduce this edition about collapse and disaster with an overview of discourses that define our understanding of collapse in recent years. These discourses have appeared in novels and movies that illustrate the "cultural memory of disaster" in the 20th and 21st centuries.

They will be presented in the following six paragraphs on war, systemic failure, terror, financial and refugee crisis, and natural disasters.

War

In the recent history of narrating collapse since 1945, post-world-war narratives about the Second World War, Nazi rule and the Holocaust dominated the content, extent and form of descriptions of collapse. The unprecedented military trials in Nuremberg in the immediate aftermath of the war established questions of guilt and responsibility as central motifs in post-war narratives. This topic had emerged in media in the aftermath of pre-WWII violent conflicts. However, the exceptional scale of murder and terror beyond military combat in WWII, in particular the Holocaust, added an unexampled severity. The first serious literary attempts to cope with post-war-collapse of German society included Wolfgang Borchert's *Draußen vor der Tür* and Heinrich Böll's *Wo warst du, Adam?* These narratives presented the heaviness of guilt and moral failing of the individual before a canvas of many unanswered questions, hereby added to the incomprehensibility of the "Weltkrieg".[1]

Loss of people and virtue determined post WWII poetry.[2] Movies like *Die Brücke*[3] ignited the question of a lost moral thinking at war in the 1950s, when suppression of war experiences and entertainment overshadowed post-war narratives. False justification, denial and forgetting characterised early "distortions"[4] in narratives of the cultural, social and ethical collapse of German society. In contrast, professional historians took a more critical and facts-based direction in the systematic reappraisal that began in the 1960s and 1970s. Backed by state institutions in Germany, historians provided the groundwork for a critical controversy about Nazi crimes and criminals in Western Germany and beyond.[5]

---

1 Wolfgang Borchert, *Draußen vor der Tür* (Hamburg: Rowohlt, 1947) (In English, *The Man Outside*, performed on stage in New York 1949); Heinrich Böll, *Wo warst du, Adam?* (Opladen: Friedrich Middelhauve, 1951).

2 Manfred Durzak, "Zwei Deutsche Literaturen nach 1945," in *Propyläen Geschichte der Literatur*, Vol. 6: *Die moderne Welt: 1914 bis heute*, ed. Erika Wischer (Berlin: Propyläen Verlag, 1982), 297–298.

3 *Die Brücke* (DE 1959), director Bernhard Wicki.

4 Manfred Gerstenfeld, "The Multiple Distortions of Holocaust Memory," *Jewish Political Studies Review* 19, no. 3–4 (2007): 36, 38–39.

5 Katrin Hammerstein, *Gemeinsame Vergangenheit – getrennte Erinnerung? Der Nationalsozialismus in Gedächtnisdiskursen und Identitätskonstruktionen von Bundesrepublik*

This controversy had its roots in detailed analyses of the structures and organisation of the Nazi regime[6] that sought to answer the question of "how could this happen?", culminating in an academic dispute about the exceptionalism of the German state formation process.[7] While historiography focused on the Nazi regime, the grand novels in post-war literature like Günter Grass's *Die Blechtrommel* and Heinrich Böll's *Gruppenbild mit Dame* addressed society and culture.[8] *Die Blechtrommel* stimulated a controversy about the roots of fascist thought in the petty bourgeois life of the 1920s, 30s and beyond.[9] Böll's novel focused on themes of social exclusion and the emotional as well as ethical hell of war.[10] Both topics had been continuously connected with pictures of combat, destruction and suffering in artistic narratives. Considering the lasting effects of war on the collective and cultural memory of societies, war provides one of the most important images of collapse.

Systemic Failure

The collapse of the Eastern bloc, of the Soviet Union and of communism radically changed the (negative) image of collapse. The falling of walls, of authoritarian regimes, their economy and of an entire ideology nurtured images of openness, freedom and new opportunities. In Thomas Brussig's *Helden Wie*

Deutschland, DDR und Österreich (Göttingen: Wallstein Verlag, 2017); Michael Beleites, "Isolierte Aufarbeitung? Zur zweigleisigen Erinnerungskultur in Deutschland und ihren Folgen," in *Aufarbeitung der Diktatur – Diktat der Aufarbeitung? Normierungsprozesse beim Umgang mit diktatorischer Vergangenheit*, ed. Katrin Hammerstein, Ulrich Mählert, Julia Trappe, and Edgar Wolfrum (Göttingen: Wallstein Verlag, 2009), 48–58.

6 Martin Broszat, *Der Staat Hitlers: Grundlegung und Entwicklung seiner inneren Verfassung* (Munich: Deutscher Taschenbuch-Verlag, 1969).

7 Ulrich von Hehl, *Nationalsozialistische Herrschaft*, 2nd edition (Munich: Oldenbourg, 2001), 110–116.

8 Günter Grass, *Die Blechtrommel* (Darmstadt: Luchterhand, 1959); Heinrich Böll, *Gruppenbild mit Dame* (Cologne: Kiepenheuer & Witsch, 1971).

9 Silke Jendrowiak, *Günter Grass und die "Hybris" des Kleinbürgers. "Die Blechtrommel", Bruch mit der Tradition einer irrationalistischen Kunst- und Wirklichkeitsinterpretation* (Heidelberg: Winter, 1979); Irmela Schneider, *Kritische Rezeption. Die Blechtrommel als Modell* (Bern: Lang, 1975).

10 Hans Joachim Bernhard, *Die Romane Heinrich Bölls. Gesellschaftskritik und Gemeinschaftsutopie*, 2nd revised and extended edition (Berlin: Rütten & Loening, 1973), 335–381; Werner Bellmann, "Die Akten der Nürnberger Kriegsverbrecherprozesse als Quelle für Heinrich Bölls Roman *Gruppenbild mit Dame*," *Euphorion* 97, no. 1 (2003): 85–97.

Wir, the collapse of the socialist system in the German Democratic Republic led to healing of the country's moribund society. Similar pictures of relief and re-emergence of historical connections after the collapse were communicated in Ericht Loest's *Nikolaikirche* or Günther Grass's *Ein Weites Feld. Ein Weites Feld*, however, introduces the inertia of a formerly disconnected cultural memory, with considerable impact on the perception of present developments and the prediction of the future.

Polish authors like Andrzej Stasiuk in *Dziewięć* or Jerzy Pilch in *Rozpacz z powodu utraty furmanki* felt the heaviness of history in the immediate aftermath of the collapse more keenly than their German colleagues. The Polish approach to collapse simultaneously was one of mental persistence and departure to a different life, which seem to have inspired Pilch to make use of the allegory of the "European in Slavic Underpants".[11] The collapse of communism initiated a search for identity in re-emerged nations like Estonia, Latvia and Lithuania. While Tõnu Õnnepalu (alias Emil Tode) in *Piiririik* situated this search in the borderland of the senseless survival of the west and the romantic idyll of the east, Jaan Kross in *Väljakaevamised* and *Paigallend* explored the traumatic past of banishment and the remediation of the first Estonian national collapse in the Soviet bombings of 1944.

For the Baltic societies, the perception of the collapse of the Soviet Union was – and remains today – irrevocably connected with collective as well as individual trauma and trauma management. Several of these traumata were suppressed for decades by official, ideologically framed narratives. The cultural memories of many societies preserve similar traumatic collapse narratives, including the post-Apartheid narratives in South Africa and the post-Khmer narratives in Cambodia.[12] Further, the collapse of ideologies has a prominent place in political and historical disaster narratives, for example, after the fall of the military dictatorship in Argentina (1976–1983), of Pinochet (1973–1990) in Chile and of Suharto (1967–1998) in Indonesia.[13]

Throughout history, the collapse of ideology and the re-emergence of historical consciousness beyond the artificial caesura of political dogma and conviction have stimulated manifold re-connections of collapse experiences. The

11 Maria Janion, "Farewell to Poland? The Uprising of a Nation," *Baltic Worlds* IV, no. 4 (2011): 4–13.

12 Martine Gosselink, Maria Holtrop, and Robert Ross, eds., *Good Hope: South Africa and the Netherlands from 1600* (Nijmegen: Uitgeverij Vantilt, 2017).

13 Mary S. Zurbuchen, "Historical Memory in Contemporary Indonesia," in *Beginning to Remember. The Past in the Indonesian Present*, ed. Mary S. Zurbuchen (Singapore: Singapore University Press, 2005), 332.

examples above show that cultural memory and foundational principles of society determine intellectual approaches to explain war and ideological collapse, including moral legitimisations and ethical thinking.

Terror

"The moment that changed your life": Post 9/11 narratives evoke this incisive and sudden observation by millions of people in response to the collapse of the World Trade Centre in New York on 11 September 2001. In *Saturday*, Ian McEwan reinforced this image, describing how disasters like 9/11 alter people's entire lives in one day. Collapse is inescapable and inhumane, according to McEwan's narrative of planes whose passengers knew their kidnappers' intended destination.[14] People were scared, shocked, traumatised, and concrete fear of terror became a definable threat in daily life. This new dimension of collapse through terror has no place, no specific country, maybe is a distorted culture of religious extremism. However, it can happen everywhere, at any time.

Other narratives explore the very nature of terror through their characters' responses to terrorist attacks. Claire Massud's *The Emperor's Children* leads up to and concludes with the collapse of the World Trade towers. Don DeLillo in *Falling Man* uses the collapse of the southern World Trade tower as the starting point of his narrative. Novels like *Saturday* and Heidi Julavits' *The Effect of Living Backwards* transfer the quality of 9/11 into comparable events in London and Morocco. The authors reflect on the mental effects of terrorism, including its ability to evoke fear everywhere and anytime it happens – for example, in the Charlie Hebdo attacks (Paris 2015), Bataclan (Paris 2015), Krudttønden (Copenhagen 2015), Charleston (2015), Erawan-Shrine (Bangkok 2015), Brussels Bombings (2016), Nice (2016), Berlin (2016), St. Petersburg (2017), Drottningsgatan (Stockholm 2017), or Manchester (2017).

Financial Crisis

Collapse became crash when, on 15 September 2008, Lehman Brothers went bankrupt and an entire line of business, the banking sector, was accused of jeopardising the finances of states and institutions around the globe. However, narratives drawing comparisons to the 1929 global world economy crisis were

14 Ian McEwan, *Saturday* (London: Vintage Books, 2006).

sparse. Rather, as shown in *The Big Short* by Michael Lewis and Vicky Ward's *The Devil's Casino*, an insular culture of greed, self-indulgence, corruption and hedonism was seen as responsible for the financial collapse.[15] The crisis continued in different facets and dimensions in Portugal, Greece, Spain, Ireland, Iceland and across the European Union. The temporal overlap of the financial crisis with terrorist attacks contributed to the idea of a crisis-ridden (global) society. Pictures of states collapsing amid wars in Afghanistan, Syria and Iraq underpinned this perception, including through images and stories of millions of refugees.

Refugee Crises

Irishness is not the first concept that comes to mind these days with respect to state, economic and social collapse. However, Ireland has one of the longest experiences of any European country with mass migration. Mass migration contributed to strong networks of Irish diasporas around the globe. Frank McCourt introduced the Irish experience of mass migration in *Angela's Ashes*.[16] Other examples of diaspora communities are the Chinese diaspora, which has existed since the 14th century,[17] and the Vietnamese diaspora in the aftermath of the Vietnam War.

"[…] we had no belongings except our stories", says the protagonist of Viet Thanh Nguyen's short story *Black-Eyed Women* in *The Refugees*.[18] Narratives about refugees are built on threatening memories that reflect the cruelty and awkwardness of the refugee experience. Knowledge of this experience separates refugees from the host society and marks them as displaced persons who do not "belong", as the mother in Nguyen's narrative points out. Flight and expulsion cause widespread individual collapses of life, which often amount to a vivid part of the cultural memory of entire societies with experience of forced migration through violence, crises and catastrophe. Several events since 1945 have forced large numbers of people to leave behind not only their home

15 Michael Lewis, *The Big Short: Inside the Doomsday Machine* (New York: W. W. Norton & Company, 2010); Vicky Ward, *The Devil's Casino: Friendship, Betrayal, and the High Stakes Games inside Lehman Brothers* (Hoboken, New Jersey: Wiley, 2010).

16 Frank McCourt, *Angela's Ashes: A Memoir* (New York: Scribner, 1996).

17 Geoffrey C. Gunn, *History without Borders. The Making of an Asian World Region. 1000–1800* (Hong Kong: Hong Kong University Press, 2011), 111–130.

18 Viet Thanh Nguyen, *The Refugees* (London: Corsair, 2017), 7.

but their way of life. These include the Second World War, the Soviet terror in the newly established Soviet Republics, the Korean War, the Vietnam War, the Yugoslav Wars, and the Syrian War.

Displacement involves collapse, first of an individual's life, then of identity and belonging to a collective and lastly, of the existence of an entire society. In *Võõras kodu* (1945), *Keegi ei kuule meid* (1948), and *Neli tuld* (1951) Valev Uibopuu dealt with the flight of Estonians from their country due to Soviet occupation in 1944. Uibopuu uses motifs such as shipwreck, collaborators and opponents to embed the transformation of Estonia in a narrative of decay and disappointment. Bernard Kangro, Valev Uibopuu and others understood the danger of flight and exile to their national culture, which had less than two decades to grow independently before displacement. The authors grasp the severity of this experience in narratives that attempt to establish a virtual place of Estonianness between the Estonian archetype Balthasar Rüssow[19] and their lost home towns.[20] These virtual places emerge from individual and collective memories of places, experiences, cultural patterns and practices combined in narratives, which serve also as markers of the refugee's belonging. These practices and narratives include refugees' efforts to cope with their fate through music.

The perspective of refugees is just one side of the story of refugee crises. The observers' perspective of the "audience" is another. The more immediate encounter with the "other" evokes as many perceptions as the refugee story told by someone else. Turning the attention to the audience of narratives, we examine a key element in the construction of disaster narratives. As mentioned before, narratives require interpretation and offer to the audience a certain liberty in applying meanings to the presented facts. In this context, the vivid images of ship wreck, of dead bodies in the sea, or the stories of virtual places of belonging depend on aesthetics, the audience and its reference points.

Natural Disasters

Collapse is destruction. Often, we view war and systemic decline as man-made and therefore distinct from natural destruction through storms, floods, earthquakes, volcano eruptions, forest fires, ice, tsunamis and hurricanes. However, in dealing with the impact of natural disasters, people seem to frame

19 Jaan Kross, *Kolme Katku Vahel* (Tallinn: Eesti Raamat, 1970, 1972, 1977, 1980).
20 Bernard Kangro, *Tartu* (Lund: Eesti Kirjanike Kooperatiiv, 1962).

and integrate catastrophic events to make sense of the collapse they caused.[21] "Naming" or "labelling" an occurrence is widely used to cope with the uncontrollable. Longstanding narratives in the disaster tradition include "Etna" for Sicily's still-active volcano, or "Eyjafjallajökull" in Iceland. Earthquakes are named after the next settlement, which they often destroyed, while hurricanes are named with female and male first names, like wind storms in Europe or typhoons in Asia.

Storms appear figuratively in our stories about grief, suffering and disruption. Narratives about storms take the perpetrators' perspective – storms appear in media before they reach communities of people in their forecasted path, which are presented along with intrinsic hopes for salvation. Through their names, storms become "actors" in a plot of destruction. In accordance with the scale of their impact, their names become part of the collective consciousness. Hurricane Katrina in the United States, or the storm Kyrill in Germany, are recent examples of natural disasters that reappear in our collective consciousness when we are faced with the threat of similar storms. Through this process, we use our experiences to understand the current impacts of storms and flooding, while updating our collective memory of Katrina and Kyrill.

Similar processes of updating the collective memory of disasters take place in our response to earthquakes, volcano eruptions and storm tides. We compare numbers of people endangered, injured, displaced and dead, as well as accounting for financial damage. Narratives of natural disasters turn quickly to the topic of recovery. Taking this kind of disaster, fixed in time and place, as a starting point of the story, its occurrence is transformed into an event with strong repercussions on social and economic structures. The threat for life demands immediate action. However, we also must deal with "developing natural disasters", often embedded in the meta-narrative of changing climate and environmental pollution. These include stories about contingency, insurance and prevention in particular.

Weather forecasts and eye-catching meteorological phenomena tell these stories in miniature. The negotiations of climate agreements like the *Paris Agreement* narrate the bigger picture. However, both employ risk analyses, and both are framed by political negotiations that produce and use these stories for economic, political and sustainability aims. In Frank Schätzing's *Der*

21 For the theory of "framing" see: Robert Entman, "Framing: Toward Clarification of a Fractured Paradigm," *Journal of Communication* 43, no. 4 (1993): 51–59.

Schwarm,[22] the macrocosm of maritime pollution develops in a disastrous apocalyptic picture. This imagery is used in real life, too, when politicians and academics describe maritime areas in seas and oceans as "dead zones". Natural disasters as much as manmade crisis nurture fear and preventive action in society, which repeatedly becomes aware of its vulnerability through stories of collapse.

Narratives of collapse are an important part of making sense of disaster and catastrophe by selecting occurrences, embedding them into a story, and making them part of the cultural memory of society. As we have seen, interpretation and updating in narrating disasters has different dimensions depending on timing. Historical distance to the occurrence allows the incorporation of a more complex interpretation history communicated through cultural memory, rather than presenting immediate or recent incidents. Reporting on current or recent collapses, therefore, tends to focus more on impacts for the future. However, distance cannot only be applied backwards. Projections of future developments – often subsumed under the umbrella of science fiction narratives – offer the same distance of decades and centuries to optimistic or semi-apocalyptic imagined futures of mankind. Both ways of constructing disaster narratives are rooted in the presence of narrator and audience, reflecting their experiences, interpretations, and collective memories, retro- and prospectively. The interrelation of narrative and cultural memory is part of the next paragraphs to illustrate that the process of making sense of collapse is rooted in narratological and cognitive processes.

The Narratological Approach: Narrative and Cultural Memory

The recognition of natural hazards as decisive events depends on the perception of such an occurrence as disaster, collapse, or crisis. While a heavy earthquake in Los Angeles like would cause enormous damage and loss of life, the same earthquake in an unpopulated desert would only excite researchers at their seismographs far away. Man-made disasters, on the other hand, usually grow out of social structures but have comparable destructive effects like geophysical hazards. Both natural and man-made collapses of social, administrative, economic and political structures show societies' vulnerability. In this way, they affect our collective approach to managing crises, shaping our strategies as well as patterns of resilience or disaster risk reduction. In reflecting disas-

22 Frank Schätzing, *Der Schwarm* (Cologne: Kiepenheuer & Witsch, 2004).

ters and disaster management strategies, recent research has highlighted geophysical hazards and man-made disasters as part of our mental representation, and storytelling as part of our way to make sense of the world.[23] Earthquakes, tsunamis and wars, financial crises, recessions or state collapses invoke our collective strategies to manage the situation. In this process, they become part of our cultural memory through the stories told, the news spread and the remediation in cases of repeated disaster experiments.

This collection of interdisciplinary essays discusses how the management of crisis is affected by previous experiences and memories and how crisis, disaster or collapse affects cultural memory and political agency. Astrid Erll suggests an ample "provisional" definition of "cultural memory", outlining "the interplay of present and past in socio-cultural contexts".[24] Event and representation, disaster and story merge in the phenomenon of "cultural memory". For the narratives analysed in this volume, this definition of cultural memory highlights the connectedness of past experience, future (precautionary) projections and acting in the immediate moment of a collapse within a specific cultural context. Cultural memory in the context of disaster management includes a process of making sense of the past, using past experiences to generate knowledge and ability to manage a crisis, and projecting an imagined future.

The narrative is the key element of these sense-making processes. Jürgen Straub states that "memory processes and recollection achievements follow in an equally important way the narrative structure".[25] From a psychological point of view, personal recollections or remembering takes place in telling a story. Any representation, including mediatisations of collapse and disaster, is not "a natural reproduction of […] events but a result of productive epistemic actions that are both cognitively *and* emotionally, or motivationally"[26] loaded.

Narration theory exemplifies how narratives are constructed through "framing" the "narrative material" and how this material is exposed to a "narrative drive", which allows textual and extra-textual stimulations to recognise a

---

23 See for example Jeffrey C. Alexander, Ron Eyeman, Bernard Giesen, Neil J. Smelser, and Piotr Sztompka, eds., *Cultural Trauma and Collective Identity* (Berkeley: University of California Press, 2004).

24 Astrid Erll, "Cultural Memory Studies: An Introduction," in *A Companion to Cultural Memory Studies*, ed. Astrid Erll and Ansgar Nünning (Berlin and New York: De Gruyter, 2010), 2.

25 Jürgen Straub, "Psychology, Narrative, and Cultural Memory: Past and Present," in *A Companion to Cultural Memory Studies*, ed. Astrid Erll and Ansgar Nünning (Berlin and New York: De Gruyter, 2010), 216.

26 Ibid, 220.

narrative.[27] Rick Altman supports our approach of researching the interrelation between collapse and cultural memory through the lens of narratives by expanding traditional narrative theory beyond classical plot-based definitions, which often even neglect characters, forget about the reader and ignore cultural contexts. Altman's approach encompasses contexts, including characters (not only actors) and narrative activity, which again implicates some motion of the reader with the character through the narrative and the framing of a story.[28]

The processes of remembering, using and shaping cultural memory function depending on the way we tell and use stories. The selection of material in performing cultural memory, which includes protagonists, their actions and their particular context, is comparable to the "narrative material" that provides the basis for storytelling. Mediatisations and actualisations of disaster and collapse through "creative" channels like news, movies, and research are analogous to the "narrative drive", which is "to make sense of social customs, ancient stones, and physical symptoms".[29] According to Altman, this is what everyone does, from researchers to doctors, and even car mechanics at a particular place and time. Erll's idea of an "interplay of present and past in cultural contexts" resembles these creative processes in storytelling and perception.

A closer look at the material used in storytelling and performing cultural memory reveals more similarities in both processes. For cultural memory, Aleida Assmann noticed a certain dynamic in the "tension between the pastness of the past and its presence".[30] Her starting point to grasp the essence of this tension is the division between canon as the "working memory" and archive as "reference memory" or store house. In her most recent study, she also applies the term "stored forgettness"[31] to the latter. However, both are still accessible, even though an archive is less in use than, for instance, a library, which Assmann says belongs to the canon. Here, information and materials are used and re-used, "re-read, appreciated, staged, performed, and commented".[32] The past events, in this way, get selected and applied to present situations and develop a different "pastness", or rather "presence".

The performance of cultural memory in this context is comparable to narration, which resembles a similar construction process and at the same time

---

27 Rick Altman, *A Theory of Narrative* (New York: Columbia University Press, 2008), 10.

28 Ibid., 9 f., 12, 15, 17 ff., 21.

29 Ibid., 19.

30 Aleida Assmann, "Canon and Archive," in *A Companion to Cultural Memory Studies*, ed. Astrid Erll and Ansgar Nünning (Berlin and New York: De Gruyter, 2010), 98.

31 Aleida Assmann, *Formen des Vergessens* (Göttingen: Wallstein Verlag, 2016), 36.

32 Assmann, "Canon and Archive," 99.

is the main medium for performing cultural memory. While the actualisation process is akin to Altman's idea of narrational activity, with its focus on perceiving and recognising a story as story, his concept of "narrative drive" resembles the actualisation process in cultural memory theory. The material is as important as the narrational activity and narrative drive, which focus on the perception of the reader and the actualisation of material. Examining the dynamics of cultural remembrance and inspired by Hayden White, Ann Rigney emphasises the importance of narrative structures in the formation process of cultural memory and the assigning of meaning to memory sites and events. Additionally, she underlines the aesthetic dimension of narratives, which support mnemonic processes and cast literary texts as "monuments" or "sites" of cultural memory.[33]

How does disaster connect to these theorisations of narrative and cultural memory? Individuals and societies make sense of the impact of disaster and manage the disaster through the stories they tell. Beginning with "news" in the immediate aftermath of the event, this "making-sense-process" continues in numerous actualisations and re-mediatisations. These serve different purposes. First, both provide a basis for survivors to work through their experiences, survive and continue life. Second, such processes help re-establish structures and re-connect lost strands of social, cultural and economic life. Third, narrating collapse helps societies work through the trauma of the unspeakable, thus creating new (cognitive) protected areas.[34]

Why did disaster cultures become such a prominent research field? In particular, the precautionary principle seems to have shifted social perceptions of collapse and its management. Kenneth Hewitt stated in his 2015 publication on the cultural framing of disaster that, "less often mentioned is the great expansion in resources and organizations devoted to disaster concerns. Of late, profitable industries have developed around disaster response in reinsurance, security technologies, relief and reconstruction".[35] Collapse and disaster seem to have

33 Ann Rigney, "The Dynamics of Remembrance: Texts Between Monumentality and Morphing," in *Cultural Memory Studies; An International and Interdisciplinary Handbook*, ed. Astrid Erll and Ansgar Nünning (Berlin and New York: De Gruyter, 2008), 347, 349.

34 Cathy Caruth, ed., *Trauma. Explorations in Memory* (Baltimore and London: The Johns Hopkins University Press, 1995); Cathy Carruth, *Unclaimed Experience. Trauma, Narrative, and History* (Baltimore and London: The Johns Hopkins University Press, 1996); Dominick LaCapra, *Writing History, Writing Trauma* (Ithaca: Cornell University Press, 2001).

35 Kenneth Hewitt, "Framing Disaster in the 'Global Village'. Cultures of Rationality in Risk, Security and News," in *Cultures and Disasters. Understanding Cultural Framings*

moved more into the centre of society's consciousness and thus into the cultural memory. The singular event of geophysical hazard or financial crisis has developed into a permanent condition of risk and danger. In this context, Isak Winkel Holm pays considerable attention to the "man-made disasters" and their circumstances, claiming that "as climate change has replaced the atomic war in the cultural imagination of disaster, it has become more and more meaningless to think of disasters as sudden concentrated events".[36]

This shift in society's perception has influenced disaster research, which "has shifted its focus from the event impacting on human society towards human society contributing to the disaster".[37] This contribution is three-fold and includes precautions, experiences and mediatisations. On the one hand, society's contribution results from the way societies proceed to build structures. This includes the establishment of emergency structures, command structures, and the implementation of safety rules and laws. In other words, the character of future disaster is connected to the prediction of disaster and the structures we have developed to prevent disaster. However, neither prediction nor structures can be observed disconnected from the actual experience of a disaster and the immediate actions taken in case of emergency.

Additionally, the continuous actualisation of experiences through (re-) mediatisations of the disaster shape our perception of disasters. Hereby, remediation through print, audio-visual and internet media, but also through academic research and for educational purposes, connects precaution measures and experience. Both refer to the cultural memory of disaster, which has been – as part of the process of overcoming a disaster – continuously updated in the immediate aftermath and later on. Often, these remediation processes of cultural memory[38] are accompanied by strategic discussion of precautions to be taken to protect society, its values, or its foundations of wealth and security.

---

in Disaster Risk Reduction, ed. Fred Krüger, Greg Bankoff, Terry Cannon, Benedikt Orlowski, and Lisa F. Schipper (Abingdon and New York: Routledge, 2015), 21.

36 Isak Winkel Holm, "The Cultural Analysis of Disaster," in *The Cultural Life of Catastrophes and Crises*, ed. Carsten Meiner and Kristin Veel (Berlin and New York: De Gruyter, 2012), 16.

37 Ibid., 16.

38 Astrid Erll and Ann Rigney, ed., *Mediation, Remediation, and the Dynamics of Cultural Memory* (Berlin and New York: De Gruyter, 2009).

Contributions to this Volume

The analyses of disaster and collapse narratives in this volume feature an overlap and entanglement of events, re-mediatisations, re-mediations and collective memories. First and foremost, these phenomena have been arranged by the object of enquiry, the event and the stories about it. However, our recognition of this overlap and entanglement is an epistemic question, comprising society's growing awareness of living under a permanent condition of risk and the collective desire for physical and moral protection. It is not sufficient to have a protective rampart against the imagined threats of society – measurements must be approved of by a majority of society and legitimised by social values and cultural traditions.

Elisabeth Oxfeldt's object of enquiry in this volume presents a convincing example of the complexity of contemporary collapse. Approaching the interpretation of Margareth Olin's *De andre* through the lens of guilt and morality, Oxfeldt discovers the interwoven experiences and memories of juvenile disasters presented in the Oslo massacre and refugee children. In addition, she highlights resemblance of guilt and moral standards of Norwegian society in the stories told by Margareth Olin. These stories about the endangered "other" threaten the "observer" through an emotional process of narration. Further, this approach touches on the question of the hidden guilt of a saturated and confined society, mentally distanced from certain events and yet, not immune to re-mediated entangled human disasters.

The dynamics and entanglements of memories in the narration of flight and expulsion after the collapse of state structures in the aftermath of the Second World War are the focus of the analysis of Uta Bretschneider, who highlights the frictions between official and individual narratives of flight experiences. She encounters the strategic and restrictive mode of the "narrative drive" behind flight stories through changing political settings from the Soviet Occupational Zone, the German Democratic Republic, and the reunited Federal Republic of Germany. While the content of these narratives refers to flight and expulsion in the context of the Second World War, the analysis focuses on the conditions of storytelling and its impact on the formation of cultural memory of collapse.

The motif of shipwreck evokes images of collapse and disaster. It has appeared in collapse narratives in literature and beyond. Its application and meanings are the focus of Philipp Wagner's analysis in this volume. Wagner focuses on authors' construction of the shipwreck motif, and its effects on readers' interpretation of events. Focusing on Lars Sund's novel *En lycklig liten ö*, Wagner encounters narrative strategies in employing a disaster motif that has been updated continuously in the cultural memory of maritime societies, and recently returned to the collective consciousness with refugee deaths in the Mediterranean. He also touches on the question of what we perceive as a disaster and what is understood as merely an accident.

Legacies, in particular political ones, are contested. Competing interpretations of events and thus competing narratives draw on different and often conflicting framings of events. Florian Peters embeds his analysis of the cultural memory of the 1980/81 movement *Solidarność* in the contemporary conflict over liberal and right-wing populist interpretations of the end of communism in Poland. His descriptions of representations of victims and masters in competing cultural memories within Polish society shed new light on the use of rupture and collapse events in shaping national consciousness and identity. In this regard, the events of 1980/81 and 1989 had been employed to different effect in master narratives of Polish history. In addition, they mark a period of transition from rebellious social activism to political movement forced to adapt narratives according to their changing political setting.

Observing an event through the lens of another comparable event influences our perception of both events. Mariëlle Wijermars examines the phenomenon of pre-mediation by comparing the narrative structures, strategies and motifs in Sergei Loznitsa's *Maidan* and *The Event*. Her analysis highlights the interconnectedness of interpretations of state collapse in the Soviet Union in 1991 and Ukraine in 2014. The social and political implications of these "revolutions" have been studied in recent decades. However, Wijermars's approach takes another turn, exploring the narrative structures and strategies in which these events were placed by Lotznitsa, and how this contributed to the formation of cultural memories of these events. In this way, Wijermars discovers interventions of established narratives, for instance from Lotznitsa's artistic arrangement of pre-existing documentary footage in the case of *The Event*.

The "narrative drive" of collapse narratives has been nurtured by the financial crises of the last decade. Beyond public responses of outrage in countries like Iceland, where the collapse of the financial sector hit the entire economy and thus the entire society, the crises also stimulated debate around the values and structures of politics, economy, society and hereby, in the case of Ireland, led to social transformations. Valur Ingimundarson approaches this collapse management process in his analysis of the politics of memory through the lens of transitional justice mechanisms. Collapses of dictatorships and post-war settings contribute to historical narratives in which the evaluation of past crimes supports the introduction of new orders and structures in society. Research on the crimes of the Stasi by the Stasi Records Agency in the aftermath of the collapse of the German Democratic Republic in 1990, or by the Truth and Reconciliation Commission in South Africa on crimes under Apartheid are examples of transitional justice mechanisms. Ingimundarson focuses on Icelandic society's search for the "truth" about the collapse of the banking sector. He shows the differences in applying transitional justice mechanisms in Iceland, which is stuck, he argues, between competing metanarratives of left-wing damnation of neo-liberal politics and right-wing white washing through oversimplified memory politics.

Two politically motivated metanarratives proposed by left and right-wing factions dominate the cultural memory of the financial crisis of 2008 in Iceland. Even more contested narratives were added to these complex structures through narratives of systemic and personal failing, betrayal by the new government, and an averted revolution. Gunnþórunn Guðmundsdóttir examines monuments and cultural memories of the Icelandic financial crisis in this contested environment of narrations. She explores the aesthetics and role of memorials in coping with the financial crisis in Iceland, focusing on Santiago Sierra's memorial *The Black Cone: Memorial to Civil Disobedience* at Austurvöllur Square in Reykjavik. Guðmundsdóttir identifies the practices and location that impart meaning to this memorial and its role in fixing the cultural memory of Icelandic crisis in society.

It is consensus in memory studies that individual memory is shaped collectively. People and media condition certain patterns of individual remembrance and premediate meanings of outstanding events like collapse and crisis. Collective memory overshadows individual life stories even more if one traumatised generation passes on fewer individual narratives due to early death or suppression. Franziska Sajdak seeks to understand these generational and trauma mechanisms in descendants of Holocaust survivors. In an approach that is novel in Scandinavian literature, Sajdak applies concepts like "telescoping" to the novel *Ett kort uppehåll på vägen från Auschwitz* (2012) by Göran Rosenberg. In the process, Sajdak describes the mechanisms of trauma transfer and narration in the context of cultural memory formation.

Bibliography

Alexander, Jeffrey C., Ron Eyeman, Bernard Giesen, Neil J. Smelser, and Piotr Sztompka, eds. *Cultural Trauma and Collective Identity*. Berkeley: University of California Press, 2004.

Altman, Rick. *A Theory of Narrative*. New York: Columbia University Press, 2008.

Assmann, Aleida. "Canon and Archive." In *A Companion to Cultural Memory Studies*, edited by Astrid Erll and Ansgar Nünning, 97–108. Berlin and New York: De Gruyter, 2010.

Assmann, Aleida. *Formen des Vergessens*. Göttingen: Wallstein Verlag, 2016.

Beleites, Michael. "Isolierte Aufarbeitung? Zur zweigleisigen Erinnerungskultur in Deutschland und ihren Folgen." In *Aufarbeitung der Diktatur – Diktat der Aufarbeitung? Normierungsprozesse beim Umgang mit diktatorischer Vergangenheit*, edited by Katrin Hammerstein, Ulrich Mählert, Julia Trappe and Edgar Wolfrum, 48–58. Göttingen: Wallstein Verlag, 2009.

Bellmann, Werner. "Die Akten der Nürnberger Kriegsverbrecherprozesse als Quelle für Heinrich Bölls Roman *Gruppenbild mit Dame*." *Euphorion* 97, no. 1 (2003): 85–97.

Bernhard, Hans Joachim. *Die Romane Heinrich Bölls. Gesellschaftskritik und Gemeinschaftsutopie*, 2nd revised and extended edition. Berlin: Rütten & Loening, 1973.

Böll, Heinrich. *Gruppenbild mit Dame*. Cologne: Kiepenheuer & Witsch, 1971.

Böll, Heinrich. *Wo warst du, Adam?* Opladen: Friedrich Middelhauve, 1951.

Borchert, Wolfgang. *Draußen vor der Tür*. Hamburg: Rowohlt, 1947. (In English, *The Man Outside*, performed on stage in New York 1949).

Broszat, Martin. *Der Staat Hitlers: Grundlegung und Entwicklung seiner inneren Verfassung*. Munich: Deutscher Taschenbuch-Verlag, 1969.

Carruth, Cathy. *Unclaimed Experience. Trauma, Narrative, and History*. Baltimore and London: The Johns Hopkins University Press, 1996.

Caruth, Cathy, ed. *Trauma. Explorations in Memory*. Baltimore and London: The Johns Hopkins University Press, 1995.

Die Brücke (DE 1959), director Bernhard Wicki.

Durzak, Manfred. "Zwei deutsche Literaturen nach 1945." In *Propyläen Geschichte der Literatur:* Vol. 6. *Die moderne Welt: 1914 bis heute*, edited by Erika Wischer, 292–333. Berlin: Propyläen Verlag, 1982.

Entman, Robert. "Framing: Toward Clarification of a Fractured Paradigm." *Journal of Communication* 43, no. 4 (1993): 51–59.

Erll, Astrid and Ann Rigney, eds. *Mediation, Remediation, and the Dynamics of Cultural Memory*. Berlin and New York: De Gruyter, 2009.

Erll, Astrid. "Cultural Memory Studies: An Introduction." In *A Companion to Cultural Memory Studies*, edited by Astrid Erll and Ansgar Nünning, 1–15. Berlin and New York: De Gruyter, 2010.

Gerstenfeld, Manfred. "The Multiple Distortions of Holocaust Memory." *Jewish Political Studies Review* 19, no. 3–4 (2007): 35–55.

Gosselink, Martine, Maria Holtrop, and Robert Ross, eds. *Good Hope: South Africa and the Netherlands from 1600*. Nijmegen: Uitgeverij Vantilt, 2017.

Grass, Günter. *Die Blechtrommel*. Darmstadt: Luchterhand, 1959.

Gunn, Geoffrey C. *History without Borders. The Making of an Asian World Region. 1000–1800.* Hong Kong: Hong Kong University Press, 2011.

Hammerstein, Katrin. *Gemeinsame Vergangenheit – getrennte Erinnerung? Der Nationalsozialismus in Gedächtnisdiskursen und Identitätskonstruktionen von Bundesrepublik Deutschland, DDR und Österreich.* Göttingen: Wallstein Verlag, 2017.

Hewitt, Kenneth. "Framing Disaster in the 'Global Village'. Cultures of Rationality in Risk, Security and News." In *Cultures and Disasters. Understanding Cultural Framings in Disaster Risk Reduction*, edited by Fred Krüger, Greg Bankoff, Terry Cannon, Benedikt Orlowski, and Lisa F. Schipper, 19–36. Abingdon and New York: Routledge, 2015.

Holm, Isak Winkel. "The Cultural Analysis of Disaster." In *The Cultural Life of Catastrophes and Crises,* edited by Carsten Meiner and Kristin Veel, 15–32. Berlin and New York: De Gruyter, 2012.

Janion, Maria. "Farewell to Poland? The Uprising of a Nation." *Baltic Worlds*, no. 4 (2011): 4–13.

Jendrowiak, Silke. *Günter Grass und die "Hybris" des Kleinbürgers. "Die Blechtrommel", Bruch mit der Tradition einer irrationalistischen Kunst- und Wirklichkeitsinterpretation.* Heidelberg: Winter, 1979.

Kangro, Bernard. *Tartu.* Lund: Eesti Kirjanike Kooperatiiv, 1962.

Kross, Jaan. *Kolme Katku Vahel.* Tallinn: Eesti Raamat, 1970, 1972, 1977, 1980.

LaCapra, Dominick. *Writing History, Writing Trauma.* Ithaca: Cornell University Press, 2001.

Lewis, Michael. *The Big Short: Inside the Doomsday Machine.* New York: W. W. Norton & Company, 2010.

McCourt, Frank. *Angela's Ashes: A Memoir.* New York: Scribner, 1996.

McEwan, Ian. *Saturday.* London: Vintage Books, 2006.

Nguyen, Viet Thanh. *The Refugees.* London: Corsair, 2017.

Rigney, Ann. "The Dynamics of Remembrance: Texts between Monumentality and Morphing." In *Cultural Memory Studies. An International and Interdisciplinary Handbook*, edited by Astrid Erll and Ansgar Nünning, 345–353. Berlin and New York: De Gruyter, 2008.

Schätzing, Frank. *Der Schwarm.* Cologne: Kiepenheuer & Witsch, 2004.

Schneider, Irmela. *Kritische Rezeption. Die Blechtrommel als Modell.* Bern: Lang, 1975.

Straub, Jürgen. "Psychology, Narrative, and Cultural Memory: Past and Present." In *A Companion to Cultural Memory Studies*, edited by Astrid Erll and Ansgar Nünning, 215–228. Berlin and New York: De Gruyter, 2010.

von Hehl, Ulrich. *Nationalsozialistische Herrschaft*, 2nd edition. Munich: Oldenbourg, 2001.

Ward, Vicky. *The Devil's Casino: Friendship, Betrayal, and the High Stakes Games inside Lehman Brothers.* Hoboken, New Jersey: Wiley, 2010.

Zurbuchen, Mary S. "Historical Memory in Contemporary Indonesia." In *Beginning to Remember. The Past in the Indonesian Present,* edited by Mary S. Zurbuchen, 3–32. Singapore: Singapore University Press, 2005.

Elisabeth Oxfeldt

Memories of Crisis and Guilt: The Oslo Massacres (22 July 2011) and Margreth Olin's *De andre* (Nowhere Home, 2012)

This article explores the current so-called refugee crisis at the intersection of memory, trauma and affective studies. I will focus in particular on guilt and guilt feelings.[1] The current refugee crisis has triggered a sizable amount of fictional and documentary texts that explore the feelings of privileged Scandinavians, as they are confronted with the crisis and trauma of others. The texts posit the Scandinavian as going through a range of emotions in her encounter with the refugee, ranging from empathy to fear. At both ends of the emotional spectrum one finds a sense that the safe, peaceful, and stable position of the Scandinavian Self may be threatened, not just by a cultural Other, but also by a traumatized Other. The refugee is imagined as victimized, tortured, and traumatized, and as someone who may consequently disturb the Scandinavian in more or less violent ways – from physically to psychologically as the Scandinavian experiences his or her traumas vicariously.

Within the literary field we find various texts exploring the Scandinavian's emotional register vis-à-vis the refugee. We have for instance Christina Hesselholdt *I familiens skød/Lykkelige familier* (In the Bossom of the Family/Happy Families, 2007/2014), Lone Aburas' *Politisk roman* (Political Novel, 2013), and Aasne Linnestå's *Morsmål* (Mother Tongue, 2012). These fictional texts are written in the mode of realism, based largely on the authors' experiences with

1 While guilt pertains to a legal realm in which one may be judged guilty, receive a punishment, and subsequently atone for one's crime, guilt feelings pertain to a moral realm in which one's conscience determines whether an injustice has occured. Philosophers who have written extensively on the various types of guilt and their social, political, and psychological functions include Martin Buber, Karl Jaspers, and Hannah Arendt. Psychologists furthermore include Sigmund Freud and Melanie Klein. For a review on this topic, see Elisabeth Oxfeldt, "Innledning," in *Skandinaviske fortellinger om skyld og privilegier i en globaliseringstid*, ed. Elisabeth Oxfeldt (Oslo: Universitetsforlaget, 2016), 9–31.

helping refugees. It may also be significant that they are all written by women and may be considered postfeminist texts.[2]

Male authors, too, take up the issue of refugees in a personal, emotional, as well as a social and political context. Examples are Lars Sund's *En lycklig liten ö* (2007; *A Happy Little Island*, 2016), Simon Stranger's so-called Emilie-trilogy (*Barsakh*, 2013; *Verdensredderne* [The World Savers, 2012]; *De som ikke finnes* [Those That Don't Exist 2014]), and Kristian Lundberg's *Vi er de döda, nu snart* (We Are the Dead Soon, 2014). These are texts that may be read as exploring the various – male and female – Scandinavian characters' social, political, and emotional engagement with refugees. They are also political texts with a purpose as they clearly seek to promote a hospitable attitude towards refugees. As Linnestå asks rhetorically: "Staten sa ja / hva sier jeg?".[3]

The encounters are furthermore explored in visual media, and within Nordic film we find, among others, Thomas Østbye's documentary *Imagining Emanuel* (2011) and Aki Kaurismäki's *Le Havre* (2011) and *The Other Side of Hope* (2017). In this chapter, however, I want to examine the work of a strong female voice in the Norwegian public debate on asylum seekers and refugees, namely that of filmmaker Margreth Olin. I have chosen to focus on her documentary film *De andre* (Nowhere Home, 2012) because of the way she draws on the very recent memory of another crisis and collapse in order to frame her story about under-age asylum seekers. This other crisis is the Oslo Massacres, commonly referred to in Norway as July 22nd. On this date in 2011, a lone perpetrator shot dead 69 participants at the annual Labour Party youth camp on Utøya after having bombed the Government buildings in Oslo, killing eight people. 77 people died in all, most of them teenagers.

This way of framing one crisis in light of another ties in with one of this book's main concerns, namely how past experiences and knowledge are re-interpreted and employed in order to overcome situations of crisis and collapse. The fact that the comparison with the Utøya Massacre turned out to be a somewhat controversial strategy, as evidenced by the reviews the film received, makes it relevant to investigate in light of Jan Assmann's understanding of communicative versus cultural memory and how his distinction is further problematized by the way the media operate to create media events immediately following

2 For a comparative analysis of these three works, see Elisabeth Oxfeldt, "'Staten sa ja, så hva sier jeg?' Flygtning og følelser i postfeministisk litteratur," in *Skandinaviske fortellinger om skyld og privilegier i en globaliseringstid*, ed. Elisabeth Oxfeldt (Oslo: Universitetsforlaget, 2016), 230–254.

3 Aasne Linnestå, *Morsmål* (Oslo: Aschehoug, 2012), 19.

terror attacks.[4] In the following I will first introduce Olin's oeuvre and *De andre* in particular. I will show how the film builds on a double framing of the Other pertaining to legal guilt on the one hand, and guilt feelings on the other. I will then explicate Olin's use of the Oslo Massacres in an attempt to understand her choice in light of E. Ann Kaplan's trauma theory and Judith Butler's notions of shared precariousness on the one hand, and the troubled reception in light of memory studies on the other. As indicated I will especially turn to Assmann's distinction between communicative and cultural memory and the way in which it was blurred by the mediatisation of the act of terror. Finally, I will discuss the film's ending by showing how Olin draws not only on cultural memories of crisis (July 22nd), but also on what we may call cultural memories of comfort, that is a well-known Norwegian lullaby, turned ugly and uncomfortable in a time of crisis. My overall argument is that Olin effectively taps into Norwegian cultural memories to evoke feelings of guilt and discomfort. However, in the case of July 22nd, traditional boundaries between the individual, communicative, and cultural memory are collapsed. Although this may be understood in terms of a personal trauma on the one hand, and contemporary mediatisation, on the other, the immediate effect of this collapse among critics was a sense of discomfort directed at Olin as a filmmaker.

Margreth Olin's Films

For Margreth Olin, her profession as a documentary filmmaker has always carried a strong ethical obligation. Olin seeks to give voice to social outsiders such as her uncle with Down's Syndrome (*Onkel Reidar* [Uncle Reidar]), immigrant children who perform poorly in school (*Ungdommens råskap* [Raw Youth]), drug addicts (*Engelen* [The Angel]), or – in the case of *De andre* (Nowhere Home) – underage asylum seekers in Norway.[5] In this film, Olin immerses herself in a participatory documentary film project based mainly on her interviews with four male underage asylum seekers in Norway. She witnesses their accounts of past traumas and observes current ones as their applications for asylum are rejected. The four young men are then institutionalized in asylum

4 The Oslo Massacres, as explained above, occured in two places. The Utøya Massacre refers to the part that took place on the island of Utøya.

5 *Onkel Reidar* (N: 1997), director Margreth Olin; *Ungdommens råskap* (N: 2004), director Margreth Olin; *Engelen* (N: 2009), director Margreth Olin; *De andre* (N: 2012), director Margreth Olin.

reception centres until their eighteenth birthdays when they can be deported as adults – no longer children. Olin follows their lives over a period of three years – through the aftermath of rejection and deportation as well.

De andre was made as a response to political changes occurring in 2009 to limit immigration. Previously, lone asylum seekers under the age of eighteen whose parents could not be tracked down in the children's home country were given residence permit on humanitarian grounds. But after the government saw a record-breaking number of lone underage asylum seekers in 2009, they decided to become more restrictive. Children over fifteen who were deemed not to be in need of protection or not to fulfil the requirements for receiving residence on humanitarian grounds were granted only a temporary residence and had to return "home" at age eighteen. Olin's clear-cut argument in the film is that Norway is breaking the United Nations' Convention of the Rights of the Child, ratified by Norway in 1991.

A Double Framing of the Other

Olin, on the one hand, uses the UN Convention of the Rights of the Child to frame her "boys" (as she calls them) and to make a logical argument pertaining to legal guilt expressed through the expository mode of the film – quoting, for instance, several articles from the UN Child Convention.[6] The boys are victims, she shows, and the state is guilty of breaking UN Conventions. This was a point audiences easily grasped. On the other hand, she frames her "boys" to make an affective argument based less on guilt than on guilt feeling combined with a sense of common precariousness. This affective argument hinges on a humanist understanding that there is no Other, separated clearly from a Self. It is an argument expressed both through the film's ambivalent title and through its participatory mode – through Olin's direct involvement with the boys and especially through the insertion of a dream sequence tied to the Oslo Massacres in the film's title sequence.

6 I am using Bill Nichols' division of documentary films into six modes: poetic, expository, observational, participatory, reflexive, and performative: Bill Nichols, *Introduction to Documentary*, 2nd edition (Bloomington: Indiana University Press, 2010). A documentary can use several of these modes simultaneously which *De andre* does.

The Oslo Massacres

The dream sequence is a reconstruction of a dream Olin claims to have had, linking the fate of her "boys" to that of the young Norwegians massacred, injured, and terrorized on Utøya on 22 July 2011. It consists of several underwater swimming scenes in which we see cropped images of bodies and body parts moving through water while Olin explains in voice over that she had a dream about participants at the Labour Party's youth camp trying to save their lives by swimming away from Utøya and being rescued by Norwegian government officials. In her dream, the image of these young people in danger of drowning merges with the image of two boat refugees swimming towards the same Norwegian government officials. At this point, age becomes a significant factor for the dream refugees who are fourteen and eighteen years old. A Norwegian policeman rescues the 14-year-old whereas the 18-year-old is denied entry and is told to swim back. "In my dream they are no longer Norwegian kids. They are the boys from my film. And they're in open sea", announces Olin.[7] We see a man floating in the ocean, the screen turns black, the title appears in white capital letters accompanied by foreboding electronic music and Olin's voice: "I make this film because I'm afraid. I'm not afraid of the others. Of the strangers. I'm afraid of what's happening with us when we no longer are capable of seeing the individual".[8] Here, Olin's focus is on a crisis pertaining to us, our values, and our national identity, rather than to "them".

As mentioned above, comparing the refugee crisis to the Utøya Massacre created a connection to a recent national trauma that made several critics uncomfortable. Film professor Bjørn Sørenssen, for instance, thought it was unnecessary and came across as an added afterthought in a film that already made a strong point. Britt Sørensen in *Bergens Tidende* saw the framing as appropriate, but found that aesthetically, the images were ill chosen since they came across as intrusive and overstated.[9] Ingunn Økland in *Aftenposten* found that the dream imagery spoiled the film in a melodramatic way and functioned

7 "I drømmen er det ikke lenger norsk ungdom. Det er guttene i filmen min. Og de er i åpent hav" (Throughout this article, I use the English subtitles on the DVD for English translations of *De andre*).

8 "Jeg lager denne filmen fordi jeg er redd. Jeg er ikke redd for de andre. For de fremmede. Jeg er redd for det som skjer med oss når vi ikke lenger er i stand til å se det enkelte menneske."

9 Britt Sørensen, "Skriften på veggen," *Bergens Tidende*, October 18, 2012.

as a noncommittal reference to the massacre.[10] My argument, however, is that the affective framing, including the dream sequence, can be understood in relation to trauma aesthetics as posited by E. Ann Kaplan and Judith Butler both of whom discuss how we frame the precariousness of ourselves and Others. At the same time, the critics' discomfort may be understood in light of Assmann's distinction between communicative and cultural memory considered in relation to a contemporary mediatisation of terror attacks.

A Traumatized Film Maker

Turning first to Kaplan and Butler, we find that they wrote *Trauma Culture* (2005) and *Frames of War* (2009), respectively, as reactions to 9/11, its media representation, and its violent political aftermath. They share a strong concern that the media's representation of trauma nourishes a culture of war and violence. Traumatic events, they underscore, also have a potential for uniting people nationally as well as globally. Yet, accounts of people's common vulnerability have to be found elsewhere than in the daily media. In *Trauma Culture*, Kaplan analyses several films from the perspective of trauma. She is interested in trauma experienced directly as well as vicariously. In a chapter on the ethics of witnessing, she writes: "One has to learn to take the Other's subjectivity as a starting point, not as something to be ignored or denied. It is only in this way that we can gain a public or national ethics"; and she adds: "Certain films may be pertinent in constructing a position for the viewer that enables him or her to take responsibility".[11]

The dream sequence may be seen as indicative of trauma. Olin's dream occurs after her intense participation in the lives of her refugee boys. She has perceived traumas through direct observation in the present and through listening to their trauma narratives about their pasts. This, as Kaplan points out, puts her in a complex position of experiencing vicarious trauma, and of passing this onto her viewers as visually mediated trauma.[12] Kaplan explains: "vicarious traumatization may be a component of witnessing, but instead of only intensifying

---

10 Inguun Økland, "Menneskekjærlig document," *Aftenposten*, October 25, 2012. Bjørn Sørensen writes about a "påklistret ettertanke," Britt Sørensen sees the images as "påtrengende" and "overtydelig," and Økland considers the references to July 22nd inappropriate, using the words "vondt," "melodramatisk" and "uforpliktende."

11 E. Ann Kaplan, *Trauma Culture. The Politics of Terror and Loss in Media and Literature* (New Brunswick: Rutgers University Press, 2005), 123.

12 Ibid., 91–92.

the desire to help an individual in front of one, witnessing leads to a broader understanding of what has been done to victims, of the politics of trauma being possible".[13] Vicariously traumatized Olin, in turn, produces a visual correlative to "the subjective, emotional, and visual experience of trauma"[14] – the dream that is passed on to the viewers of her film. In terms of aesthetics, trauma aesthetics tend to reflect the way in which traumatized people experience their memories of trauma – memories that are repressed, but surface by means of the subconscious, through dreams and various forms of dissociation and fragmentation.

There is another important aspect to Olin's linking the national trauma of July 22nd with the refugee situation, pertaining to grief and precariousness. In addition to blurring the boundaries between "us" and "them", and asking us to broaden our perspectives on young victims who need our help, Olin taps into recent cultural memories by inserting iconic black-white photographs documenting the public grief expressed after July 22nd into her dream sequence. We thus move from a personal, participatory mode to a more expository film mode as Olin shows us stills commemorating the grief felt after the Oslo Massacre, in particular photographs of flowers placed all over the city, and of people in tears.

Turning to the aftermath of July 22nd, Olin reminds her viewers of their values of tolerance and compassion – values that were attacked on July 22nd and strongly expressed and reasserted in the following weeks. As Svein Østerud puts it in his introduction to an anthology on July 22nd: "Official Norway countered the one-man terror of July 22nd with appeals for more democracy and more openness. By supporting common values and through political engagement the fight against terror was to be won".[15] These are values that Olin wants viewers to keep in mind when watching the film about her refugee boys. As documentary film theorist Bill Nichols puts it, the documentary maker has to know "how to enlist an audience's pre-existing values and beliefs for specific ends".[16] Yet, in addition to reminding us of what are widely perceived as national, Norwegian values and virtues, Olin also taps into strong emotions of grief and vulnerability. As such, her opening can be viewed as an extraordinary example of creating a counter-narrative to the media's dominating us-them portrayals. This is done

13 Ibid., 123.

14 Ibid., 125.

15 Svein Østerud "'Oslo, 22. juli 2011," in *22. juli. Forstå – forklare – forebygge*, ed. Svein Østerud (Oslo: Abstrakt forlag, 2012), 13. "Det offisielle Norge møtte enmannsterroren 22. juli med appeller om mer demokrati og mer åpenhet [...]. Gjennom oppslutning om felles verdier og gjennom politisk deltakelse skulle kampen mot terroren vinnes" (my English translation).

16 Nichols, *Introduction to Documentary*, 98.

based on what Butler reminds us is our common "grievability" and precariousness.[17] Clearly Olin and Butler are of the same opinion that we are not just individual beings, or singular social groups, such as nations; instead all human lives are interdependent. As Butler puts it regarding the aftermath of 9/11:

> "War seeks to deny the ongoing and irrefutable ways in which we are all subject to one another, vulnerable to destruction by the other, and in need of protection through multilateral and global agreements based on the recognition of shared precariousness".[18]

Olin uses July 22nd not only to evoke feelings of guilt, reminding us that our grief and concern is distributed unequally, or unjustly – we mourn our "own" children, but seem not to care about those of other nations. She also uses July 22nd to remind us of our common vulnerability, and to stress the fact that although precarity is distributed unequally, we all live precarious lives. As individuals, we are part of greater social networks, and also within our nations we are bound to people "whom one never chose and never knew".[19]

Framing the Oslo Massacres as a national moment of grief and vulnerability, evoking tolerance, compassion and non-violence, Olin seeks to situate us once more in a situation of strong affect supporting a stance of non-violence. She then uses this as a platform to expand the circle of concern, to make us see young, male asylum seekers as equally vulnerable, grievable and human. It becomes an example of a film, as Nichols would put it: "activating our predispositions and tap[ping] into emotion we already have toward certain values and beliefs" to enhance its "affective powers".[20]

Memory and Media

As indicated above, Jan Assmann's distinction between communicative and cultural memory may provide a key to why critics were uncomfortable with Olin's use of July 22nd. We are, in fact, left in what seems to be an uncomfortable borderland between communicative and cultural memory – or worse yet,

17 Butler coins the term "grievable" to discuss how we find the loss of some human lives worthy of grief while the loss of lives of others seems not to affect us.

18 Judith Butler, *Frames of War. When Is Life Grievable?* (London: Verso, 2010), 43.

19 Ibid., 179.

20 Nichols, *Introduction to Documentary*, 97–98.

between three types of memory: individual, communicative and cultural.[21] Most significantly this is an issue of time compression. As Assmann summarizes it, a communicative memory lasts 80–100 years (three to four generations) and has not yet been institutionalized.[22] It is expressed informally through everyday conversation, through vernacular language.[23] Yet, July 22nd and its aftermath were quickly institutionalized, with the media focusing on the speeches and reactions of the heads of the most significant national institutions: the prime minister Jens Stoltenberg and the royal family. As representatives of an "official Norway", Østerud points in particular to Jens Stoltenberg's advocating democracy, openness, and humanity[24] as well as crown prince Håkon Magnus who stated that "the streets are filled with love and compassion".[25] In addition came an abundance of celebrity artists, and as Unni Langås explains in her recent book on trauma in Norwegian literature: "The poems that were sung and written after July 22nd advocated unity and love (or compassion) as a collective response".[26]

Viewed from the perspective of media studies, this expression of collective grief and reassertion of common values constituted the second phase of mediatisation and news coverage of the event. The first phase, in Svein Brurås' analysis of the mediatisation of July 22nd, consisted of direct reporting on the shocking event – a phase that lasted a little less than 24 hours – when it became clear exactly how many had died.[27] The second phase started on the 23rd of July and was that of comforting, stabilizing, and assuaging the nation through arranged media events. The media took on a ceremonial and unifying role – broadcasting performances like the rose demonstration ("rosetog"),

21 Jan Assmann, "Communicative and Cultural Memory," in *A Companion to Cultural Memory Studies*, ed. Astrid Erll and Ansgar Nünning (Berlin: De Gruyter, 2010), 109. Assman's main focus is on communicative versus cultural memory, but he also discusses three types of memory as individual, social, and cultural.

22 Ibid., 113.

23 Ibid., 117.

24 Østerud, "22. Juli," 10, 14.

25 Ibid., 13. "gatene er fylt av kjærlighet" (my English translation).

26 "Diktene som ble sunget og skrevet etter 22. juli, mante til samhold og kjærlighet som et kollektivt svar." Unni Langås, *Traumets betydning i norsk samtidslitteratur* (Bergen: Fagbokforlaget Vigmostad & Bjørke, 2016), 12. (my English translation).

27 Svein Brurås, "'Det er en tid for alt.' Nyhetsdekning i tre faser," in *Mediene og terroraksjonen. Studier av norske mediers dekning av 22. Juli*, ed. Svein Brurås (Oslo: Unipub, 2012), 13. In his discussion of media events, Brurås refers mainly to: Daniel Dayan and Elihu Katz, *Media Events. The Live Broadcasting of History* (Cambridge Mass.: Harvard University Press, 1992).

memorials, and funerals. This phase lasted two to three weeks and was characterized by a tone of gravity and veneration.[28] It was a phase when the nation's broadcasting corporations and social institutions cooperated to unite people and create a social common understanding of the traumatic event.[29] During a third phase, critical, investigative journalism set in, which had previously been considered inappropriate.[30]

If we examine these three media phases through the lens of Assmann's division between communicative and cultural memory, we see a set of potential clashes. Whereas communicative memories pertain to a time structure consisting of nearly a century, encompassing three or four interacting generations, cultural memories pertain to an absolute past, or at least one that extends beyond the aforementioned 80 years. The cultural memory is mediated ceremonially, in a "classical" or "otherwise formalized language", while the communicative memory is a living, embodied memory, communicated in a vernacular language, informally, through genres of everyday communication.[31] A conceptual problem arises when a traumatic event is treated as a cultural memory within a mere 24 hours through ceremonial communication; July 22nd was, as Bruräs points out, already considered "historical" at this early stage. It may then seem irreverent or gratuitous for a filmmaker – who is not just talking in an informal everyday setting, but making a film, aimed at a national audience – to locate the traumatic event within the sphere of an individual or communicative memory, relating it through a personal dream. In addition, the second phase is about rebuilding a sense of unity within a specific community, in this case Norway. It is about "our" loss, grief, trauma, and standing united in the face of terror. It may then seem "wrong" and improperly transgressive of boundaries to involve those who are conceptualized as not part of "us" in this memory. Yet, as I have argued, this may nevertheless be understood in the context of trauma and trauma aesthetics, building precisely on dissociations, fragments, and new associations appearing through the subconscious of a vicariously traumatized filmmaker.

28 Ibid., 13, 18, 20.
29 Ibid., 14, 18.
30 Ibid., 21.
31 Assmann, "Memory," 117.

Black-and-White Photographs

A similar, yet less problematic, collapse of the border between the personal and the public arises with Olin's use of iconic photos. Jens Ruchatz distinguishes between the photograph as externalization and trace. A central point is that "private photographs tend to be used as traces [...] whereas collective memory favours photographs that support a symbolical reading and thus can be appropriated for externalization".[32] Public photographs may serve an iconic role: "the term 'photographic icon' [...] designates pictures that attract strong collective attention and emotional reactions", and "iconic photographs foreground symbolic values".[33] When Olin inserts black-and-white stills of grief expressed in Oslo immediately after the massacres, they are presented as something that could be personal photographs. After all, Olin informs us that she, herself, was there with her daughter. As a filmmaker she may very well have brought her camera. At the same time, we recognize the scenes as those from the second phase of media coverage. We know they symbolize the common grief and values of democracy and tolerance that were reasserted as a reaction to the act of terror. Again, with Assmann we might say that the boundaries between individual, communicative, and cultural memory are blurred. When this caused less of a critical reaction, however, it may be because it came across as less "melodramatic", "overstated", and "intrusive" since it to a lesser degree tapped into something that was clearly an individual memory. In terms of affect, it set the stage for feeling connected through a common sense of vulnerability without also guilt-tripping viewers.

It furthermore ties in with the film's overall use of black-and-white stills. After the opening sequence, the film follows Olin's young male refugees, especially three Afghans and an Iraqi Kurd, allowing us to witness their past and present traumas as well as their intermittent hopes for a brighter future. Throughout the film, Olin employs the aforementioned aesthetics of trauma. She uses black-and-white stills and extreme close-ups of faces and body parts to interrupt the flow of her film, and she uses uncanny disassociations between voices and bodies as trauma victims narrate their primary traumas. The black-and-white still photography has been interpreted as providing a sense of sadness, gloom,

32 Jens Ruchatz, "The Photograph as Externalization and Trace," in *A Companion to Cultural Memory Studies*, ed. Astrid Erll and Ansgar Nünning (Berlin: De Gruyter, 2010), 372.

33 Ibid., 374.

and fear.[34] They may, however, also have to be understood in terms of trauma. The first time, for instance, Olin uses black-and-white stills is when Kurdish Goli is deported and loses hope for the future, stating that he would rather die in the process of fleeing, than live in Iraq. The stills showing him sitting in the airplane, interrupt the flow of the film and appear to mirror an inner state of mind in which life at best, is put on hold. The inner state of mind appears to be Goli's as well as, empathically and vicariously, Olin's.

The fourth and final main story presented in the film belongs to Husein, a refugee from Afghanistan. Here, too, Olin uses an elaborate aesthetics of trauma including the black-and-white stills, extreme close-ups of faces and (scarred) body parts, as well as uncanny dissociations between voices and bodies. When Husein's application for asylum is turned down, the rejection evidently constitutes a new trauma, evoking the memories of his prior trauma, an incident in which all his family members – except his brother Hassan who accompanies him to Norway – were killed and during which he was stabbed with a bayonet. In a live recording in colour we hear Husein narrating his account to Olin in a broken, soft voice. When Husein gets to the point in his story in which everything turns black and he wakes up at the hospital with severe injuries, he pauses for a moment. To reflect his traumatized state of mind, Olin continues to show him sitting quietly. Meanwhile his account is further narrated as a voice over, still using Husein's voice. The effect is uncanny and jarring as body and voice are disassociated. How can Husein talk without moving his lips? What does this cinematic technique mean? On the one hand, Husein appears to dissociate himself from his own story, which is accentuated as being simultaneously unspeakable and spoken. In shock, he seems mentally alienated from his own body. The scene thus provides a visual correlative to the experience of trauma – with its "terrifying dissociations and splitting", the "uncanny intertwining of inside and outside", and the "crossing of borders normally held firm in ordinary life".[35] At the same time, the cinematic technique may reflect Olin's own sense of vicarious trauma – which, as in the case of Goli, she passes on, "leaving the situation uncertain or to be deduced by the viewer".[36]

34 Økland, "Menneskekjærlig document." Kjersti Juul, "Vond og bevegende film," *Vårt Land*, October 25, 2012.

35 Kaplan, *Trauma Culture*, 125.

36 Ibid., 125.

An Open-Wound Ending – Memories of Comfort

The ending of the film, in which Olin once more frames the refugee crisis as a crisis of children, evokes a sense of injustice and guilt as well as a sense of common precariousness. In a final scene, she again taps into Norway's collective memory, this time by juxtaposing homeless refugee children in Athens, sleeping in public places with and without their families, with a classic Norwegian lullaby, Margrethe Munthes "Dear God, I am well taken care of".[37]

Earlier in the film we have seen similar bedtime scenes accompanied by Greek folk music. Now the soundtrack brings the scenes home, so to speak, yet the well-known lullaby is performed in an unfamiliar version, sung in a dreary and melancholy manner (arranged by Rebekka Karijord and performed by the Stockholm Boys' Choir). What this song evokes in the viewer is presumably a parent singing the lullaby in the intimacy of a child's bedroom. The safe child – through a simple hymn – thanks God for his love and everything else he has given the child, and prays that God will keep looking after the child and her family. Olin, by contrast, uses a version full of musical and intertextual dissonance, compared to the traditional version. In addition, the visual context enhances an uncomfortable sense of contrast between the viewer's musical associations and the images on the screen. There is no bedroom for these children, and neither God nor anybody else seems to be giving them and their families what they need. The combination of song and imagery creates cognitive dissonance and psychological discomfort. In this way, the film's participatory, affective mode has what Kaplan calls an open-wound ending.

According to Kaplan, an open-wound ending may urge viewers to take an active, ethical stance on the matter: "Art that takes trauma for its topic but does not allow the spectator so easily to 'survive' the protagonist's death or wound, refuses the safe closure that melodrama perhaps vainly seeks".[38] Such films have "power to move the audience ethically, to expose the structure of injustice and to invite viewers to take responsibility for related specific injustice" (ibid.). Clearly, Olin's film mobilizes audience emotions of guilt, precariousness, and injustice, suggesting that the primary way to heal the wound is to act politically. The last point is made as the open-wound affective framing of *De andre* is followed by the expository framing anchoring the film in several articles from the UN Convention of the Rights of the Child with which Norwegian government institutions is not complying, according to Olin.

37 "Kjære Gud jeg har det godt" (my English translation).

38 Kaplan, *Trauma Culture*, 135.

Conclusion

Overall, the film was well received, also by those who were otherwise critical to Olin's references to the Utøya Massacres. Bjørn Sørenssen, for instance, writes in the film journal *Montages* that:

> "*De andre* is an appeal that mobilizes rather than satisfies emotions. While similar films are content to leave the viewer in a teary catharsis, Olin sets out to use emotions politically. Instead of just pointing at the sad fact that we live in an evil world, she directs a clear appeal at her audience, demanding action".[39]

Sørenssen's conclusion is that this makes the film "entirely necessary in the Norwegian asylum debate".[40] The film, in addition, is important from several other perspectives. It illustrates the public function of documentaries as a counter-voice to other media presentations (on refugees); it builds on trauma aesthetics that have attracted new interest internationally after 9/11; and it enters into a Scandinavian discourse on guilt and privilege with a focus on guilt as well as guilt feeling. As such it constitutes a unique voice that assumes the point of view of the Other without fearing anything but the integrity – not the collapse – of the Self. Yet as I indicated at the beginning of this article Olin's voice is just one of many; a good deal of these express ambivalence regarding Scandinavian guilt, while others express a more explicit defence of Scandinavian privilege.

From the point of view of memory studies, it is interesting that crossing the boundaries between representing individual, communicative, and cultural memories may prompt audience discomfort – probably more so upon the film's immediate release than now, five years later. Conversely, we may turn the problem around and ask whether Assmann's distinction between the three types of memory remains valid, once the event remembered is of such critical magnitude as is an act of terror. This is an act that government institutions, artist celebrities, and the media in general devote vast amounts of energy to quickly consolidate and provide meaning as a cultural memory. Assmann's three cat-

39 Bjørn Sørenssen in *Montages*, November 5th, 2012. "*De andre* er en appell som mobiliserer, heller enn å tilfredsstille følelser. Der lignende filmer nøyer seg med å etterlate tilskueren i en tårevåt katharsis, satser Olin på bruke [sic.] følelsene politisk. I stedet for bare å påpeke det sørgelige faktum at vi lever i en ond verden, retter hun en klar og tydelig appell til tilskuerne med krav om handling" (my English translation).

40 Ibid., "helt nødvendig i den norske asyldebatten" (my English translation).

egories nevertheless help explain the sense of discomfort that may arise when contemporary media contribute to a collapse between classifications that have traditionally been kept distinct for generations.

Bibliography

Assmann, Jan. "Communicative and Cultural Memory." In *A Companion to Cultural Memory Studies*, edited by Astrid Erll and Ansgar Nünning, 109–118. Berlin: De Gruyter, 2010.

Brurås, Svein. "'Det er en tid for alt.' Nyhetsdekning i tre faser." In *Mediene og terroraksjonen. Studier av norske mediers dekning av 22. Juli*, edited by Svein Brurås, 9–22. Oslo: Unipub, 2012. https://bruraas.wordpress.com/forskning/det-er-en-tid-for-alt-nyhetsdekning-i-tre-faser/.

Butler, Judith. *Frames of War. When Is Life Grievable?*. London: Verso, 2010.

Dayan, Daniel and Elihu Katz, *Media Events. The Live Broadcasting of History.* Cambridge Mass.: Harvard University Press, 1992.

De andre (N 2012), director Margreth Olin.

Juul, Kjersti. "Vond og bevegende film." *Vårt Land*, October 25, 2012.

Kaplan, E. Ann. *Trauma Culture. The Politics of Terror and Loss in Media and Literature.* New Brunswick: Rutgers University Press, 2005.

Langås, Unni. *Traumets betydning i norsk samtidslitteratur.* Bergen: Fagbokforlaget Vigmostad & Bjørke, 2016.

Linnestå, Aasne. *Morsmål.* Oslo: Aschehoug, 2012.

Nichols, Bill. *Introduction to Documentary.* 2nd ed. Bloomington: Indiana University Press, 2010.

Økland, Ingunn. "Menneskekjærlig document." *Aftenposten*, October 25, 2012.

Østerud, Svein. "Oslo, 22. juli 2011." In *22. juli. Forstå – forklare – forebygge*, edited by Svein Østerud, 9–29. Oslo: Abstrakt forlag, 2012.

Oxfeldt, Elisabeth. "'Staten sa ja, så hva sier jeg?' Flygtning og følelser i postfeministisk litteratur." In *Skandinaviske fortellinger om skyld og privilegier i en globaliseringstid*, edited by Elisabeth Oxfeldt, 230–254. Oslo: Universitetsforlaget, 2016. https://www.idunn.no/skandinaviske-fortellinger/12-staten-sa-ja-sa-hva-sier-jeg.

Oxfeldt, Elisabeth. "Innledning." In *Skandinaviske fortellinger om skyld og privilegier i en globaliseringstid*, edited by Elisabeth Oxfeldt, 9–31. Oslo: Universitetsforlaget, 2016. https://www.idunn.no/skandinaviske-fortellinger/1-innledning.

Ruchatz, Jens. "The Photograph as Externalization and Trace." In *A Companion to Cultural Memory Studies*, edited by Astrid Erll and Ansgar Nünning, 367–378. Berlin: De Gruyter, 2010.

Sørensen, Britt. "Skriften på veggen." *Bergens Tidende*, October 18, 2012.

Sørenssen, Bjørn. "Analysen: *De andre* (2012)." *Montages*, November 5, 2012. http://montages.no/2012/11/analysen-de-andre-2012/ (read 10.06.2014).

Uta Bretschneider

Flight and Expulsion after World War II as Collapse: Official and Individual Memories in Eastern Germany

In the spring of 2016 the *Sudetendeutsche Landmannschaft*, an organisation of German expellees from Bohemia, changed their by-laws. The "right to homeland" and their goal of "winning back" was taken out of the statutes.[1] This symbolic step occurred more than seven decades after the end of World War II. The change in the statutes was both a political shift (that was criticised on the one hand and welcomed on the other) and a symptom of the current German 'culture of remembrance' concerning flight and expulsion.

In 1945, around 14 million Germans were affected by the forced migration out of Germany or German-settled territories in Eastern Europe, such as Silesia, East Prussia, Pomerania and Bohemia. They experienced the end of the war as the beginning of a collapse. Over four million refugees or expellees wound up in the Soviet Occupied Zone. They made up a quarter of the population there, yet they were only able to hang on to their status as a distinct group for a very short time. The "resettler policy" (*Umsiedlerpolitik*) was a firm assimilation policy marked by repression. It aimed at a one-sided adjustment of the new arrivals to the receiving society and negated their particular body of experience. In this policy the authorities aimed to gain quick social cohesion, or something even stronger: a mostly homogeneous society based on their ideological perspective. In this "socialistic" society (*Sozialistische Gesellschaft*) there was neither space for thousands of people hoping to leave the country and return home to Eastern Europe nor for groupings that did not accept the legitimacy of the political system. And so, only a few years after the end of World War II the so-called "resettlers" (*Umsiedler*) were declared to be integrated.

Against this background, this paper focuses on the individual and collective modes of remembrance concerning flight and expulsion after World War II.[2]

---

1 See e. g., "Sudetendeutsche verzichten auf 'Wiedergewinnung der Heimat'," *Zeit online*, February 2016, http://www.zeit.de/gesellschaft/zeitgeschehen/2016-02/vertriebene-sudetendeutsche-verzicht-wiedergewinnung-heimat.

2 The data (qualitative interviews, records, and contemporary journals) were collected inter alia during the research on the doctoral dissertation project "Vom Ich zum Wir?" (2011–2014), which analyses the processes of integration of the "resettlers" in the context of transformation in rural areas of the Soviet Occupied Zone/GDR; Uta Bretschneider,

Changes and challenges of memory in the unique setting of the Soviet Occupied Zone and the German Democratic Republic (GDR) are analysed, and the following questions are approached: How successful had the displacement from the public been? How do contemporary witnesses who have experienced flight or expulsion in childhood remember this time now? And what was the impact of the German reunification – the so-called *Wende* – in the years 1989 and 1990 on the processes of remembrance?

"Resettler Policy"

In the closing days of World War II, millions of Germans fled from the German or German-settled territories in Eastern Europe as the eastern front moved closer and closer. Soon, the flight merged into the wild expulsion that continued even after the allies' Potsdam Conference in the summer of 1945.

Belongings, packed in haste by the so-called resettlers, soon disappeared in the confusion of the flight westward – whether through plundering, exchange, or sale. Upon reaching their final destination, they had as good as nothing.

Against the background of a newly formed bureaucracy and an infrastructure destroyed by the war, it was determined that the survival of these people had to take priority. Often it was the native population that assisted with food or a place to stay in the direst situations. Help from the state only came gradually. The most important institution was the Central Administration for German Resettlers (*Zentralverwaltung für deutsche Umsiedler*).[3]

It was already determined in the autumn of 1945 that the refugees and expellees were to be officially designated as "resettlers" in the Soviet Occupation Zone. The terminology reduced the forced migration of people in their millions to a "resettlement". It masked the involuntariness of having to leave their homes and was intended to emphasise the irreversibility of the situation.[4]

In 1947, the Socialist Unity Party (*Sozialistische Einheitspartei Deutschlands*)[5] politician Paul Merker offered a definition of the term:

'Vom Ich zum Wir'? Flüchtlinge und Vertriebene als Neubauern in der LPG (Leipzig: Leipziger Universitätsverlag, 2016), 23–31.

3 Manfred Wille, "Die Zentralverwaltung für deutsche Umsiedler. Möglichkeiten und Grenzen ihres Wirkens (1945–1948)," in *Sie hatten alles verloren. Flüchtlinge und Vertriebene in der Sowjetischen Besatzungszone Deutschlands*, ed. Manfred Wille, Johannes Hoffmann, and Wolfgang Meinicke (Wiesbaden: Harrassowitz, 1993), 27–54.

4 Bretschneider, *'Vom Ich zum Wir'?*, 23–31.

5 Socialist Unity Party (*Sozialistische Einheitspartei Deutschlands*).

> "Resettlers are those people, who, due to international decisions, had to leave their places of origin because they are German – to the extent that these areas now lay outside the current German border – and are now being taken in as resettlers in the areas of today's German occupation zones".[6]

The politics of language concerning flight and expulsion was ideologically and symbolically heavily laden. Within a few years, the "resettlers" were proclaimed to be "new citizens" (*Neubürger*) and then finally "former resettlers" (*ehemalige Umsiedler*).

"Resettler" was a euphemism. The terminus was introduced to avoid words like "expellees" or "refugees" (*Vertriebene und Flüchtlinge*) or, as they were called in the Western part of Germany, "homeland expellees" (*Heimatvertriebene*). "New citizens" described the progress of integration and "former resettlers" marked the process of assimilation as complete. At the beginning of the 1950s, integration was already declared to be successfully completed. The existence of a particular group of people with broken biographies, no belongings, and the desire to return was negated.

As examples, the "resettler"-political program comprised financial support, preferred credit grants, participation in land reform, and also included special support for job re-training. Paul Merker outlined the goals for 1947 as follows:

> "The fact that we are nearing the end of the resettlement has to serve as an occasion to force us to review our collective experiences and to find ways of promoting the assimilation of the resettlers in their new homes along with a merging with the native population. This should be done to facilitate the final naturalization, and to provide them with housing, furniture, and suitable employment".[7]

Merker's proposal makes it clear that the "resettler policy" in the Soviet Occupation Zone – and after 1949 in the GDR – was above all an assimilation policy, the goal of which was rapid integration into the so-called receiving society. However, due to the collapse of the national socialist regime and the so-called anti-fascist democratic revolution, this process came at a time of profound transformation: the so-called receiving society was in a flux. This meant that everyone, long-time natives and new arrivals alike, had to deal with various forms of adjustment. In the process, especially for the "resettlers", there dominated a "compulsion

6 Paul Merker, *Die nächsten Schritte zur Lösung des Umsiedlerproblems* (Berlin: Dietz, 1947), 24.

7 Ibid., 7.

for the future".[8] They were not to look back; instead, they were to invest all of their energies into building the new – socialistic – society. According to historian Michael Schwartz, the efforts towards making certain themes taboo were "all the more effective, in that [they] not only concentrated on repression, but also on ideological indoctrination".[9] It contained an "anti-fascist loaded 'guilty conscious' and produced a corresponding self-control [...]".[10] Those "resettlers" who were susceptible to socialist ideas gained social rise, but they paid for it with their personal lack of the past. The integration history, therefore, is to be understood as a "necessary and long-term history of conflict".[11]

Until the end of their lives, many "resettlers" hoped for a de facto return to their so-called "old homeland" (*alte Heimat*). There were more than a few who always kept a packed suitcase on hand – they wanted to be ready at all times for the return trip to their home region. Even political decisions, such as the recognition of the Oder-Neisse border by the GDR in 1950, were hardly able to shake their determination. On the one hand, there was a refusal by the "resettlers" to settle into their new surroundings; on the other, the "strangers" were marginalised and discriminated against again and again.

In the first few years of the post-war period, the refugees and expellees were competitors for scarce resources, such as food, accommodation and work. In addition, various daily habits became symbols of "being strangers". There often followed – after their experience of total collapse and professional and social relegation – the realisation of not being wanted. Although, as Germans, the "resettlers" belonged to the same nationality as the locals, they were often labelled "gypsies" or "Russians". In doing so, the locals denied them solidarity. For many years the "resettlers" remained "foreigners". Only in the long-term (inter alia through generational change) could the tension be attenuated.

Nevertheless, the so-called process of integration was brought – at least officially – to a formal end in September 1950 with the *Act for the Continued Improvement of the Situation of the Former Resettlers* (*Gesetz über die weitere Verbesserung der Lage der ehemaligen Umsiedler in der Deutschen Demokratischen*

8 Michael Schwartz, "Umsiedlerpolitik in der Krise? Das Vertriebenenproblem in der Gründungsphase der DDR 1948–1950," in *Das letzte Jahr der SBZ. Politische Weichenstellungen und Kontinuitäten im Prozeß der Gründung der DDR*, ed. Dierk Hoffmann and Hermann Wentker (Munich: Oldenbourg, 2000), 186.

9 Michael Schwartz, "'Zwangsheimat Deutschland.' Vertriebene und Kernbevölkerung zwischen Gesellschaftskonflikt und Integrationspolitik," in *Nachkrieg in Deutschland*, ed. Klaus Naumann (Hamburg: HIS Verlag, 2001), 133.

10 Ibid.

11 Ibid., 146.

Republik). Only five years after the end of World War II, the refugees and expellees were officially considered to be integrated. The so-called resettler problem (*Umsiedlerproblem*), at least in official contemporary interpretation, was solved.[12] A veritable mythology of a successful integration was staged, disseminated, and politically manipulated. Consequently, the refugees and expellees then disappeared from official statistics.

Example Case: The Moor Family's Way to Thuringia

The example of a family (the pseudonym 'Moor' has been given) is chosen here to illustrate the "resettler policy" and the individual processes of adaption. The following is based on interviews with the two daughters of the Moor family: Bärbel Lohner (born Moor) and Ingeborg Lösch (born Moor). At the beginning of 1945, Gertrud Moor fled with her mother and her three children from the area around Landsberg an der Warthe (today, Gorzów Wielkopolski in Poland). At first they set out in a westerly direction, but then soon returned to their house, which in the meantime had been plundered. They were finally driven out for good in May, 1945. They landed in a camp somewhere in Brandenburg. Then the Moors were shipped off to Thuringia in a freight wagon. Until the father was released from a prisoner-of-war camp in 1948, they lived in a village in the south of Thuringia.

On June 18th, 1948, the Moor family arrived in Kloster Veßra, a small village in the south of Thuringia with approximately 300 inhabitants, and there they took over a land reform farm that had failed. At this point the Moors belonged to the ten new farm families in the village who were settled in the area of the former manorial farm estate.

In September of 1945, a land reform was introduced in the Soviet Occupied Zone. Owners of property larger than 100 hectares, as well as the (supposed) profiteers of national socialism, were dispossessed without compensation. Their possessions – land, buildings, livestock, and agricultural equipment – fell to the agricultural land fund and were newly distributed. Thus, 210,000 new farms were created, each containing between five and ten hectares of land. In addition to this, numerous small pieces of land were distributed as garden allotments.

---

12 Michael Schwartz, "Staatsfeind 'Umsiedler'," in *Die Flucht. Über die Vertreibung der Deutschen aus dem Osten*, ed. Stefan Aust and Stephan Burgdorff (Bonn: Bundeszentrale für politische Bildung, 2003), 224–235.

Among the new farmers were more than 90,000 "resettled" families.[13] The goal was the destruction of traditional hierarchies and the elimination of the great land owners and their families. The new farmers (*neubauern)* were to be 'planted' as a new social group in the villages. Furthermore, the land reform served to ensure the food supply. Not least of all, this was intended as a form of aid for the "resettlers" towards becoming self-sufficient. The land reform, therefore, can be seen as one of the state measures to support the refugees and expellees.

Bärbel remembers an episode from a period in the beginning: a sack of wheat that had been allocated to the family for the seed was instead immediately ground into flour. At that moment, bread was more important than seed for the next year.[14] This example illustrates that taking over a land reform business may have promised – in the best case – a secure existence in the long run, but the lack of basic necessities in the beginning still had to be overcome.

After only five months for construction, the Moor family moved into their farm house in October of 1948. There still remained no electricity and the walls were not yet painted. Furniture was collected piece by piece.[15] For Erich Moor, who had been working as a butcher with a small farm in his home village, the land reform – and therefore, the possibility of a "land grab" (*Landnahme*)[16] – had particular significance. It meant a return to the older, more familiar ways of doing things they had known before the war.[17]

However, running an agricultural business in Thuringia meant a host of other challenges to confront. Among other problems, for example, the Moors had to become accustomed to the different soil and weather conditions. They had to adapt themselves to the area. In the interview with Ingeborg, she emphasised

13 Altogether, the expropriation encompassed 3.3 million hectares of land. 560,000 people were involved in the land distribution: Michael Schwartz, *Vertriebene und "Umsiedlerpolitik". Integrationskonflikte in den deutschen Nachkriegs-Gesellschaften und die Assimilationsstrategien in der SBZ/DDR 1945–1961* (Munich: De Gruyter, 2004), 652.

14 Lohner, Bärbel (born Moor), born in 1940. She was driven out of the Landsberg an der Warthe district, Brandenburg (today Gorzów Wielkopolski, Poland) along with her family (her father was a prisoner of war). After many stops along the way, they landed in Kloster Veßra (Thuringia) in 1948. Interview by the author Uta Bretschneider, November 4, 2011, line 203.

15 Lösch, Ingeborg (born Moor), born in 1939. She was the sister of Bärbel Lohner and was driven out of the Landsberg an der Warthe district, Brandenburg (today Gorzów Wielkopolski, Poland) along with her family (her father was a prisoner of war). After many stops along the way, they landed in Kloster Veßra (Thuringia) in 1948. Interview by the author Uta Bretschneider, May 12, 2011, line 5.

16 Christoph Hein, *Landnahme* (Frankfurt: Suhrkamp, 2004).

17 Interview by the author Uta Bretschneider and Ingeborg Lösch, 2011, line 5.

that her parents had proved – in the long term after overcoming enormous problems – that they could run a business by themselves, and that they were indeed farmers despite their numerous set-backs.[18] In any case, the Moor family was able to stabilise their farm business. What sounds like one of those often-told stories of success was indeed a story of failure and individual struggle. Erich Moor, for example, refused until the end of his life to be buried far from his home. We will return to the Moors later.

Policy of Forgetting

"Historical memory is always a political act".[19] Of course, this also applies in particular to the avoidance of historical remembrance. Making certain themes taboo was widely practised in the GDR. Here, the "alliance between regime and memory",[20] as described by the cultural expert Aleida Assmann in reference to forced forgetting, is particularly relevant – that is, the refugee and expellee interest groups that emerged in West Germany as important associations of remembrance were forbidden in the GDR. At first, they fell under the so-called coalition ban that the four occupation zones had passed in 1945.[21] Until the summer of 1948, there was a general ban for the refugees and expellees to establish coalitions. It was thought this ban would help to stabilise the political system as well as the borders in the East. At the end of the 1940s, however, this ban was lifted in West Germany. In the GDR it remained in effect.[22] On top of this, the

18 Ibid., line 13.

19 Edgar Wolfrum, "Erinnerungskultur und Geschichtspolitik als Forschungsfelder. Konzepte – Methoden – Themen," in *Reformation und Bauernkrieg. Erinnerungskultur und Geschichtspolitik im geteilten Deutschland*, ed. Jan Scheunemann (Leipzig: Evangelische Verlagsanstalt, 2010), 15.

20 Aleida Assmann, *Erinnerungsräume. Formen und Wandlungen des kulturellen Gedächtnisses* (Munich: C. H. Beck, 1999), 138.

21 Heike Amos, *Vertriebenenverbände im Fadenkreuz. Aktivitäten der DDR-Staatssicherheit 1949 bis 1989* (Munich: De Gruyter, 2011), 27.

22 "Gesetz zum Schutze des Friedens vom 15. Dezember 1950," law text, accessed September 6, 2017, http://www.verfassungen.de/de/ddr/friedensgesetz50.htm; Michael Schwartz, "Vertriebenenproblem und Umsiedlerpolitik in der SBZ/DDR," Friedrich-Ebert-Stiftung, accessed September 6, 2017, http://www.fes.de/magdeburg/pdf/6_10_14_schwartz.pdf; Heike Amos, *Die Vertriebenenpolitik der SED 1949 bis 1990* (Munich: Oldenbourg, 2009), 257; Ute Bretschneider, "Zwangsmigration und Neubeheimatung. 'Umsiedler' als 'Neubauern' in der SBZ/DDR," in *Aufbrechen, Arbeiten, Ankommen. Mobilität und*

West German associations for the "homeland expellees" (*Heimatvertriebenen*) were designated in East Germany as backward-looking and revanchist – which to a large extent they actually were.[23] The 'Remembering Culture' on the one side and the 'Forgetting Culture' on the other side of the inner-German border served a key function in the propaganda battle of the Cold War. Historian Edgar Wolfrum assessed the situation as follows:

> "For the Federal Republic, the GDR was always the negative-comparison society. For their part, the GDR could never entirely pull themselves away from the magnet field of the great western brother, although the SED-Regime permanently strove to. The SED-Regime tried to offset their lack of democratic legitimation through a secondary legitimacy – and it is here where the development of a socialist historical picture played a crucial role".[24]

And within this picture, the "resettler's" history, their experiences, fears, and the harm done were mostly excluded. Although they initially disappeared from official statistics in the 1950s, they did not disappear from the GDR media. It is with this that the historian Bill Niven speaks of a "supposed taboo"[25] - that is, for years researchers stated that the theme was completely taboo. However, subsequent years have offered the knowledge that it was a taboo with certain gaps. Even if the "resettlers" did not entirely disappear from East German media, the mode of their presentation was nevertheless strictly prescribed: a history of achievement was presented. This consisted of economic as well as social integration, which corresponded to professional and personal success. This is illustrated above with the example of the Moor family. The fact that a particular person was profiled as a "resettler" only underscored the achievement of reconstruction and therefore increased the overall balance of success.[26] This

---

Migration im ländlichen Raum seit 1945, ed. Rita Garstenauer and Anne Unterwurzacher (Innsbruck et al.: Studienverlag, 2015), 37–52.

23 The book "Kreuzritter in Trachten" was published in the GDR in 1984 against Western German associations of the so-called *Heimatvertriebenen*. Its language represents typical elements of the Cold War period and shows the GDR's attitude towards the Western German resettler policy: Werner Flach and Christa Kouschil, *Kreuzritter in Trachten. Organisierter Revanchismus und seine Macher* (Leipzig: Urania-Verlag, 1984).

24 Wolfrum, "Erinnerungskultur und Geschichtspolitik," 25.

25 Bill Niven, "On a supposed taboo: Flight and refugees from the East in GDR film and television," *German life and letters* 65, no. 2 (2012): 216–236.

26 Uta Bretschneider, "'Die Bodenreform wurde auch für sie die Rettung.' 'Umsiedler' als Neubauern in der zeitgenössischen Presse (1945–1960)," in *Fremde – Heimat – Sachsen.*

was to be especially emphasised since the number of "resettlers" that had fled East Germany to West Germany up to 1961 offered a more obvious explanation: among the total of 2.7 million so-called "Republic refugees" (*Republikflüchtlinge*), no less than 900,000 were former refugees and expellees from the German or German-settled territories in Eastern Europe.[27]

The order to write about success stories and the enforcement of an official speaking and memory ban was only partially successful on the private level. Although the "resettlers" were supposed to be transformed into "people without a past",[28] they nevertheless used forms and means of private memory, founded niches, or created their own individual scopes of action.[29] In many cases, therefore, the circles of friends and family provided areas for remembering. One interviewee thus distinguished between public and inner-family recollections:

> "So, amongst ourselves, when we were all together, we would talk about everything. Here, there were no taboos. However, on the outside, it was very noticeable; I would like to say, it was like a ban because you had to keep quiet about it. You couldn't say anything. Because, if someone did say something, then there was immediate trouble. Therefore, in the outside world, we did not dare to say too much about the flight or the expulsions – no way".[30]

Neubauernfamilien in der Nachkriegszeit, ed. Ira Spieker and Sönke Friedreich (Beucha and Markkleeberg: Sax-Verlag, 2014), 369–396.

27 Schwartz, "Vertriebenenproblem und Umsiedlerpolitik." According to the differing statistic data, see also: Helge Heidemeyer, *Flucht und Zuwanderung aus der SBZ/DDR 1945/1949–1961. Die Flüchtlingspolitik der Bundesrepublik Deutschland bis zum Bau der Berliner Mauer* (Düsseldorf: Droste, 1994), 44; Michael Schwartz, "Kriegsfolgelasten und 'Aufbaugesellschaft'. Vertriebene, Bombengeschädigte und Kriegsbeschädigte in den langen fünfziger Jahren der DDR," in *Vor dem Mauerbau. Politik und Gesellschaft in der DDR der fünfziger Jahre*, ed. Dierk Hoffmann (Munich: Oldenbourg, 2003), 184–185.

28 Uta Bretschneider, "Menschen ohne Vergangenheit? Zum Umgang mit Flucht und Vertreibung in der SBZ/DDR," conference paper presented at "Unsichtbares Gepäck. Zur Bewältigung von Kriegs- und Fluchterfahrungen seit 1945," Project at Museum Friedland, September 18–19, 2014, Friedland.

29 The illegal meetings of "Umsiedler" in the zoo of Halle are well-known, but everyday situations offered possibilities of communication as well.

30 Peters, Rudolf, (born 1940). Fled with his family in January 1945 from Waldheide, Silesia (today Świętoszyn, Poland). After many stops along the way, they settled in Altenhain (Saxony). Interview by the author Uta Bretschneider, March 8, 2013, line 59.

For many areas of life in the GDR, such a double standard of speaking was typical. This form of communication strategy was in particular a result of the regime's surveillance system. A focus for the State Security Service always included the "resettlers". This hampered attempts at speaking of memories and experiences all the more.[31]

The partial taboo, with which the forced migration at the end of World War II was stamped, ran throughout public life in the Soviet Occupation Zone and the GDR. Forms of remembrance such as monuments, commemorations, and associations with a focus on regional identity were banned. The emotional baggage of over four million people – their experiences, customs, traditions, values, and biographical development – was to have as little influence on the new society as possible.

The only exception to references to the past concerned their professional qualifications and training, which were absolutely needed (and used) for building the new socialist society after the war. A processing of the flight experience beyond the private context hardly occurred and, as a result, there came no treatment. The emergence of any sort of identity promotion – or at least of any sort of 'identity-stabilising communities of remembrance' – was therefore prevented. The flight and expulsion experience was undesirable as an aspect of identity.

Historian Günther Lottes has stated that:

> "In totalitarian systems, memory is quite simply decreed. There exists a prevailing (and official) memory that can assert itself through broadly reaching control. Alternative memories are either not allowed, or, in the best case, are marginalised".[32]

This finding precisely corresponds to the 'policy of forgetting' in the Soviet Occupation Zone and the GDR.

---

31 Heike Amos, "Feindliche Organisationen. Die Sicht des MfS auf die Vertriebenenverbände in der Bundesrepublik Deutschland," *Zeitschrift des Forschungsverbundes SED-Staat* 20 (2006): 20–35.

32 Günther Lottes, "Erinnerungskulturen zwischen Psychologie und Kulturwissenschaft," in *Erinnerung, Gedächtnis, Wissen – Studien zur kulturwissenschaftlichen Gedächtnisforschung*, ed. Günter Oesterle (Göttingen: Vandenhoeck & Ruprecht, 2005), 180.

Culture of Remembrance

It was not until the 1980s that the situation of the GDR's policy of forgetting would gradually start to relax. This would prove to have an impact on the Moor family story: after the death of her husband in the early 80s, Gertrud Moor sold the farm house to the new open-air museum in Kloster Veßra. She then moved to a small city close by. The "resettler's" farm house became a museum. Today, it is still a part of the Open-air Museum Kloster Veßra. It has been preserved and essentially remains the same as it was presented 30 years ago. The house does not explain the Moor family's history, with all its twists and turns; instead, it shows how a small farming establishment looked in the 1950s. With this, the stereotype of the success story of the "resettlers" in the GDR is perpetuated – that is, in accordance with contemporary terminology, they became 'normal citizens' within a very short period. In coming years, the exibition is to be supplemented by quotations from the Moor's daughters and by further information according to the GDR's resettler policy.

Individual memories are based on personal experiences that are influenced by external factors such as the politics of memory in restrictive state systems, and they can compete, contradict, or complement one another.[33] Simultaneously, there occurs a sort of 'over-formation' of one's own existing memories through hearing the stories of others, and through official memory narratives as they were told, for example, by monuments and in official memorial ceremonies, as well as through media. These meanings of history, situations, experiences, and stories then seep into one's own memory bank. In these processes, a changing political imprint (such as after the end of the Cold War period) also changes parts of the personal ideas of memories. Memories are always in a state of flux. In addition, there occurs reinterpretations and re-codings shaped by subsequent experiences because we are constantly looking back from a current present to an occurred present.[34] With the passing of time and subsequent life experiences, an experience will be assessed and told differently than it would be directly after the event. For this reason, so many native witnesses, for example, in our present topic remember the integration of the so-called resettlers as seamless and largely free of conflict:

---

33 Assmann, *Erinnerungsräume*, 16.

34 Angela Keppler, "Soziale Formen individuellen Erinnerns. Die kommunikative Tradierung von (Familien)Geschichte," in *Das soziale Gedächtnis*, ed. Harald Welzer (Hamburg: HIS Verlag, 2001), 137.

> "Since the resettlers were so quickly taken in by us into our village life, we did not have any trouble. Although it often happened that the resettlers stole things, we ourselves never had any trouble with that. They were able to integrate themselves without being offended, either religiously or any other way. They were very hard-working and that was very much respected by the villagers".[35]

Here, all of the points of conflict, disputation, and confrontation have fallen into oblivion. The interview partner is today still recounting the myth of rapid integration. And – as most of the interviewees – she uses the topos of the acquisition of recognition through work. At the same time, this also reflects the self-perception of many expellees as "poor but hard-working".

Only with the end of the SED state in 1989 could flight and expulsion in the eastern part of Germany also become a public "place of memory" (*Erinnerungsort*),[36] as defined by the French sociologist Pierre Nora. Homeland trips, associations, monuments, and publications established themselves as memory and media forms. In the beginning, however, they found many of the established practices of similar organisations in West Germany to be very strange. The traces of the 40 years of GDR's policy of forgetting are not to be removed in a relatively short period.

Aleida Assmann believes that a memory culture, in reference to traumatic events, ceases after about a 15- to 30-year period.[37] In the territory of the former GDR it lasted for more than four decades. Only after the upheaval of 1989/90 was work on the catching up of memory able to begin. In particular, it was the former "resettler children" – a group who had previously distanced themselves from the 'expellee status' of their parents – who became actively engaged in examining their past.[38] Thus, a new "remembering space" unfolded.[39] Now an explanation of state repression in the memory culture was possible.

However, the new possibilities nonetheless had to consider and adapt to the changes in the collective German situation of the time. Furthermore, it can be

---

35 Schenk, Jutta, born 1941 in Kloster Veßra (mother was a housewife and part-time farmer, as well as a seasonal worker on the estate). Parents took over a new farmstead in 1945 and were founding members of the agricultural cooperative "Vorwärts" ("onwards!") in Kloster Veßra in 1953. Members of cooperative until resigning in 1965 and moving out of Kloster Veßra. Interview by the author Uta Bretschneider, May 10, 2011, line 302.

36 Pierre Nora, *Zwischen Geschichte und Gedächtnis* (Berlin: Wagenbach, 1990).

37 Aleida Assmann, *Der lange Schatten der Vergangenheit. Erinnerungskultur und Geschichtspolitik* (Munich: Beck, 2006), 28.

38 Schwartz, "Vertriebenenproblem und Umsiedlerpolitik."

39 Assmann, *Erinnerungsräume.*

assumed that the process involved in the establishment of the theme into public memory culture to this day is yet to be completed. Currently, the generational change in reference to the 'memoria' is showing itself to be particularly active, reaching down to the grandchildren of the "children of flight and expulsion".[40]

On the one hand, it will likely lead to a partial loss in meaning, while on the other it may lead to a new-codification and likewise to a new engagement of changed memory keepers and media. Thus, the homeland books of the expellees, in which mental maps, photographs and documents are gathered together, will more than likely find their form onto Internet sites. Even the practice of taking 'home trips' (*Heimatreisen*) has changed. For some time now, the grandchildren of the refugees and expellees have been researching the regions of their family's origin in Eastern Europe from the point of view of a tourist.[41]

Around the year 2000 there was much talk about a "memory boom" as well as "Pastifying".[42] In general, what goes for remembrance culture also largely applies to the thematic areas of flight and expulsion – that is, the memory landscape is still growing. It has been transforming and changing since the reunification of Germany. The anniversary of the end of World War II in particular has been accompanied with a veritable memory boom. In the eastern part of Germany today things may now be expressed, which had previously not been allowed. However, it should not be forgotten that *the one* memory of flight, expulsion, and the new beginning in the Soviet Occupation Zone does not exist.

The statute alterations by the *Sudetendeutsche Landsmannschaft*, as described at the beginning of this paper, is a further symptom that the memory of (and the dealing with) flight and expulsion is constantly in flux – even, and especially, over the 70 years since the end of World War II.

Not least of all, the character of the process embodied by the memorial culture is shown by the establishment of a new memory marker in the year 2015. Since this time, the 20th of June has been known as the "Memorial Day for the Victims of Flight and Expulsion" (*Gedenktag für die Opfer von Flucht und Vertreibung*). The introduction of this national Memorial Day was preceded by protracted and tedious debates dating back to 2011.The opponents argued that there was no need to offer memory spaces to this topic. They saw a danger of

40 Silke Satjukow, *Kinder von Flucht und Vertreibung* (Erfurt: Landeszentrale für Politische Bildung Thüringen, 2007).

41 Sabine Marschall, "'Homesick tourism': Memory, Identity and (be)longing," *Current Issues in Tourism* 18, no. 9 (2015): 876–892.

42 Wolfrum, "Erinnerungskultur und Geschichtspolitik," 14; Pierre Nora, "Gedächtniskonjunktur," *Transit. Europäische Revue* 22 (2002): 18–31, here 18–19.

revanchist tendencies becoming strong again. The Memorial Day, one could say, is a controversial "memorial in time".[43]

However, this has hinted at a new dimension of the commemoration of the forced migration in 1945, as this date is also simultaneously known as "World Refugee Day". Therefore, this pushes the memory of the collapse of 1945 – and the fate of the German refugees and expellees – into a transnational and a transtemporal connection. In addition, it can be seen that those who experienced flight and expulsion at the end of World War II have not been known to show great empathy for the millions of people who are refugees today. In truth, it is just the opposite: the witnesses of that time have developed various narrative patterns in order to distance themselves from the refugees of today. However, that is a topic for a separate paper.

Bibliography

Amos, Heike. "Feindliche Organisationen. Die Sicht des MfS auf die Vertriebenenverbände in der Bundesrepublik Deutschland." *Zeitschrift des Forschungsverbundes SED-Staat*, 20 (2006): 20–35.

Amos, Heike. *Die Vertriebenenpolitik der SED 1949 bis 1990*. Munich: Oldenbourg, 2009.

Amos, Heike. *Vertriebenenverbände im Fadenkreuz. Aktivitäten der DDR-Staatssicherheit 1949 bis 1989*. Munich: De Gruyter, 2011.

Assmann, Aleida. *Erinnerungsräume. Formen und Wandlungen des kulturellen Gedächtnisses*. Munich: C. H. Beck, 1999.

Assmann, Aleida. "Jahrestage – Denkmäler in der Zeit." In *Jubiläum, Jubiläum … Zur Geschichte öffentlicher und privater Erinnerung*, edited by Paul Münch, 305–314. Essen: Klartext-Verlag, 2005.

Assmann, Aleida. *Der lange Schatten der Vergangenheit. Erinnerungskultur und Geschichtspolitik*. Munich: C. H. Beck, 2006.

Bretschneider, Uta. "'Die Bodenreform wurde auch für sie die Rettung'. 'Umsiedler' als Neubauern in der zeitgenössischen Presse (1945–1960)." In *Fremde – Heimat – Sachsen. Neubauernfamilien in der Nachkriegszeit*, edited by Ira Spieker and Sönke Friedreich, 369–396. Beucha and Markkleeberg: Sax-Verlag, 2014.

Bretschneider, Uta. "Zwangsmigration und Neubeheimatung. 'Umsiedler' als 'Neubauern' in der SBZ/DDR." In *Aufbrechen, Arbeiten, Ankommen. Mobilität und Migration im ländlichen Raum seit 1945*, edited by Rita Garstenauer and Anne Unterwurzacher, 37–52. Innsbruck et al.: Studienverlag, 2015.

43 Aleida Assmann, "Jahrestage – Denkmäler in der Zeit," in *Jubiläum, Jubiläum … Zur Geschichte öffentlicher und privater Erinnerung*, ed. Paul Münch (Essen: Klartext-Verlag, 2005), 305–314.

Bretschneider, Uta. *'Vom Ich zum Wir'? Flüchtlinge und Vertriebene als Neubauern in der LPG*. Leipzig: Leipziger Universitätsverlag, 2016.
Flach, Werner and Kouschil, Christa. *Kreuzritter in Trachten. Organisierter Revanchismus und seine Macher*. Leipzig: Urania-Verlag, 1984.
Heidemeyer, Helge. *Flucht und Zuwanderung aus der SBZ/DDR 1945/1949–1961. Die Flüchtlingspolitik der Bundesrepublik Deutschland bis zum Bau der Berliner Mauer*. Düsseldorf: Droste, 1994.
Hein, Christoph. *Landnahme*. Frankfurt: Suhrkamp, 2004.
Keppler, Angela. "Soziale Formen individuellen Erinnerns. Die kommunikative Tradierung von (Familien-)Geschichte." In *Das soziale Gedächtnis*, edited by Harald Welzer, 137–159. Hamburg: HIS Verlag, 2001.
Lottes, Günther. "Erinnerungskulturen zwischen Psychologie und Kulturwissenschaft." In *Erinnerung, Gedächtnis, Wissen – Studien zur kulturwissenschaftlichen Gedächtnisforschung*, edited by Günter Oesterle, 163–184. Göttingen: Vandenhoeck & Ruprecht, 2005.
Marschall, Sabine. "'Homesick tourism': Memory, Identity and (be)longing." *Current Issues in Tourism* 18, no. 9 (2015): 876–892.
Merker, Paul. *Die nächsten Schritte zur Lösung des Umsiedlerproblems*. Berlin: Dietz, 1947.
Niven, Bill. "On a supposed taboo: Flight and Refugees from the East in GDR Film and Television." *German Life and Letters* 65, no. 2 (2012): 216–236.
Nora, Pierre. *Zwischen Geschichte und Gedächtnis*. Berlin: Wagenbach, 1990.
Nora, Pierre. "Gedächtniskonjunktur." *Transit. Europäische Revue* 22 (2002): 18–31.
Satjukow, Silke. *Kinder von Flucht und Vertreibung*. Erfurt: Landeszentrale für Politische Bildung Thüringen, 2007.
Schwartz, Michael. "Umsiedlerpolitik in der Krise? Das Vertriebenenproblem in der Gründungsphase der DDR 1948–1950." In *Das letzte Jahr der SBZ. Politische Weichenstellungen und Kontinuitäten im Prozess der Gründung der DDR*, edited by Dierk Hoffmann and Harald Wentker, 185–205. Munich: Oldenbourg, 2000.
Schwartz, Michael. "'Zwangsheimat Deutschland'. Vertriebene und Kernbevölkerung zwischen Gesellschaftskonflikt und Integrationspolitik." In *Nachkrieg in Deutschland*, edited by Klaus Naumann, 114–48. Hamburg: HIS Verlag, 2001.
Schwartz, Michael. "Staatsfeind 'Umsiedler'." In *Die Flucht. Über die Vertreibung der Deutschen aus dem Osten*, edited by Stefan Aust and Stephan Burgdorff, 224–235. Bonn: Bundeszentrale für politische Bildung, 2003.
Schwartz, Michael. "Kriegsfolgelasten und 'Aufbaugesellschaft'. Vertriebene, Bombengeschädigte und Kriegsbeschädigte in den langen fünfziger Jahren der DDR." In *Vor dem Mauerbau. Politik und Gesellschaft in der DDR der fünfziger Jahre*, edited by Dierk Hoffmann, 165–190. Munich: Oldenbourg, 2003.
Schwartz, Michael. *Vertriebene und "Umsiedlerpolitik". Integrationskonflikte in den deutschen Nachkriegs-Gesellschaften und die Assimilationsstrategien in der SBZ/DDR 1945–1961*. Munich: De Gruyter, 2004.
Wille, Manfred. "Die Zentralverwaltung für deutsche Umsiedler – Möglichkeiten und Grenzen ihres Wirkens (1945–1948)." In *Sie hatten alles verloren. Flüchtlinge und Vertriebene*

in der Sowjetischen Besatzungszone Deutschlands, edited by Manfred Wille, Johannes Hoffmann, and Wolfgang Meinicke, 27–54. Wiesbaden: Harrassowitz, 1993.

Wolfrum, Edgar. "Erinnerungskultur und Geschichtspolitik als Forschungsfelder. Konzepte – Methoden – Themen." In *Reformation und Bauernkrieg. Erinnerungskultur und Geschichtspolitik im geteilten Deutschland*, edited by Jan Scheunemann, 13–32. Leipzig: Evangelische Verlagsanstalt, 2010.

Interviews

Lohner, Bärbel (born Moor), born 1940. She was driven out of the Landsberg an der Warthe district, Brandenburg (today Gorzów Wielkopolski, Poland) along with her family (her father was a prisoner of war). After many stops along the way, they landed in Kloster Veßra (Thuringia) in 1948. Interview by the author Uta Bretschneider. November 4, 2011.

Lösch, Ingeborg (born Moor), born 1939, sister of Bärbel Lohner. She was driven out of the Landsberg an der Warthe district, Brandenburg (today Gorzów Wielkopolski, Poland) along with her family (her father was a prisoner of war). After many stops along the way, they landed in Kloster Veßra (Thuringia) in 1948. Interview by the author Uta Bretschneider. May 12, 2011.

Peters, Rudolf, born 1940. Fled with his family in January 1945 from Waldheide, Silesia (today Świętoszyn, Poland). After many stops along the way, they settled in Altenhain (Saxony). Interview by the author Uta Bretschneider, March 8, 2013.

Schenk, Jutta, born 1941 in Kloster Veßra (mother was a housewife and part-time farmer, as well as a seasonal worker on the estate). Parents took over a new farmstead in 1945 and were founding members of the agricultural cooperative *Vorwärts* ("onwards!") in Kloster Veßra in 1953. Members of cooperative until resigning in 1965 and moving out of Kloster Veßra. Interview by the author Uta Bretschneider, May 10, 2011.

Internet Sources

Law text. "Gesetz zum Schutze des Friedens vom 15. Dezember 1950." Accessed September 6, 2017. http://www.verfassungen.de/de/ddr/friedensgesetz50.htm.

Zeit. "Sudetendeutsche verzichten auf 'Wiedergewinnung der Heimat'." Accessed September 6, 2017. http://www.zeit.de/gesellschaft/zeitgeschehen/2016-02/vertriebene-sudetendeutsche-verzichtwiedergewinnung-heimat.

Schwartz, Michael. "Vertriebenenproblem und Umsiedlerpolitik in der SBZ/DDR." Accessed September 6, 2017. http://www.fes.de/magdeburg/pdf/6_10_14_schwartz.pdf.

Philipp Wagner

Death at Sea as Accident or Disaster: The Case of the Missing Shipwreck in Lars Sund's *En lycklig liten ö* (2007)

In 2015 a global public was confronted with the effects of the European Union's migration politics. An increasing number of sunken boats and drowned migrants in the Mediterranean Sea came to be acknowledged as the so-called 'European Migrant Crisis' and caused temporary medial attention on the events. In particular, the picture of Alan Kurdi, a drowned boy lying on the beach, became iconic at the time and was widely disseminated through both traditional and social media. The incident of Alan Kurdi's death illustrates that nowadays new kinds of "moral spectatorship" emerge in a transnational public sphere provided by the Internet's social networks. Aesthetic traditions are thereby still relevant when it comes to appeal audiences in social media.[1] In the case of the recent events in the Mediterranean, the shipwreck motif can be considered the most important tradition and reference point. This paper aims to approach the shipwreck motif in the context of the 'European Migration Crisis' from a literary studies perspective.

European art and literature have depicted ships in distress for centuries. One notable outcome of this long history is that shipwrecks became "potent metaphors for some supposed larger truth such as the state of the nation, the workings of Providence, or the human condition", as defined by the literary scholar Carl Thompson in his introduction to the anthology *Shipwreck in Art and Literature: Images and Interpretations from Antiquity to the Present Day*.[2] Théodore Géricault's painting *The Raft of the Medusa* (1818/19), Daniel Defoe's novel *Robinson Crusoe* (1719) and Homers *Iliad* are prominent examples. Brigitte LeJuez and Olga Springer, who are also from the field of literary studies, even go so far as to say the shipwreck motif, with regard to its meta-

---

1 Mette Mortensen and Hans-Jörg Trenz, "Media Morality and Visual Icons in the Age of Social Media: Alan Kurdi and the Emergence of an Impromptu Public of Moral Spectatorship," *Javnost: The Public* 23, no 4 (2016): 348–349.

2 Carl Thompson, "Introduction," in *Shipwreck in Art and Literature: Images and Interpretations from Antiquity to the Present Day*, ed. Carl Thompson (London: Routledge, 2013), 2.

phorical potential, is "atemporal and universal".[3] When faced with this scholarly praise of the motif's potential, we are also intrigued by artistic and literary reactions to shipwreck in the Mediterranean today. It would take more than one paper to answer this question. Alternatively, one particular text, which configures the motif of shipwrecks with regard to Europe's migration politics in the Mediterranean Sea, is the main focus: the novel *En lycklig liten ö* [A Happy Little Island] by the Finland-Swedish author Lars Sund.[4] The novel's publication date shows that the 'European Migrant Crisis' cannot be reduced to the events of 2015.

Sund's novel is set on a fictional island in the Archipelago on Finland's Coast. Almost 100 water corpses are found on the island's beach. Their origin remains a mystery, because there is no news about a missing ship and the corpses are hard to identify. The reactions of the island's inhabitants are the main theme of the novel. Life in a maritime environment causes the inhabitants to become used to people dying at sea – for example, in the case of minor accidents. As more and more corpses arrive, a new feeling of discomfort spreads and theodical as well as existential questions are raised. Given the number of victims, a disaster must have occurred. Classical coping mechanisms fail in the face of this particular incident, because the search for the wrecked ship proves to be unsuccessful.

For this reason, *En lycklig liten ö* is analysed here with regard to its configuration of the shipwreck motif. First, two frames to interpret the usage of shipwrecks in art and literature from the theoretical discourse within cultural studies are outlined. In both cases, the mode of perspective presented to the audience has interpretative consequences for the classification of a shipwreck event as either an outstanding disaster or a mere (usual) accident. It depends on whether the position of spectator[5] or observer[6] is taken. After a short discussion of ways to perceive and interpret shipwrecks, the medialisation and communication of such events is thematised. Furthermore, the specificalities

3 Brigitte Le Juez and Olga Springer, "Introduction: Shipwrecks and Islands as Multilayered, Timeless Metaphors of Human Existence," in *Shipwreck and Island Motifs in Literature and the Arts*, ed. Brigitte Le Juez and Olga Springer (Leiden: Brill, 2015), 3.

4 Lars Sund, *En lycklig liten ö* (Helsinki: Söderström, 2007). All Swedish quotes are my own translation.

5 Hans Blumenberg, *Schiffbruch mit Zuschauer. Paradigma einer Daseinsmetapher*, 6th edition (Frankfurt: Suhrkamp, 2014).

6 Burkhardt Wolf, "Schiffbruch mit Beobachter. Zur Geschichte des nautischen Gefahrenwissens," in *Die Unordnung der Dinge. Eine Wissens- und Mediengeschichte des Unfalls*, ed. Christian Kassung (Bielefeld: Transcript, 2009), 19–48.

of the narrator in Sund's *En lycklig liten ö* are examined. It is important to note that Sund's narrator is inspired by Walter Benjamin's[7] 1936 theoretical Essay, *The Storyteller* [*Der Erzähler*], which gives to the reader a special twist to his position as mediator. A close reading demonstrates the narrator's attempts to provide an alternative point of view on shipwrecks for the reader. The outcome is a configuration of the shipwreck motif that opens up a new perspective on literature's role in coping with collective traumas in today's media culture. In this article it is argued that Lars Sund's Novel *En lycklig liten ö* promotes a perspective of agency for the reader.

Spectators of Disasters or Observers of Accidents? Perspectives on Shipwrecks from Cultural Studies

One of the most prominent books on the iconic and metaphoric significance of shipwrecks in the field of cultural studies is Hans Blumenberg's (2014 [1979]) *Schiffbruch mit Zuschauer* [Shipwreck with Spectator], a philosophical essay on the phenomenon of shipwrecks. The essay also offers a short history of ideas about shipwrecks, which makes it a central reference point within academic discourse dedicated to the topic.

In the present context Blumenberg's remarks on the peak of shipwreck depictions in the 18th century are most relevant here. Blumenberg argues that during the enlightenment metaphors from the field of theatre were combined with the notion of shipwreck as a philosophical thought experiment. The modern – mostly metaphorical – understanding of shipwrecks was thereby coined.[8] It is important to note that a spectator [Zuschauer] in German is an aesthetic category and is thought of as being part of an audience. In the scenario described by Blumenberg, the spectator watches the wrecking of a ship from a safe distance similar to people in chairs at a theatre or cinema. The event of a shipwreck, therefore, has characteristics of a thrilling show with a moral. Such shows are intended to remind the spectator of their safety. A good show should give reason for the contemplation of life's challenges. For this reason, Blumenberg has a specific scenario in mind: the shipwreck figures act as a metaphor for the precarity of life. While safe, the position of the spectator grants the opportunity

7 Walter Benjamin, "The Storyteller: Reflections on the Works of Nikolai Leskov," in *The Novel: An Anthology of Criticism and Theory 1900–2000*, ed. Dorothy J. Hale (Malden, Mass.: Blackwell Publishing, 2006), 362–378.

8 Blumenberg, *Schiffbruch mit Zuschauer*, 51.

to draw lessons about the constitution of human life. In this way, the wrecking of a ship in the eyes of a spectator is always a disaster.

Blumenberg's history of ideas offers an initial method to frame shipwrecks for cultural analysis. Pictures and narratives where shipwrecks feature as disasters intend to depict life changing moments. In literature, shipwreck scenes can easily rely on this metaphorical background. Shipwrecks function as narratological devices to indicate turning points within a story.[9] This function applies the "shipwreck-with-spectator" scenario in a condensed form: the horrors of a shipwreck are sufficient as explanation for extreme changes in a protagonist's way of life.

In the German discourse on shipwrecks a second method of framing an analysis on the cultural significance of them has occurred. The literary scholar Burkhardt Wolf[10] outlined in his paper *Schiffbruch mit Beobachter* the "shipwreck-with-observer" scenario, which provides an alternative perspective in cultural studies:[11] Being a "Beobachter" is something different to being a "Zuschauer", because "Beobachter" means observer. Observers are different, because they have an analytical task. The observer is searching for the traces of a shipwreck; he is also safe but not at all interested in entertainment. For this reason, the observer only counts the evidence of a shipwreck, because they want to calculate real risks and thereby avoid these risks in the future. It is the observer's social task to evaluate and clarify security questions. The wrecking of a ship always features in the observer's perspective as an accident. If the wrecking of a ship is an accident, then there might be mistakes that can be fixed. Accidents happen in routines and these routines can be improved.[12]

The scenario described by Wolf merely occurs on an extratextual level. It is nevertheless important in analysing depictions of shipwrecks in literature, because it underlines a parallel approach towards the scene of a shipwreck in modern times. Wolf focuses on the mnemonic function of texts. This function means that literary texts contain and distribute important memories. Rather than being a reminder of the precarity of life, the telling of shipwreck narratives

---

9 Thompson, "Introduction," 5–7; Le Juez and Springer, "Introduction," 2.

10 Wolf, "Schiffbruch mit Beobachter."

11 In total Wolf offers four categories for the classification of shipwreck scenarios. He favours the "shipwreck-with-observer" scenario, but also includes Blumenberg's "shipwreck-with-spectator" scenario. Besides these two, Wolf develops the "shipwreck-without-spectator" scenario and the "shipwreck-without-witnesses" scenario: Ibid., 22. The former means a dramatic account of a shipwreck missing, while the latter describes a case where almost no trace and only short records exist.

12 Ibid., 38–39.

shows a need for revision. Using the example of Homer's *Odyssey*,[13] Wolf argues that a literary text itself could be used as a tool in this revision. This ancient Greek text can be considered a source of knowledge with regard to seafaring. Going to sea is then considered something quite ordinary and not primarily a transgression of natural boundaries, as Blumenberg suggests.[14]

Based on the theoretical scenarios just presented, a shipwrecking is either a disaster or an accident. The classification depends on which perspective applies. 'Disaster' and 'accident' are not interchangeable terms. In his cultural history of disaster, *Katastrophen: Eine Kulturgeschichte vom 16. bis ins 21. Jahrhundert*, historian Francois Walter explains that accidents are a phenomenon of industrialisation.[15] Accidents occur under daily routines and in working processes – they can be avoided by optimisation. On the other hand, disasters have an older history that originally connected them to the thought of a divine incident: if something ends in a disaster, the reason could be metaphysical. Furthermore, a disaster could be God's punishment for human wrong-doing.[16] Similarly, Walter suggests that the occurrence of World War I blurs the dividing line between these categories. As the first transnational catastrophe, World War I is considered to be caused by humanity itself and not by nature or God alone. The consequence still today is that feelings of guilt have a collective dimension, not an individual one.[17]

The Medialisation and Communication of Disasters

At the beginning of the 21st century a cultural pessimism about the role of media in the perception of disasters can be noted. Walter argues that the medialisation of disasters is the major cultural technique to cope with collective traumas.[18] For Walter, novels and especially movies are very helpful in processing disastrous events. During the 20th century, this cultural technique was increasingly used and in Walter's opinion led to reduced effectiveness: limited to a screen, the medialisation of disasters nowadays lacks aesthetics and theodicy. The

13 Ibid., 12–21.
14 Blumenberg, *Schiffbruch mit Zuschauer*, 9.
15 François Walter, *Katastrophen: Eine Kulturgeschichte vom 16. bis ins 21. Jahrhundert* (Stuttgart: Reclam, 2010), 158.
16 Ibid., 52.
17 Ibid., 180.
18 Ibid., 183.

public is left in a state of disorientation and uncertainty.[19] One can apply to Walter's opinion the two perspectives on shipwrecking offered by Blumenberg and Wolf.[20] Walter would certainly agree that the "observer" perspective, as described by Wolf, is the dominant method of perceiving disasters in all media nowadays. Not only shipwrecking, but every kind of disaster is more or less treated like an accident. Consequently, every difference in the representation of real and imaginary disasters on the level of visual media, especially, makes for example television news and motion pictures almost indistinguishable. For Walter, a feeling of safety is no longer guaranteed, because neither the observer nor the spectator is able to identify disastrous events as dangerous and process the experience accordingly.

In a less alarming tone than expressed by Walter[21] but also with concern for today's handling of traumatic events by the media, is the Collaborative Research Centre 923, "Threatened Order – Societies under Stress" at the University of Tuebingen (funded by the German Research Foundation DFG, 2011–2015).[22] The Collaborative Research Centre was established in 2011 for the purpose of researching scenarios of threats, their social impact from a cultural studies perspective, and aims for new approaches to understand rapid social change.

One conclusion presented by the Collaborative Research Centre from the first funding period is that researching threats means evaluating how societies communicate them. The discourse about threats is labelled by the Collaborative Research Centre as threat-related communication ("Bedrohungskommunikation"). According to the historians Ewald Frie and Mischa Meier[23] (from the team at the Collaborative Research Centre), a special focus on the conditions of success of such threat-related communication should be the object of study, because its establishment goes hand in hand with the declaration of threats by certain actors. Once a threat is declared, it is communicated in an effective manner, rapidly receives more attention than other topics, and discussions are mainly focused on arguments about (the lack of) time.[24] These identified

19 Ibid., 285.

20 Blumenberg, *Schiffbruch mit Zuschauer*; Wolf, "Schiffbruch mit Beobachter."

21 Walter, *Katastrophen*.

22 The Collaborative Research Centre, "Threatened Order – Societies under Stress" continues its work in a second funding period from 2015–2019.

23 Ewald Frie and Mischa Meier, "Bedrohte Ordnungen. Gesellschaften unter Stress im Vergleich," in *Aufruhr – Katastrophe – Konkurrenz – Zerfall. Bedrohte Ordnungen als Thema der Kulturwissenschaften*, ed. Ewald Frie and Mischa Meier (Tübingen: Mohr Siebeck, 2014), 1–30.

24 Ibid., 20–25.

steps of communicating threats could be used to structure and compare case studies as well as to identify recurring patterns. The Collaborative Research Centre aims for such patterns, especially, in order to provide a data basis for future projects on the optimisation of threat-related communication patterns.[25]

The role of media has to be evaluated, as the corresponding arguments by Frie and Meier[26] and Walter[27] show. Both sides focus primarily on the news coverage. Literary Studies, however, can see this interest in medialisation as a chance to take a closer look at the literary representations of news and disasters. Literature, as a special form of media, has the potential for medial self-reflection. The variety of narrative devices and their creative combination is literature's strength. In this way, the analysis of motifs and their configuration – for example, the shipwreck – is of special interest.

Literature has a crucial part in shaping the way disasters are remembered. Astrid Erll, a scholar of literature and memory studies, argues in her introduction to *Memory in Culture*:

> "The level of configuration is [...] the key to literature's role as a medium of cultural memory. It is here, that literary works bring together, reshape and restructure real and imaginary practices of remembering and forgetting. With their transition into the literary text, elements of cultural memory are separated from their original contexts and can be combined and arranged in novel ways, into new and different memory narratives".[28]

On the one hand, in literature it follows that the recurring patterns of threat-related communication in the sense of "real and imaginary practices of remembering and forgetting" might be present and identifiable. On the other hand, there is always the possibility that these patterns are also altered in literature in a lasting way. The "new and different memory narratives" result from such alterations and can be analysed by paying attention to the structures and methods of presentation in a literary text. This approach is favoured in the following close reading of Lars Sund's[29] novel.

25 Ibid., 27.
26 Ibid.
27 Walter, *Katastrophen.*
28 Astrid Erll, *Memory in Culture* (Houndsmills: Palgrave Macmillan, 2011), 154.
29 Sund, *En lycklig liten ö.*

Storytelling against Death: The Importance of the Narrator in Lars Sund's *En lycklig liten ö*

Already, the motto of Lars Sund's[30] *En lycklig liten ö* indicates that this novel was written with some consciousness about literature's self-reflexive potential and therefore offers a solid case to trace the configuration of the shipwreck motif. In Walter Benjamin's[31] *The Storyteller*, the following is quoted in Swedish translation at the beginning of the novel: "Death is the sanction of everything the storyteller can tell".[32]

At first glance, Benjamin's essay seems as culturally pessimistic as the recent research about media and disaster. The essay is written under the impression of World War I. This war was still a historical singularity for Benjamin, and he argues that this singular event initiated the decline of narrating. For Benjamin, narrating consists mainly of the exchange of lived experience, but the war proved that lived experience is false. Nobody could imagine the war as it was on the basis of his or her previous lived experience.[33]

Benjamin claims that the emergence of information contributes to the decline of narrative. When everything is information and therefore a verified fact, not much remains (and might be fictionalised by the imagination of a narrator). The presence and accessibility of news media devalues the social relevance of narrative.[34] These assumptions by Benjamin might be considered proof for Walter's[35] analysis of the historical development of news coverage and the perception of disasters in the 20th century. On the other hand, Benjamin follows another agenda in his essay. A culturally pessimistic commentary on the state of today's world, as it is presented at the end of Walter's *History of Disaster*, is not what Benjamin is aiming for. Rather, he sets out in an attempt to reanimate narrative by making a poignant argument: narrative is not supposed to die; narrative is alive by telling about death and mortality.[36]

In keeping with Benjamin, the social relevance of narrating is kept alive in the modern form of the novel. Novels, then, are an instrument of survival for

---

30 Ibid.

31 Benjamin, "The Storyteller."

32 "Döden ger sanktion åt allt som berättaren kan skildra."

33 Benjamin's argument could be considered confirmation for Walter's thesis, that World War I was a historical turning point for the perception of disasters, as mentioned above (Walter, *Katastrophen*, 180; Benjamin, "The Storyteller," 362–363).

34 Benjamin, "The Storyteller," 365–366.

35 Walter, *Katastrophen*.

36 Benjamin, "The Storyteller," 373.

the modern individual. Reading about another person's life and death is what enables the modern individual to go on with his own life:

> "The novel is significant, therefore, not because it presents someone else's fate to us, perhaps didactically, but because this stranger's fate by virtue of the flame which consumes it yields us the warmth which we never draw from, our fare. What draws the reader to the novel is the hope of warming his shivering life with a death he reads about".[37]

In Benjamin's view, the novel does not primarily have an educative function. Benjamin would probably refuse an all-too-clinical understanding of literature as 'medicine' to cope with collective traumas. In any case, Benjamin would not assume that recovery from trauma is possible; rather, the novel nourishes the hope of the modern individual to not be alone in the world.

Therefore, Benjamin does not aim for the optimisation of threat-related communication. From his point of view, identifying patterns for a better understanding of social change is not a main goal from a literary studies perspective on the narrator. The approach to literature as presented by the "shipwreck-with-observer" scenario would also be beyond the scope of such a perspective. Information about historical circumstances are secondary when it comes to close reading and its focus on structures and modes of presentation. Alternatively, Benjamin might favour the "shipwreck-with-spectator" scenario, because the 'thrill' of the show might nourish hope for the modern individual. Speaking less in a metaphorical sense, one could also say that presenting an old motif in a new and altered way might appeal to a novel's audience as well as provide a thought-provoking impulse.

Looking out for the Shipwreck in Lars Sund's *En lycklig liten ö*

Lars Sund's[38] novel *En lycklig liten ö* offers an interesting case with regard to the frames outlined in analysing cultural representations of shipwrecks, because an actual shipwreck is missing in the story. Neither the "observer" nor the "spectator" scenario is easily applicable; rather, feelings of disorientation and uncertainty in today's medialised world are addressed in the novel using a complex

37 Ibid.

38 Sund, *En lycklig liten ö.*

narrative structure – inspired by Benjamin's[39] *The Storyteller* – and references to several mythological and religious plot elements.

A complex and multi-referential piece of literature is already indicated by the novel's original title: in Swedish, the title *En lycklig liten ö* sounds similar to the term 'Lycksalighetens Ö', which means *fortunate island*. The title bears another meaning besides the air of an idyll. This could be read as an important hint to ancient myths, where the fortunate isles are paradise-like places. Access to these mythological islands is exclusive to the not-living, who earned their place there through an exemplary or heroic lifestyle.[40] Therefore, the island in the novel might not only be a place for a happy community, but might also be associated with an otherworld.

The novel starts with a separated introduction. In this introduction the making of the following story is located on a computer screen. Rather than being just a technical device for receiving information, the computer screen is thereby also presented as a site of production. A third-person narrator describes how a person – called the scribe ["skrivaren"] – creates an imaginary world. In this way, the reader is presented at least two different possible sources for the story: a) the narrator, and b) the scribe. The narrator is the source of the story. This source does not seem to be identical to a second entity in the text, the so-called scribe; otherwise, the narrator would not, for example, talk about the scribe in the third person. On the other hand, it is apparent that the scribe writes the story. As indicated by the job description, his task is writing *only*. A scribe's profession was always just to copy or lay down the words of others. Overall, the reader does not know who is responsible for the story that has been told.

This complex narrative structure becomes even more confusing because of an added layer of references, especially to the Bible. For example, the first sentence of the introduction echoes Genesis: "In the beginning, the screen was blank and empty and the scribe's fingers rested on the keyboard".[41] Analogies like this are expanded on throughout the following pages of the introduction. As the text proceeds, a description is given of how the scribe types and in doing so first creates the sky of an imaginary place. Then the sea is created before the land, and the plants and all the animals come into being Finally, the first human in the narrative is set in place and called Adam. The introduction ends

39 Benjamin, "The Storyteller."

40 Volkmar Billig, *Inseln. Geschichte einer Faszination* (Berlin: Matthes & Seitz, 2010), 27–28.

41 "I begynnelsen låg datorskärmen öde och tom och skrivarens fingrar vilade på tangentbordet." Sund, *En lycklig liten ö*, 7.

with Adam lying unconscious on the beach. The scribe or the narrator or both, therefore, have explicit god-like features in this story.

Following the introduction, the first chapter begins with an e-mail that contains a police report about the discovery of a male corpse. It is easy for the reader to conclude that the corpse is the deceased Adam, who is known from the introduction of the novel.

There are several e-mails in the narrative, which are marked typographically. These e-mails enable the narrator to show his ambiguity and his detachment from the scribe as in the scene, for example, where the narrator comments on the e-mails written by a policeman:

> "With the help of electronic devices, we can intercept and read his messages in the police's internal network, even if such an act is illegal and the scribe risks a charge for hacking. Sheriff Riggert von Haartman's thoughts we are by contrast not able to intercept with electronic or other devices. We can't see through his eyes".[42]

In this quote, the narrator explicitly claims he is not identical to the scribe, because only the scribe could face prosecution for hacking. At the same time, the narrator includes the reader using the personal pronoun "we" in his misdeeds of privacy violation. By using "we", the narrator implies that he witnesses scenes in the novel along with the reader. Furthermore, the narrator states his inability to give insight into the policeman's thoughts. The narrator's statement about his inability to look inside the head also shows the unreliability of the narrator. In other instances, the narrator is able to tell completely what the characters are thinking about.

Throughout the novel in its entirety, the narrator uses markers of reality to provide a feeling of familiarity with the narrated world in a two-fold way. On the one hand, the narrator refers to a contemporary state of technology and consequently, to the daily life of the reader. On the other hand, he addresses the collective memory. It is part of the narrative strategy in Lars Sund's *En lycklig liten ö* to confront the reader with elements of the past. Several disastrous events such as the sinking of the ferry *Estonia* for example, and also the reactor breaking down in Chernobyl occurred in the narrated world. This strategy

---

42 "Med hjälp av elektronisk utrustning kan vi fånga upp och läsa hans meddelanden i polisens interna datornät, trots att ett dylikt förfarande är lagstridgt och skrivaren riskerar åtal för dataintrång. Länsman Riggert von Haartmans tankar är vi däremot inte i stånd att uppfånga med elektroniska eller andra medel. Vi kan inte se genom hans ögon." Ibid., 125.

becomes most apparent in a chapter about the dreams of the island inhabitants.[43] At this point in the story the islanders show a clear tendency towards racist attitudes as more and more corpses arrive on the island.

Accordingly, when a politician dreams of being visited by a man speaking German, a reference to the Shoah might at first be implicit for the reader: "KD Mattson dreamed about a man with a white long beard and black suit, who entered his kitchen, bowed and uttered: *Wie Sie sind, waren wir auch einmals* [sic!]. The man bowed again and just stood and waited".[44] The phrase 'like you, we once have been' could be understood as a comparison to the population of Nazi Germany, which may be the most present entity of collective memory at this point in the narration. Close to the end of the novel another explanation is revealed in a speech by a chaplain:

> "On medieval pictures that depict the devastating plague you see often the dead greeting the still-alive with the words: 'Like you, we once have been. Like us, you will once be'. In front of Death we humans are all alike, death is our common fate no matter where we are from, which skin color we have, what language we speak. We all have the right to be treated equal, regardless being dead or alive".[45]

The sentence in German, which is already familiar to the reader from the dreaming scene, is reproduced in Swedish by the chaplain. This central sentence is followed by another: "Like you, we once have been. Like us, you will once be". Both sentences together point to the universality of death, as the chaplain explains. It is the tradition of the late medieval Dance of Death that comes into play and is reactivated in order to advertise the ideas of equality and Christian love.

As a motif, the Dance of Death is far more important than the shipwreck in Lars Sund's *En lycklig liten ö.* This twist is important to note – that is, tension is built up through the entire novel as the search for the missing shipwreck

43 The corpses in this chapter are called "strangers." The term "strangers" marks not only the alterity between the living and the dead but also the opposition between the island's 'own' people and the 'others' from outside the island.

44 "KD Mattsson drömde om en karl med vitt tovigt skägg och svart kostym, som steg in hans kök, bugade sig och yttrade: *Wie Sie sind, waren wir auch einmals* [sic!]. Mannen bugade sig en gång till och ställde sig att vänta." Sund, *En lycklig liten ö,* 145–146.

45 "På medeltida bildar som skildrar pestens härjningar ser man ofta de döda hälsa de ännu levande med orden: 'Såsom ni är har vi också varit. Såsom vi är ska ni också bli'. Inför döden är vi människor lika, döden är vårt gemensamma öde oberoende av varifrån vi kommer, vilken hudfärg vi än har, vilket språk vi än talar. Vi har alla rätt att bli behandlade lika, oavsett om vi är döda eller levande." Ibid., 278.

is followed. The reader accompanies the characters and probably identifies with them, as one is likely to want to know the reason for the corpses on the beach. While identifying with the characters and searching for a metaphysical or technological reason, the reader is free to choose to take either the role of the "spectator",[46] the "observer"[47] or both alternately. Descriptions of an awful disaster are nevertheless missing, so the reader as a spectator may become disappointed from time to time. Hard evidence, which enables the avoidance of further accidents, is also not present in the narrative. Every investigation performed by an observer leads to nothing.

Regardless of with whom the reader identifies and which role is taken, the active search for an explanation may result in frustration. An explanation is already given in the introductory chapter, when the first dead body is created by the scribe without any shipwreck. In this god-like act the first character is simply created without life.

Even if death is omnipresent in the entire novel and, according to its motto, giving sanctions to everything the narrator might tell, the assumption of a pessimistic world view would not fit. Rather, the exposure of the Dance of Death motif points more towards an attempt to create a memento mori through the telling of this story. For a memento mori, not only is consciousness regarding death central, but remembering the dead also becomes a meaningful demand. In the context of the novel this demand is executed by way of the several references to collective memory. These references are crucial for the configuration of both motifs: the Dance of Death and the shipwreck.

At the same time, the novel follows Benjamin's essayistic thought that memory is the opposite to death and therefore an important part of narration. According to Benjamin, a narration always contains memory, which has a counteracting effect on the power of death: "Only by virtue of a comprehensive memory can epic writing absorb the course of events on the one hand and, with the passing of these, make its peace with the power of death on the other".[48] Through traditions, as Benjamin continues, an intertextual web is created, which entails memory and is characteristic of literature. The narrator's speech in *En lycklig liten ö* can be considered a plea for the social relevance of literature, because the traditions of the shipwreck and Dance of Death motif, and also their humanistic potential are reactivated.

46 Blumenberg, *Schiffbruch mit Zuschauer.*
47 Wolf, "Schiffbruch mit Beobachter."
48 Benjamin, "The Storyteller," 370–371.

The Prospect of Agency for the Reader

Lars Sund's[49] novel *En lycklig liten ö* offers what the news on the screen lacks, according to Francois Walter's[50] cultural history of disaster. The several references to religious motifs open up theodical questions – for example, why does evil exist in this world? Why do people have to suffer? And why do the god-like narrator and scribe create a paradisiacal 'happy little island' just to confront its inhabitants with the horror of death? Herein the aesthetic dimension arises: the nominated questions result on the one hand from the novel's intertextual references to the Bible; on the other, the explicit comments on the almightiness of the writer are part of a metaperspective on narrativity. The novel provides such a perspective in order to highlight problems of contemporary news coverage and threat-related communication. For example, one journalist in the story even doubts her profession. In place of informing people, she has the feeling of contributing to a never-ending flood of Information: "Besides, I have started wondering, if reporting has any benefit. Sure, people become indignant, if one exposes injustice and suffering, but they forget so quickly. We are overwhelmed by information, but at the same time it seems that we know less and less".[51] This journalist expresses a feeling of powerlessness. It seems that the narrator of the novel literally takes the reader by the hand in order that they overcome their feelings of disorientation and uncertainty. The use of "we" by the narrator draws the reader up to the level of his metaperspective – to see the events 'from above'. Nevertheless, the reader faces a complex narrative structure that calls attention to the way these events are represented. It remains unclear whoever tells the story. Therefore, the theodical question – traditionally tied to disasters like shipwrecks – gets transformed in Lars Sund's *En lycklig liten ö*. The question is not who or what is responsible for the suffering; rather, it is who or what is causing attention to it. A question such as this points towards an analysis of the ways threats and disasters are communicated, as suggested by the Collaborative Research Centre – that is, "threatened order".[52] However, the metaperspective offered by the novel is not necessarily a good source for generalisations regarding such communication, because it imitates this com-

49 Sund, *En lycklig liten ö.*

50 Walter, *Katastrophen.*

51 "Dessutom har jag börjat undra om alla reportage tjänar någonting till. Visst blir folk upprörda när man exponerar orättvisor och lidande, men de glömmer lika snabbt. Vi överöses med information, men samtidigt verkar det som om vi vet allt mindre." Sund, *En lycklig liten ö,* 243.

52 Frie and Meier, "Bedrohte Ordnungen."

munication for aesthetic purposes. As an alternative, the novel offers an essayistic approach, which is in keeping with Benjamin's[53] thoughts on narrating.

In *En lycklig liten ö* the narrator draws from collective memory in several ways to pose and transform theodical questions. At the same time, the traditions of the shipwreck and Dance of Death motif are revived and configured. A close reading illustrates that the reader can neither take the role of the 'spectator'[54] nor the 'observer'[55]. Mortality levels the hierarchy between the 'spectator'/'observer' and the victims of a sinking ship. This levelling of hierarchies confronts the reader with his/her own agency, because without the established roles the reader must actively look for a new perspective to take hold of. Perhaps the memento mori even motivates one to engage politically with the issue of the drowning migrants in the Mediterranean Sea. A change of perspectives is the prospect, which fictional genres like the novel can provide.

Bibliography

Benjamin, Walter. "The Storyteller: Reflections on the Works of Nikolai Leskov." In *The Novel: An Anthology of Criticism and Theory 1900–2000*, edited by Dorothy J. Hale, 361–378. Malden: Blackwell Publishing, 2006.

Billig, Volkmar. *Inseln. Geschichte einer Faszination.* Berlin: Matthes & Seitz, 2010.

Blumenberg, Hans. *Schiffbruch mit Zuschauer. Paradigma einer Daseinsmetapher.* 6th edition. Frankfurt: Suhrkamp, 2014.

Erll, Astrid. *Memory in Culture.* Houndsmills: Palgrave Macmillan, 2011.

Frie, Ewald, and Mischa Meier. "Bedrohte Ordnungen. Gesellschaften unter Stress im Vergleich." In *Aufruhr – Katastrophe – Konkurrenz – Zerfall. Bedrohte Ordnungen als Thema der Kulturwissenschaften*, edited by Ewald Frie and Mischa Meier, 1–30. Tübingen: Mohr Siebeck, 2014.

Le Juez, Brigitte, and Olga Springer. "Introduction: Shipwrecks and Islands as Multilayered, Timeless Metaphors of Human Existence." In *Shipwreck and Island Motifs in Literature and the Arts*, edited by Brigitte Le Juez and Olga Springer, 1–16. Leiden: Brill, 2015.

Mortensen, Mette, and Hans-Jörg Trenz. "Media Morality and Visual Icons in the Age of Social Media: Alan Kurdi and the Emergence of an Impromptu Public of Moral Spectatorship." *Javnost: The Public* 23, no. 4 (2016): 343–362.

Sund, Lars. *En lycklig liten ö.* Helsinki: Söderström, 2007.

Thompson, Carl. "Introduction." In *Shipwreck in Art and Literature: Images and Interpretations from Antiquity to the Present Day*, edited by Carl Thompson, 1–26. London: Routledge, 2013.

---

53 Benjamin, "The Storyteller."

54 Blumenberg, *Schiffbruch mit Zuschauer.*

55 Wolf, "Schiffbruch mit Beobachter."

Walter, François. *Katastrophen: Eine Kulturgeschichte vom 16. bis ins 21. Jahrhundert.* Stuttgart: Reclam, 2010.

Wolf, Burkhardt. "Schiffbruch mit Beobachter. Zur Geschichte des nautischen Gefahrenwissens." In *Die Unordnung der Dinge. Eine Wissens- und Mediengeschichte des Unfalls,* edited by Christian Kassung, 19–48. Bielefeld: Transcript, 2009.

Florian Peters

Rethinking History and Memory in the Transformation Era: How Solidarity's Struggle for History Shaped Recent Polish Conflicts over the Past

"The best thing would be if we never had to hear about that guy anymore".[1] This recent comment on Lech Wałęsa by Jacek Bartyzel, a Polish sociologist and former activist of the anti-communist opposition movement, may come as a surprise for many who remember the legendary Solidarity chairman and Nobel Peace Prize laureate as an icon of Polish self-liberation from communist rule. But Bartyzel is anything but alone with this view: since new documents on Wałęsa's cooperation with the communist state security service surfaced in January 2017, right-wing media and academics supporting the current government of Jarosław Kaczyński's "Law and Justice" (PiS) party have launched a full-blown smear campaign against the country's former president. Taking opportunity of the long-known fact that Wałęsa, then a politically inexperienced 27-year-old electrician, had been registered as informer "Bolek" by state security after the bloody crushing of the Gdańsk uprising in December 1970, and deliberately ignoring that he had terminated cooperation by 1976 at the latest, they eagerly attempt to question his place in history books.[2]

What is at stake in these attacks on Wałęsa is much more than the personal integrity of the erstwhile Solidarity leader; it is the established legacy of the democratic opposition movement of the 1980s as a whole. Thus, the campaign reflects a fundamental division in Polish society about how the collapse of communism and the creation of post-socialist Poland are to be interpreted and remembered. While liberals take pride in Poland's leading role in the fall of Eastern European communism and see the unprecedented Round Table negotiations between government and opposition representatives in 1989 as

1 Jacek Bartyzel, "Oni bronią siebie, swojej fałszywej legendy," wPolityce.pl, February, 2017, http://wpolityce.pl/polityka/325780-prof-bartyzel-o-obroncach-walesy-oni-bronia-siebie-swojej-falszywej-legendy.

2 Wałęsa had apparently tried, more or less skilfully, to outwit state security, but still got entangled in its nets, at least temporarily. For a matter-of-fact review of new information on Wałęsa's early cooperation with the security service, see Jan Skórzyński, "Od informatora do kontestatora. Akta "Bolka" – próba lektury," *Wolność i Solidarność* 9, (2016), 7–25.

the door opener to peaceful transition throughout the region, more and more conservatives tend to believe that the Polish way out of communism was in fact overshadowed by treason. They take the Round Table talks for an elite conspiracy driven by secret police and the subsequent economic "shock therapy" for a betrayal of the heroic anti-communist workers' upheaval staged by Solidarity in 1980/81.[3]

Although such views have only gained the status of a government-supported master narrative after the coming to power of PiS in 2015,[4] they are by no means new. Already back in 1989, more radical opposition activists felt betrayed by the Solidarity elites' decision to negotiate with the communists, because they were longing for a true anti-communist revolution that would see the "commies" hanging on the trees rather than sitting at negotiation tables. Additional doubts were raised by the hardships of the neoliberal transformation pursued by the first non-communist government of Tadeusz Mazowiecki and Leszek Balcerowicz, which struck most harshly the industrial working class employed in big state factories, while offering a lot of new business opportunities for former communist nomenclature members. As David Ost has pointed out, social conflicts aroused by the economic transformation failed to find representation in the emerging political culture of post-socialism, so popular anger frequently turned into clashes over identity issues.[5] History and memory, which had been major fields of political combat between the opposition movement and the communist party-state before 1989, resurfaced as a divisive political cleavage at the end of the 1990s, when right-wing parties throughout East-Central Europe promoted lustration as a means to bring to an end the anti-communist revo-

---

3 For an overview of the divisive politics of memory of 1989 throughout East-Central Europe, see James Mark, Muriel Blaive, Adam Hudek, Anna Saunders, and Stanisław Tyszka, "1989 After 1989. Remembering the End of State Socialism in East-Central Europe," in *Thinking through Transition. Liberal Democracy, Authoritarian Pasts, and Intellectual History in East Central Europe After 1989*, ed. Michal Kopeček and Piotr Wciślik (Budapest and New York: CEU Press, 2015), 463–503.

4 In August 2016, the official promotional website Poland.pl run by the Polish Ministry of Foreign Affairs with the objective to show foreigners "all that is fascinating, extraordinary and beautiful about our country", did not hesitate to publish an English version of the lengthy article, "A controlled revolution" by Rzeczpospolita journalist Konrad Kołodziejski, who explained that there may have even been something like a revolution in 1989, but if so, it was initiated and controlled by the KGB aiming at securing economic power for the communist elites: Konrad Kołodziejski, "A controlled revolution," Poland.pl, August, 2016, https://poland.pl/politics/foreign-affairs/controlled-revolution/.

5 David Ost, *The Defeat of Solidarity: Anger and Politics in Post-communist Europe* (Ithaca: Cornell University Press, 2005).

lution that many of their voters considered unfinished before.[6] Evidently, this cleavage continues to provide resources for right-wing populists like Viktor Orbán in Hungary and Jarosław Kaczyński in Poland until today: both succeeded in channelling unfulfilled ambitions by promising a radical break not only with communism, but also with anything looking or seeming alike – that is, the whole post-socialist democratic system allegedly built on compromise with "the reds", including former opposition leaders and liberals who had been ready for such temporary compromises.

In order to understand why such radical re-interpretations of the Polish way out of communism – which may seem to be obscure conspiracy theories when seen from outside – indeed appear convincing to noticeable parts of Polish society, I propose a closer look at how Poles perceived history and memory on the eve of the transformation era. During the 1980s, which saw both the most powerful collectivist mass mobilisation in contemporary European history (1980/81) and the swiftest turn to a neoliberal transformation strategy (1989), social perceptions and concepts of historical agency had been seriously challenged and reconfigured. I argue that these radical shifts in perception of the ongoing crisis have set the stage for the ways Poles think of the transformation era to date.

My point of departure, therefore, is the considerable change taking place in Polish society during the last decade of state socialism, which separates Solidarity of 1980/81 from the Round Table transformation in 1989, but which is hardly present in the liberal master narrative of national self-liberation that has been dominating Polish public discourse for the last 25 years. If you walk through the main exhibition of the flagship European Solidarity Centre, which was opened in Gdańsk in 2014, you will experience a smooth trajectory of progress leading from Solidarity in 1980 to the "triumph of freedom" in 1989 (as the exhibit's final room is called). The years of martial law and thereafter, when Solidarity had been effectively crushed and the underground opposition was fading, are presented in a mode of dramatic suspense – that is, as a time of persistence, not of transition and reconfiguration. Yet, Solidarity in 1989 was not the same as it had been before martial law. From a trade union deeply rooted in collectivist working class culture, it had transformed into a political movement dominated by reform-minded liberal intellectuals. It is this improbable evolution from collapse to victory, and the ambiguous and contradictory devel-

6 James Mark, *The Unfinished Revolution: Making Sense of the Communist Past in Central-Eastern Europe* (New Haven: Yale University Press, 2010).

opments that made it possible, that have made these years of crisis a subject of political contestation to date.

Instead of suggesting a story of the betrayal of "true Poles" by liberal intellectuals, or indulging in speculations on a conspiracy between opposition leaders and the communist secret service (as it is commonplace in right-wing discourse), I propose an investigation into the fissured evolution of the contemporary interpretation frameworks of social change, which I consider crucial for the course of events preceding 1989. They become most obvious when focussing on history and memory culture, the political significance of which makes for much of the specificity of the demise of communism in Poland. More generally, this approach tries to illuminate how the remembrance of the past can influence the construction of political agency, and how both modes of remembering and concepts of historical change may change in response to crisis.

Solidarity's Struggle for History

Historical consciousness had been at the cradle of Solidarity. While vast majorities of society in the Soviet Union under Brežnev, in "normalised" Czechoslovakia under Husák, or in the GDR under Honecker experienced late socialism as an era of stagnation where "everything was forever, until it was no more", as Alexei Yurchak has put it retrospectively,[7] the Polish opposition movement could build upon markedly different perceptions of time and historicity prevalent in Polish society. By modelling itself on the experiences of Polish uprisings and resistance movements from the 19th century to communist times, it succeeded to break up what Václav Havel had considered the most important means of power in late socialism: the omnipresent feeling of timeless powerlessness.[8] History facilitated the integration of diverse social groups like workers and intelligentsia, and helped to articulate the widespread but somewhat diffuse discontent stemming from the deep economic crisis in a genuinely political way. Since the late 1970s, the rather elitist counter-culture of *drugi obieg* (second circulation) pioneered in replacing experiences of powerlessness by offering *podmiotowość* (subject agency) to its participants, and from August 1980 millions of Poles from all spheres of society were provided with a sixteen-month

7 Alexei Yurchak, *Everything Was Forever, Until It Was No More: The Last Soviet Generation* (Princeton: Princeton University Press, 2006).

8 Vaclav Havel, *The Power of the Powerless* (1978), accessed January 23, 2018, http://vaclavhavel.cz/showtrans.php?cat=clanky&val=72_aj_clanky.html&typ=HTML.

experience of collective agency by the nationwide grass-roots movement of Solidarity. Historical remembrance became part and parcel of the struggle between the opposition movement and the communist regime.[9]

The urge to defy the state's monopoly on interpreting national history was not a compensatory side effect of oppositional activities – quite the contrary. When opposition activists dared to make their first steps out of private flats into the public space of Polish cities, they did so by organising alternative remembrance ceremonies dedicated to Poland's Independence Day, to the Warsaw Uprising of 1944, and to the Gdańsk Workers' upheaval of December 1970.[10] When the Gdańsk shipyard workers started to negotiate with regime representatives in August 1980, one of their first demands was to erect a monument for their colleagues killed ten years before.[11] When sociologists asked rank-and-file members of the "independent, self-governed trade union", which had been established after the Gdańsk agreements, about Solidarity's most burning issues, 77 % of respondents answered that the union should give special priority to spreading "knowledge on the true history of Poland". Support for this goal was only slightly outnumbered by postulates for "economic reform" (80 %) and "sovereignty of the country" (79 %). In contrast, both the core issues of Eastern European dissidents, human and civic rights, and typical labour objectives like material advancements and self-governance by workers, ranked considerably lower.[12]

Generally speaking, Solidarity supporters did not dream of liberal democracy or even capitalism, nor did they reject socialist values, especially working-class values. Rather, they sought to combine the latter with religious and national elements in an eclectic melange, advocating some kind of "socialism with a divine face".[13] Solidarity was not a lobby group for economic or political inter-

9 Jan Kubik, *The Power of Symbols against the Symbols of Power: The Rise of Solidarity and the Fall of State Socialism in Poland* (University Park: Penn State University Press, 1994); Barbara Törnquist-Plewa, *The Wheel of Polish Fortune: Myths in Polish Collective Consciousness during the First Years of Solidarity* (Lund: Lund University, 1992).

10 Kubik, *Power of Symbols*, 163–182; Aandrzej Friszke, *Czas KOR-u. Jacek Kuroń a geneza Solidarności* (Krakow: Znak, 2011), 458–473.

11 Florian Peters, *Revolution der Erinnerung. Der Zweite Weltkrieg in der Geschichtskultur des spätsozialistischen Polen* (Berlin: Ch. Links Verlag, 2016) 120–121.

12 These opinion polls were carried out in August 1981 by a group of Warsaw sociologists involved with the union's Centre for Social Research: Andrzej Radźko, *Sprawy podstawowe w oczach członków Związku. Badania opinii członków Związku sierpień 1981* (Warsaw: Ośrodek Badań Społecznych, 1981), I.

13 Michał Łuczewski, "Solidarność: socjalizm z boską twarzą," in *Polska Solidarności. Kontrowersje, oblicza, interpretacje*, ed. Jacek Kloczkowski (Krakow: Ośrodek Myśli Politycznej, 2011), 217–244.

ests of particular societal groups, but conceived of itself as a collective subject of history. It called for no more or no less than the restoration of its right to self-governance – primarily in the sphere of production, but at least implicitly on a national level too. Its historical thinking was inclusive, collectivist and deeply rooted in the linear concept of history characteristic of modernity. When philosopher and priest Józef Tischner preached to the delegates of the first nationwide congress of Solidarity in September 1981 that "at the turning points of history, the basic truths are common ones", it was more than obvious to everyone present that the pure existence of the union was to be seen as such – a "turning point of history".[14]

Consequently, most union members would have had great difficulty in understanding the taunting undertone of Timothy Garton Ash's contemporary assessment that "Solidarity's best product were monuments", whereas its achievements in terms of economic reform and manifest material improvements turned out meagre.[15] For millions of Solidarity supporters, the monument projects initiated by the union immediately after its legalisation, especially the Monument of the Fallen Shipyard Workers erected at the gates of the Gdańsk Lenin shipyard in December 1980, were much more than just symbolic representations of past events; rather, they bridged the past and present by reassuring the notion of the historicity of present events. By establishing a direct link between Solidarity and Polish national history, these monuments served as permanent manifestations of the historic subjectivity of the movement. Their purpose was to counter the state monopoly on history, which was rightly considered a cornerstone of state socialism's "superstructure". It is no wonder, then, that the gigantic crosses erected in Gdańsk and Poznań did not fall short of the monumentality typical for state socialist cultures of remembrance.

But Solidarity's remarkable commitment to history resembled communist references to the past not only with regard to aesthetics. Ironically enough, it drew heavily from a concept of collective agency that had been most ardently promoted by Marxism – before it had been frozen in the authoritative discourse of late socialism. Communists always strove to legitimate their rule in historical terms, and they did so with special devotion in Poland, consistently mixing up national and class elements.[16] Their efforts in historical legitimation

---

14 Józef Tischner, "Czas zakorzenia," *AS. Agencja Solidarności* 40 (1981), 26–28.

15 Timothy Garton Ash, *The Polish Revolution: Solidarity 1980–82* (London: Cape, 1983), 278.

16 Marcin Zaremba, *Komunizm, legitymizacja, nacjonalizm. Nacjonalistyczna legitymizacja władzy komunistycznej w Polsce* (Warsaw: Trio, 2001).

reached new peaks towards the end of the 1970s, since both the future-oriented promises of Stalinism and the presentist paradigm of consumer socialism had failed. Solidarity challenged communist politics of history with a fresh belief in collective agency, but essentially it shared the party's deeply collectivist vision of history. Both communist and oppositional master narratives merged class and nation into one single principal subject of historical change, with the working class as a prime mover, but the nation gradually getting the upper hand.[17]

The more polarised the political conflict between Solidarity and the party-state grew, the fiercer both sides competed for the title of the better advocate of the Polish nation by referring to traditional heroic-martyrological narratives. Namely, the communist regime sought to link the national self-image of Polish fighting "for your and our freedom" to the foundation myth of "People's Poland" based on Soviet liberation from fascism as well as on the "regaining" of former German territories in the West and North. Oppositional counter-narratives emphasised the long-standing Polish tradition of resistance against any foreign domination and demanded investigation into the so called "blank spots" in Polish-Soviet history. Instead of questioning the way Polish communists approached history, the opposition activists fought for the integration of new elements into the old discursive framework. Most notably, they sought to integrate Soviet oppression (like the massacre of Katyń) into the martyrological narrative that was until then focused on Nazi oppression, and also to include the record of the non-communist *Armia Krajowa* into the heroic narrative of Polish wartime resistance.

This polarisation of official and alternative politics of history grew even deeper after general Jaruzelski's imposition of martial law in December 1981, which effectively crushed Solidarity as a working-class mass organisation. The forced retreat of the opposition from open labour unionism to clandestine structures suggested diverse references to experiences in Polish national history deemed more or less comparable, especially to the underground resistance movement during the Second World War. At the same time, the sudden fall of Solidarity reinforced romanticist notions of continuous fighting in spite of successive material defeats. These historical references gave consolation and offered a shelter for intellectual retreat, thus contributing significantly to the remarkable persistence of the opposition spirit throughout the 1980s.

---

17 The insightful discussion of nation and class as converging subjects of post-Stalinist historical narratives by Pavel Kolář, *Der Poststalinismus. Ideologie und Utopie einer Epoche* (Cologne: Böhlau, 2016), 143–177.

On the other hand, the generals of Jaruzelski's martial law regime did not even attempt a substantial roll-back in the politics of history, but rather reacted to the evident lack of popular support with a further shift from socialist traditions towards the national paradigm. In reaction to bottom-up initiatives that had popped up in 1980/81 and demanded adequate remembrance of the Warsaw Uprising of 1944, the Jaruzelski regime tried to take over the initiative and allowed for various activities in this field. Among these was a large-scale photo exhibition with ambient sound and light installations, which attracted more than two million visitors in 1982 and the erection of the iconic Monument of the Little Insurgent at the Warsaw Old Town walls in 1983. The competition between official and alternative remembrance culminated in sustained quarrels on the establishment of a museum and a prestigious monument for the uprising.[18] While the monument was finally erected in 1989, the museum was not opened until 2004, after future Polish president Lech Kaczyński had launched an initiative to fulfil this idea. There is good reason to conclude that the struggles and the overall convergence of interpretations during the last decade of state socialism were crucial in facilitating the ascension of the Warsaw Uprising to an undisputed cornerstone of post-socialist politics of remembrance.

The Rise of Memory as a Response to Crisis

For the time being, however, the competing historical narratives contributed to deepen the impasse Polish society found itself in after martial law: the regime was in power but lacked popular support to cope with the deep economic and social crisis, while the underground opposition succeeded in retaining the myth of Solidarity but remained unable to challenge the regime's power base. As time passed since the suppression of the legal Solidarity union and hopes for its reconstruction dwindled, the underground's incessant references to the national insurrection tradition tended to turn into empty pathetic formula, thus increasingly resembling the phraseology of party-state rituals of remembrance. The efforts of both sides to outperform the other in terms of historical remembrance turned increasingly compensatory and showed but a lack of real political options and ideas. History had transformed from a major instigator of social mobilisation to a symptom of stagnation.

Around the middle of the decade, the reactions to the evident crisis of the opposition's political project started to diverge: some fractions of opposition

18 Peters, *Revolution der Erinnerung*, 311–337.

supporters barricaded themselves in grim defence of the national collective they had seen embodied in Solidarity and demonstrated their anti-Soviet radicalism with increasing ostentation. Others grew more and more weary of the deadlocked national-romantic conceptions of past and present prevalent in both official and alternative culture. Intellectual elites as well as some of the younger opposition activists disbanded the revolution myth repeated by the older generation and resorted to new, individualist conceptions of identity and historical agency. The discovery of "I" offered an attractive way out of the clear-cut distinctions of "them" and "us".

This paradigm shift had varied disguises: it became visible in the growing appeal of subcultures like rock and punk, in ironic attitudes cultivated by art students at the happenings of the *Pomarańczowa Alternatywa* (Orange Alternative), but also in the graffiti and slogans painted onto the walls of Polish towns. An attentive observer stated that, while political slogans had definitely dominated up until the mid-1980s, "nowadays it is individuals who doodle on the walls, longing to express their individualism".[19] The radical rejection of any collectivist concept of agency was summarised by a slogan painted on a Gdańsk wall in 1989: "There won't be any revolution here – down with everybody!".[20]

A more sophisticated way of opposing the collectivism cultivated by the older opposition milieus was developed by intellectuals, who adapted ideas of neoliberal thinkers like Friedrich August von Hayek or Milton Friedman and propagated individual entrepreneurship as a way to regain agency vis-à-vis the overwhelming power of the communist state.[21] This shift of attention to economic problems went along with a resolute rejection of both revolutionary conceptions of collective action and the historically-grounded underground rhetoric dominant during martial law. Instead, opposition liberals like the Cracow philosopher Mirosław Dzielski and the Gdańsk liberals group led by Donald Tusk argued for a compromise between the opposition and the communist regime, which was to be based on economic liberties rather than on political freedom. Others, like historian of ideas Marcin Król, adapted the concept of "civil society" that circulated among Western social scientists of the

---

19 The anonymous author conceded that this trend did not affect the issues of "erotics, adolescence, military service and football," the frequency of which, as could be expected, was not subject to any noteworthy changes: R., "Czas alternatywy. O napisach na murach," *Brulion* (1989): 144–145.

20 Ibid., 145.

21 Konrad Knoch, *Pisma liberalne drugiego obiegu w Polsce w latach 1979–1990* (Warsaw: IPN, 2015) 233–234, 261 ff.

time, and envisaged it as a realm of fresh air sharply opposed to the musty fug of "historic-symbolic community". As Król put it in a 1987 essay:

> "A person who has once breathed in fresh air, who has learned to live as a citizen, may admittedly be ready to visit a Polish historic-symbolic stage performance one more time, but the time he has to spend between church and national theatre will be empty and lost for him".[22]

While this intellectual re-orientation marked a turning away from history as a dimension of present-day politics, it added momentum to individualist and subjectivist approaches to the past that transcended the frames of national collectivity. One of the most visible aspects of this change was the distinct trend to rediscover the forgotten history and culture of the Polish Jews in the second half of the 1980s.[23] Many students and young academics began to learn Yiddish, delved into Jewish literature, or got involved in cleaning up Jewish cemeteries. Sociologist Paweł Śpiewak explained in a clear-sighted contemporary article:

> "First of all, the new generation longs to be free and feels free – from tradition, from the heritage of their ancestors, from the sanctuaries of their fathers. […] The young people who submerge into Jewish culture also want to be free from celebrating Polishness, from its priests and iconoclasts. […] They want to be inside this culture the same way they want to get to know the cultures of India or America; they want to know Judaism the same way they want to get to know Buddhism or medieval Christian mysticism. They want the world to be their home, not Poland".[24]

These young Poles consciously disengaged themselves from the notion of historical continuity, which dominated both official and alternative visions of history. They did not cling to the concept of history as a linear, meaningful link between past, present, and future, but conceived it as a loose combination of manifold individual experiences, the directions and ends of which were neither defined nor known. Rather than heroes and martyrs, whose posthumous fame rested upon their outstanding contributions to their own collectivities, their interest instead was directed towards the victims of history. In short, the nascent

22 Marcin Król, "Inny kraj," *Res Publica* (1987): 23.

23 Michael C. Steinlauf, *Bondage to the Dead: Poland and the Memory of the Holocaust* (Syracuse: University Press, 1997), 98–106.

24 Paweł Śpiewak, "Dlaczego Żydzi," *Res Publica* (1987): 20.

remembrance of Polish Jewry and the Holocaust in late socialist Poland can be seen as a precursor of the emergence of a self-reflective, victimising culture of *memory*. Paralleling similar processes taking place in Western Europe and North America at the same time, this new, subjectifying mode of referring to the past challenged the universalistic, objectifying concept of *history*, which had been characteristic of modernity by that time.[25]

Indeed, developments in Poland were partly instigated by impulses from abroad as, for example, Claude Lanzmann's controversial documentary *Shoah*, which was screened in Polish cinemas (partly even on public television) and sparked a heated public debate in 1985.[26] In order to arouse more than an indignant defensive reaction, however, such impulses had to meet with endogenous change inside Polish society and genuine readiness for open debate. And for that matter, the established discursive order began to erode in the second half of the decade. While regime propagandists continued to present themselves in their newly-acquired favourite role as faithful defenders of the honour of the Polish nation, debates were more complicated in the opposition milieus. Opposition intellectuals like Jan Józef Lipski repeatedly argued for transcending limited national perspectives on difficult issues of the national past, but their position was not at all commonplace within the opposition movement. This became evident when literary critic Jan Błoński, in a now famous essay published in the liberal Catholic weekly *Tygodnik Powszechny* in January 1987, called for a self-critical re-evaluation of collective Polish witnessing and bystanding of the Holocaust.[27] Błoński's most pronounced opponent in the ensuing debate was not a regime historian, but the renowned Solidarity advocate Władysław Siła-Nowicki, who sought to defend the good name of the Polish nation in a

---

25 Reinhart Koselleck, "Geschichte, Historie," in *Geschichtliche Grundbegriffe. Historisches Lexikon zur politisch-sozialen Sprache in Deutschland*, Vol. 2: *E-G*, ed. Otto Brunner, Werner Conze, and Reinhart Kosselleck (Stuttgart: Klett-Cotta, 1975), 593–717; Martin Sabrow, "Erinnerung als Pathosformel der Gegenwart," in *Der Streit um die Erinnerung*, ed. Martin Sabrow (Leipzig: Akademische Verlags-Anstalt, 2008), 9–24; Enzo Traverso, *Gebrauchsanweisungen für die Vergangenheit. Geschichte, Erinnerung, Politik* (Münster: Unrast, 2007).

26 Piotr Forecki, *Od Shoah do Strachu. Spory o polsko-żydowską przeszłość i pamięć w debatach publicznych* (Poznań: Poznańskie, 2010), 132–149; Piotr Forecki, *Reconstructing memory: The Holocaust in Polish public debates*, trans. Marta Skowsronska (Frankfurt: Lang, 2013).

27 Jan Błoński, "Biedni Polacy patrzą na Getto," *Tygodnik Powszechny* 2 (1987): 1, 4; Antony Polonsky, ed. *"My brother's keeper?," Recent Polish debates on the Holocaust*, trans. Institute for Jewish Studies (London: Routledge, 1990), 34–52.

way not dissimilar to rationales typically used by the nationalist wing of the communist party.[28]

Such unexpected cleavages running across the regime-opposition divide showed that the battle lines of Solidarity's struggle for history had definitely started to disperse. They indicated the change that came along with the transnational paradigm shift from history to memory. The calling into question of the classical universalistic understanding of history and its partial substitution by the particularistic counter-concept of memory was to have major consequences for the Polish conflict so firmly entrenched in historical frames of interpretation. While Solidarity of 1980/81 can be seen as a last attempt at historical revolution rooted in the symbolic universe of modernity, the subtle revolution of individualist memory was in fact about to shake the foundations of that symbolic universe.

It is important to note here that this new approach to the past did not render the dominant collectivist modes of remembrance obsolete – quite the contrary. In contrast to the collective struggle for history led by Solidarity in 1980/81, the emergence of memory was anything but a mass phenomenon. Its humble beginnings and subtle symptoms were limited mainly to the academic intelligentsia, whereas the public sphere continued to be dominated by homogenising collectivist master narratives. The function of history as a reservoir of collectivist identity patterns in Polish society had by no means come to an end in the late 1980s. Underground publications on historical topics enjoyed lasting popularity amongst anti-communist audiences, public conflicts over significant historical monuments continued with undiminished rigour, and the clash over the Katyń massacre grew fiercer than ever after the establishment of a Polish-Soviet commission of party historians in 1987.[29] Rather than initiating a smooth transformation, the discovery of individualism established a new line of differentiation and conflict within the opposition, and within society in general. Not everybody shared the joy Marcin Król felt about living in a "world without form, the future of which I do not know",[30] and not everybody rated individual liberties so high that he was ready to abandon collectivist certainties known for decades. Tadeusz Łepkowski, a Warsaw historian actively supporting Solidarity, commented on the ambivalence of these new prospects:

28 Ewa Koźmińska-Frejlak, "Świadkowie zagłady – Holocaust jako zbiorowe doświadczenie Polaków," *Przegląd Socjologiczny* 49, no. 2 (2000): 181–206; Forecki, *Od Shoah do Strachu*, 149–165.

29 Peters, *Revolution der Erinnerung*, 248–274.

30 Król, "Inny kraj," 24.

"The world, which was perceived in two colours in the age of revolution [in 1980/81], more precisely: as black-and-white, slowly becomes colourful, but the dominant colour is grey".[31]

Still, the rise of individualist concepts of agency proved instrumental in overcoming black-and-white perceptions of past and present conflicts. Namely, the concept of civil society offered a bridge over the deep gap between communist and non-communist elites by marginalising the notion of historicity of change that had prevailed before. Conceptualising social change not as the outcome of collective action but as the object of permanent negotiation amongst competing players, civil society complied with the growing yearning for individual liberties and served as a means of neutralising the historical overload of the current political conflict. Its implicit promise was tempting for anyone tired of the deadlock of antagonistic collectivities based on national-historical imagery: history in general, and revolution all the more, would be superseded by an ever-progressing balancing of particularistic interests. Significantly, in Poland it was not the democratic opposition but the party leadership and its intellectual masterminds who had the major share in putting the concept of civil society onto the political agenda in the run-up to the Round Table negotiations.[32] Since the ideological core values of socialism had been embodied more plausibly by Solidarity in 1980/81, the communist party evidently lacked a meaningful idea of collective agency that would have transcended the defence of its own power. What, therefore, could be more obvious than to drop the old disavowed legitimation frames in favour of a dehistoricising model that promised to outmanoeuvre the opposition's superior collectivist identity narrative?

Hence, Solidarity's struggle for history and the rise of memory and civil society in the late 1980s provided both necessary and sufficient preconditions for negotiations and compromise at the Round Table. On the one hand, it was the persistence of historically grounded oppositional identities that finally forced the Jaruzelski regime to accept the Solidarity representatives as negotiation partners, although they had been defeated in terms of power politics long before. On the other hand, the window of opportunity to overcome the cleavage stemming from collectivist historical culture did not open until the individualist backlash against the omnipresence of that culture had gained momentum. Only the dialectic interaction of both factors added up to a setting

31 Tadeusz Łepkowski, "Rewolucja polska 1980 roku," *Warszawskie Zeszyty Historyczne* 3 (1989): 25.

32 Paweł Stefan Załęski, *Neoliberalizm i społeczeństwo obywatelskie* (Toruń: Naukowe Uniwersytetu Mikołaja Kopernika, 2012), 122–141.

that facilitated a peaceful, evolutionary transition from authoritarian socialism to parliamentarian democracy and capitalism.

History Returning

The interplay of collectivist and individualist concepts of historical change that had eventually proved successful in paving the Polish way out of state socialism did not, however, resolve the inherent contradictions between them. Moreover, the essential contributions of both approaches, and therefore the legitimacy of both collectivist beliefs in history and individualist confidence in memory have hardly been recognised by their respective opponents. Instead, two contradictory narrations of what was decisive for the change brought about in 1989 emerged, as did two divergent claims to the recognition of agency – and to power.

This conflict, the aftermath of which we observe today, was no doubt deepened by the predominantly elitist character of the Polish transformation. It is no wonder that almost nobody speaks of the Polish events of 1989 as a revolution – in striking contrast to the talk on "peaceful", "velvet" or "singing" revolutions in East-Central European neighbouring countries. Unlike the Solidarity rising in 1980/81, the Polish transformation of 1989 was in fact accompanied by a very low level of democratic mass participation. The Round Table negotiations took place in an atmosphere of societal exhaustion and were carried out mainly, as Włodzimierz Borodziej put it, by "tired men around 60".[33] Even the first semi-free elections of the 4th of June 1989, which were to add the ultimate spark to the collapse of state socialism in Poland and, subsequently, all over Eastern Europe, did not attract more than 62 % of eligible voters to the ballot boxes. This profound demobilisation of society prevailed not only during the epoch-making months of 1989 but also throughout the years to come.

Under these circumstances, former opposition activists turning into democratic politicians and government officials were happy to avoid the effort to moderate between the identity frames and expectations that had been raised by the collectivist insurgence of the early 1980s and the individualist concepts that came to dominate public discourse later. Instead of reviving Solidarity's substantial legacy in deliberative democracy practices, the new government took

33 Włodzimierz Borodziej, "Vom Warschauer Aufstand zum Runden Tisch. Politik und Gewalt in Polen 1944–1989," in *1989 und die Rolle der Gewalt*, ed. Martin Sabrow (Göttingen: Wallstein, 2012), 303.

advantage of the leap of faith to the Solidarity myth that had been built up since 1980 in order to push through the radical transformation strategy advocated by Leszek Balcerowicz.[34] The absence of major protests to the project of "building capitalism" from scratch enabled many members of the new elite to keep quiet about the rapid ideological transition to (neo)liberalism they had gone through in the late 1980s. In effect, triumphalist myths of national resurrection and a "return to Europe" took hold, which precluded a serious debate over the multifaceted legacies of Solidarity and the Round Table negotiations. This created a fertile ground for distrust and suspicion not only amongst those who experienced a less smooth passage from old to new socio-economic realities, but also amongst numerous rank-and-file members of the opposition movement, many of whom still adhered to the hopes and ideals that had mobilised them into action in 1980.[35] Soon, such suspicions were to be purposefully nourished and exploited by the political right.

In the long run, the trust in the timeless rationalities of the market prescribed by the shock therapists did not keep its promise of transcending antagonistic interests and resolving social problems by an "invisible hand", that is, outside the sphere of politics. Neither did liberal intellectuals succeed in offering a consistent narrative of the transformation era that would have integrated the regaining of political and individual freedom with the loss of economic security and the depreciation of lifetime achievements experienced by a broad section of Polish society. Consequently, seemingly old-fashioned, collectivist perceptions of agency and identity reappeared with considerable might a decade later. And again, it was history that returned to the centre of Polish political debates.[36] The controversies over the role of Poles as bystanders and, to a smaller degree, even co-perpetrators of the Holocaust, which had been initiated by Błoński and others in the late 1980s, resurfaced fiercer than ever with Jan Tomasz Gross' book on the Jedwabne pogrom at the turn of the century. The first PiS government of the Kaczyński brothers (2005–2007) spared no effort to make "historical policy" *(polityka historyczna)* a founding element of the self-proclaimed "Fourth Republic". Under the impression of the tragic crash of the

34 For (self-)critical retrospective appraisals from contrary political positions see Marcin Król, *Byliśmy głupi* (Warsaw: Czerwone i Czarne, 2015), 34–37; Karol Modzelewski, *Zajeździmy kobyłę historii. Wyznania poobijanego jeźdźca* (Warsaw: Iskry, 2013), 399–405.

35 Adam Mielczarek, "Przemiany roku 1989 w oczach szeregowych działaczy podziemia," in *Interpretacje upadku komunizmu w Polsce i w Europie środkowo-wschodniej*, ed. Krzysztof Brzechczyn (Poznań: IPN, 2011), 251–62.

36 Paweł Machcewicz, *Spory o historię 2000–2011* (Krakow: Znak, 2012).

Polish presidential plane at Smolensk in 2010, PiS radicalised its manichaeic interpretation of national history even further before the party's returning to power in 2015, now openly resorting to dubitable conspiracy theories, where "traitors" and hidden evil seem to be responsible for everything. Simultaneously, the heated emotions and the antagonistic styles of debating and politicising history well known from the opposition-regime conflict of the last decade of state socialism resumed their prominent places in Polish political culture.

No less than in the 1980s, recent Polish quarrels over the past reveal a clear division between traditionalist parts of society holding fast to a heroic-martyrological narrative of Polish history, and liberals showing more openness towards accepting responsibility for negative or disturbing aspects of the past and advocating historical reconciliation with former enemies. These competing attitudes towards the past can be traced back to the collectivist notion of history and the individualist concept of memory respectively. The origins of this cleavage are to be found in the contrary conceptions of historicity and social agency, which divided the inclusive, collectivist project of Solidarity in 1980/81 from the elitist, individualist outlook of the Round Table transformation. For those remaining in the revolutionary paradigm of 19th century historicism, the negotiated transformation from communism to democracy lacked the stark systemic break they had hoped for. For others, the "triumph of freedom" seemed so impressive that they did not even feel the need to engage with the experiences of powerlessness, which returned now in a capitalist disguise, as the social world people were familiar with rapidly broke apart due to shock therapy and deindustrialisation. As long as a viable arrangement between the notions of history and memory coined during Polish transformation is out of sight, their contradictory legacies will persist.

Bibliography

Ash, Timothy Garton. *The Polish Revolution: Solidarity 1980–82*. London: Cape, 1983.

Bartyzel, Jacek. "Oni bronią siebie, swojej fałszywej legendy." *wPolityce.pl*, February, 2017. http://wpolityce.pl/polityka/325780-prof-bartyzel-o-obroncach-walesy-oni-bronia-siebie-swojej-falszywej-legendy.

Błoński, Jan. "Biedni Polacy patrzą na Getto." *Tygodnik Powszechny* 2 (1987): 1–9.

Borodziej, Włodzimierz. "Vom Warschauer Aufstand zum Runden Tisch. Politik und Gewalt in Polen 1944–1989." In *1989 und die Rolle der Gewalt*, edited by Martin Sabrow, 278–303. Göttingen: Wallstein, 2012.

Forecki, Piotr. *Od Shoah do Strachu. Spory o polsko-żydowską przeszłość i pamięć w debatach publicznych*. Poznań: Poznańskie, 2010.

Forecki, Piotr. *Reconstructing Memory: The Holocaust in Polish Public Debates*. Translated by Marta Skowsronska. Frankfurt: Peter Lang, 2013.
Friszke, Aandrzej. *Czas KOR-u. Jacek Kuroń a geneza Solidarności*. Krakow: Znak, 2011.
Havel, Václav. *The Power of the Powerless*. 1978, http://vaclavhavel.cz/showtrans.php?cat=-clanky&val=72_aj_clanky.html&typ=HTML.
Knoch, Konrad. *Pisma liberalne drugiego obiegu w Polsce w latach 1979–1990*. Warsaw: IPN, 2015.
Kolář, Pavel. *Der Poststalinismus. Ideologie und Utopie einer Epoche*. Cologne: Böhlau, 2016.
Kołodziejski, Konrad. "A controlled revolution." *Poland.pl*, https://poland.pl/politics/foreign-affairs/controlled-revolution/.
Koselleck, Reinhart. "Geschichte, Historie." In *Geschichtliche Grundbegriffe. Historisches Lexikon zur politisch-sozialen Sprache in Deutschland*, Vol. 2: E-G, edited by Otto Brunner, Werner Conze, and Reinhart Kosselleck, 593–717. Stuttgart: Klett Cotta, 1975.
Koźmińska-Frejlak, Ewa. "Świadkowie zagłady – Holocaust jako zbiorowe doświadczenie Polaków." *Przegląd Socjologiczny*, 49, no. 2 (2000): 181–206.
Król, Marcin. "Inny kraj." *Res Publica* 1 (1987): 19–24.
Król, Marcin. *Byliśmy głupi*. Warsaw: Czerwone i Czarne, 2015.
Kubik, Jan. *The Power of Symbols against the Symbols of Power: The Rise of Solidarity and the Fall of State Socialism in Poland*. University Park: Penn State University Press, 1994.
Łepkowski, Tadeusz. "Rewolucja polska 1980 roku." *Warszawskie Zeszyty Historyczne* 3 (1989): 13–28.
Łuczewski, Michał. "Solidarność: socjalizm z boską twarzą." In *Polska Solidarności. Kontrowersje, oblicza, interpretacje*, edited by Jacek Kloczkowski, 217–244. Krakow: Ośrodek Myśli Politycznej, 2011.
Machcewicz, Paweł. *Spory o historię 2000–2011*. Krakow: Znak, 2012.
Mark, James, Muriel Blaive, Adam Hudek, Anna Saunders, and Stanisław Tyszka. "1989 After 1989. Remembering the End of State Socialism in East-Central Europe." In *Thinking through Transition. Liberal Democracy, Authoritarian Pasts, and Intellectual History in East Central Europe After 1989*, edited by Michal Kopeček and Piotr Wciślik, 463–503. Budapest and New York: CEU Press, 2015.
Mark, James. *The Unfinished Revolution: Making Sense of the Communist Past in Central-Eastern Europe*. New Haven: Yale University Press, 2010.
Mielczarek, Adam. "Przemiany roku 1989 w oczach szeregowych działaczy podziemia." In *Interpretacje upadku komunizmu w Polsce i w Europie środkowo-wschodniej*, edited by Krzysztof Brzechczyn, 251–262. Poznań: IPN, 2011.
Modzelewski, Karol. *Zajeździmy kobyłę historii. Wyznania poobijanego jeźdźca*. Warsaw: Iskry, 2013.
Ost, David. *The Defeat of Solidarity: Anger and Politics in Post-communist Europe*. Ithaca: Cornell University Press, 2005.
Peters, Florian. *Revolution der Erinnerung. Der Zweite Weltkrieg in der Geschichtskultur des spätsozialistischen Polen*. Berlin: Ch. Links Verlag, 2016.
Polonsky, Antony, ed. *"My brother's keeper?" Recent Polish debates on the Holocaust*. Translated by the Institute for Jewish Studies. London: Routledge, 1990.

R. "Czas alternatywy. O napisach na murach." *Brulion* 11–12 (1989): 141–145.

Radźko, Andrzej. *Sprawy podstawowe w oczach członków Związku. Badania opinii członków Związku sierpień 1981.* Warsaw: Ośrodek Badań Społecznych, 1981.

Sabrow, Martin. "Erinnerung als Pathosformel der Gegenwart." In *Der Streit um die Erinnerung*, edited by Martin Sabrow, 9–24. Leipzig: Akademie Verlags-Anstalt, 2008.

Skórzyński, Jan. "Od informatora do kontestatora. Akta "Bolka" - próba lektury." *Wolność i Solidarność* 9 (2016): 7–25.

Śpiewak, Paweł. "Dlaczego Żydzi." *Res Publica* 2 (1987): 17–20.

Steinlauf, Michael C. *Bondage to the Dead: Poland and the Memory of the Holocaust.* Syracuse: University Press, 1997.

Tischner, Józef. "Czas zakorzenia." *AS. Agencja Solidarności* 40 (1981): 26–28.

Törnquist-Plewa, Barbara. *The Wheel of Polish Fortune: Myths in Polish Collective Consciousness during the First Years of Solidarity.* Lund: Lund University, 1992.

Traverso, Enzo. *Gebrauchsanweisungen für die Vergangenheit. Geschichte, Erinnerung, Politik.* Münster: Unrast Verlag, 2007.

Yurchak, Alexei. *Everything Was Forever, Until It Was No More: The Last Soviet Generation.* Princeton: Princeton University Press, 2006.

Załęski, Paweł Stefan. *Neoliberalizm i społeczeństwo obywatelskie.* Toruń: Naukowe Uniwersytetu Mikołaja Kopernika, 2012.

Zaremba, Marcin. *Komunizm, legitymizacja, nacjonalizm. Nacjonalistyczna legitymizacja władzy komunistycznej w Polsce.* Warsaw: Trio, 2001.

Mariëlle Wijermars

Framing the Revolution: Memory and the Medialisation of Crisis in Loznitsa's *Maidan* and *The Event*

In times of political crisis, the experience and memory of previous crises can "premediate"[1] the understanding of its causes, significance and expected outcomes. Memories of, for example, revolutionary upheavals and the concomitant experience of the collapse of political order can, at the same time, provide the basic framework for initial attempts to memorialise the ongoing or recently concluded crisis and may influence how its meaning is interpreted. To examine the complex interplay between the memory of collapse and the interpretation and initial memorialisation of a recent state of crisis, this chapter explores the dynamics between two documentary films by Ukrainian director Sergei Loznitsa: *Maidan* (*Maidan* 2014) and *The Event* (*Sobytie* 2015). While the first film documents the street protests in Kiev in 2013–2014 and their tragic unfolding, and thereby forms an early contribution to the memorialisation of "Euromaidan", the latter, through a montage of archival footage, revisits the mass protests in the Soviet city of Leningrad during the August 1991 Putsch. This failed coup-d'état by communist hardliners against Secretary-General Mikhail Gorbachev, in an attempt to halt his reformist policies, is generally seen as having dealt a final blow to the authority of the Soviet government; it was the point of no return that culminated – within several months – in the disintegration of the Soviet Union and the independence of Ukraine.

The two films are worthy of our attention in their own right for their cinematic qualities; yet, it is particularly productive to read them in combination. In this approach, I take a cue from the director himself: Loznitsa had come across the Soviet-era archival footage already some years earlier but, in his opinion, the events in Ukraine invested the images with particular significance ("Q&A session" 2016).[2] Indeed, it was the most recent Maidan revolution that inspired him to revisit the revolution of 1991 in *The Event*. As I demonstrate in this chapter, in the hands of Loznitsa, documentary footage shot on the

1 Astrid Erll, "Literature, Film, and the Mediality of Cultural Memory," in *Cultural Memory Studies: An International and Interdisciplinary Handbook*, ed. Astrid Erll and Ansgar Nünning (Berlin and New York: De Gruyter, 2008), 389–398.

2 Sergei Loznitsa, "Q&A session." Interview on *Rotterdam Film Festival*, January 30, 2016.

eve of the Soviet Union's collapse is turned into a means of understanding the origins and nature of the 2014 Ukrainian crisis and of assessing the possible outcomes of Euromaidan.

My analysis is guided by the following set of questions: In what way does watching *The Event* influence our understanding of *Maidan* (the film) and Maidan (the crisis)? why does Loznitsa feel that it is necessary to revisit this particular episode in history to fully assess contemporary political conflict and vice versa, how does approaching the films in combination affect how we can or should interpret the political message of *The Event*? Directing attention to the depiction of information flow and medialisation during both crises, I argue that the reworking of the memory of a previous state of emergency in *The Event* serves to validate the Euromaidan revolution as a *grassroots* revolution by positing it – in the perception of Loznitsa – in contrast with the top-down revolution of 1991.

The following chapter is structured as follows: first, I provide a brief account of the two crises, how they are remembered and their significance for Ukraine; second, I introduce both films in more detail, where I place them within the context of the (documentary) oeuvre of Loznitsa and the filmmaker's preoccupation with memory, witnessing and revisiting the past; third, I delve deeper into how the films (re)mediate the respective political crises; and finally, I focus on the chemistry between both historical events, which are brought about by Loznitsa, and his framing of the two revolutions.

Two Revolutions

During the August 1991 Putsch, the most dramatic and well-known confrontations took place in Moscow where Boris Yeltsin, the president of the Russian Soviet Federative Socialist Republic (RSFSR), led a civil resistance to oppose the governmental takeover. While Gorbachev was held under house arrest in his holiday residence on Crimea, the coup-makers – having declared themselves the State Committee of the State of Emergency (GKChP)[3] – launched an armed attack on the parliament building (the White House) to where Yeltsin and his supporters had retreated. In the subsequent confrontation with the civil defenders of the White House, three men were killed. Within two days from its beginning, the coup collapsed and Gorbachev returned to power. The episode nevertheless severely destabilised the Soviet Union. In fact, the attempted

3 Gosudarstvennyi komitet po chrezvychainomu polozheniiu.

coup was a landslide event in terms of political and public opinion in several of the Soviet Republics (Estonia and Latvia declared their independence during its course) including Ukraine, where it marked a political turning point. The general stance on the question whether to pursue independence was, for a long time, more ambiguous in Ukraine than in the Baltic States, for instance. But on the 24th of August, some days after the failed coup, the Ukrainian Soviet Socialist Republic legislature voted in favour of the declaration of independence. According to Serhii Plokhy:

> "The event that triggered the change of heart among the conservative deputies of the Ukrainian parliament and, in time, throughout the world was the hard-liners' coup against Mikhail Gorbachev in Moscow on August 19, 1991".[4]

In the subsequent popular referendum, organised on the 1st of December, an overwhelming majority voted in favour of independence, whereas in March that year some 70 percent had voted to remain part of a (reformed) Soviet Union.[5] As Plokhy points out, the failure of the Putsch and Yeltsin's role in its collapse had demonstrated the weakness of the Union's center vis-à-vis its republics, in particular Russia. With power relations now shifted in favour of the Russian president, the appeal of remaining part of the Union was diminished.[6]

Seeking an improvement of the republic's economic situation was the dominant driving force behind popular support for independence, combined to lesser or larger extent with nationalist convictions and a desire for ideological freedoms in different regions. The subsequent economic collapse and protracted process of political transformation, which dashed the hopes for significantly improved living conditions and freedoms, meant that the revolution of 1991 soon came to be viewed in a more negative light. In part, such discussions also questioned the nature of the revolution itself:

> "Was Ukrainian state independence, gained in 1991, a culmination of decades (or even centuries) of a 'national-liberation' struggle by Ukrainian patriots? Or was it merely a present granted by largely external events and persons? Was it liberation from the Soviet-Russian yoke and the attainment of a 'natural' nation-state status for an objectively existing distinct Ukrainian nation, or was it a historical

4 Serhii Plokhy, *The Gates of Europe: A History of Ukraine* (New York: Basic Books, 2015), 318.

5 Ibid., 320.

6 Ibid., 319.

> tragedy, [...] because it separated not just a single communist state but tore apart an 'authentic' Slavic nation composed of Russians, Ukrainians, and Belarussians?".[7]

In Russia, the memory of August 1991 and the hopes for democratisation it represented – iconised by the image of Yeltsin standing on top of a tank near the White House – were equally quickly tarnished, especially in October 1993, when Yeltsin himself ordered Russian tanks to fire at the White House after dissolving the Russian Supreme Soviet.[8]

On the 20th anniversary of the Putsch and Ukraine's independence, their commemoration was once again overshadowed by a revolution that, as it had by then become apparent, failed to deliver on its promises: Ukraine's 2004 Orange Revolution. Mass protests, which erupted in response to fraud in the presidential elections, had prevented Viktor Yanukovych from taking power back then, and the presidential seat was occupied instead by the reformist, westward-leaning Viktor Yushchenko. By 2010, however, Yanukovych became president and restored the presidential republic, thereby undoing the "victory" of 2004. Meanwhile, the country's socio-economic state was poor: "Given the hopes and expectations and grim socioeconomic reality twenty years after independence, the twentieth anniversary was more of a somber milestone than a cause for celebration".[9]

It should be noted that the memory landscape in Ukraine in recent years is particularly dynamic – that is, there are marked regional differences and, while there is a noticeable top-down dynamics of memory politics and relatively little space for alternative narratives, the regime changes that have marked recent Ukrainian politics have also involved dramatic turns in how Ukraine's Soviet past is interpreted.[10] These largely alternated between staunchly anti-Soviet positions, in particular under President Yushchenko, and more centrist tendencies:

> "Even if one could argue that during Yushchenko's tenure the national mnemonic field was particularly contentious, during all periods (pre-Orange revolution, the Orange period, and post-Orange revolution) the mnemonic field was fractured

7 Oxana Shevel, "Memories of the Past and Visions of the Future: Remembering the Soviet Era and its End in Ukraine," in *Twenty Years After Communism: The Politics of Memory and Commemoration,* ed. Michael Bernhard and Jan Kubik (Oxford: Oxford University Press, 2014), 149–150.

8 Kathleen E. Smith, *Mythmaking in the New Russia: Politics and Memory during the Yeltsin Era* (Ithaca: Cornell University Press, 2002), 30–56.

9 Shevel, "Memories of the Past," 151.

10 Ibid., 152, 158.

> and contentious due to the consistent articulation of two distinct, coherent, and contradictory historical narratives by elite actors who saw themselves as proprietors of the 'true' vision of the Ukrainian past".[11]

The renegotiation of memory, most importantly in connection to the Soviet past, was also a central element of Euromaidan – the protests that erupted in November 2013 following Yanukovych's decision to postpone the signing of the Association Agreement with the European Union. Among other things, these actions targeted the remaining visual traces of the Soviet Union. Indeed, "[a] symbolic farewell to the Soviet past – the demolition of remaining monuments to Lenin, more than hundred altogether, in a few weeks – accompanied the Revolution of Dignity" (the name given to the most recent protests).[12] Yet, the conflict on memory is but one aspect of the mass protests on Kiev's Independence Square and elsewhere in Ukraine, and of their violent repression by state security forces (the Berkut) in February 2014. Having finally succeeded in overthrowing the government on the 22nd of February (Yanukovych had by then fled the country), the protests had claimed some 100 lives.[13]

Loznitsa and the Negotiation of Cultural Memory

The unfolding of Ukraine's most recent revolution is documented in *Maidan* – a largely uncommented and rather slow montage of footage that Loznitsa and his team of two additional camera operators shot of the events as they were unfolding – from the very beginning of the street protests through their violent outcome. A total volume of some 100 hours of film was edited back to a running time of two hours. In extremely long, static takes – at times resembling security-camera footage – the camera takes on the role of observer. The chosen style suggests impartiality, which imparts the documentary with an authoritative feel; it appears to be documenting the uprising, rather than interpreting it. The viewer witnesses the events as they unfold, including the less eventful moments, particularly during the first half of the film. While directorial decisions such as camera placement, choice of depicted locations, persons and

---

11 Ibid., 158–159.

12 Plokhy, *The Gates of Europe*, 352.

13 For a detailed account and analysis of the events, see, e. g., David R. Marples and Frederick V. Mills *Ukraine's Euromaidan: Analyses of a Civil Revolution* (Stuttgart: Ibidem Verlag, 2015).

objects, subtly guides the viewers' perception of the shown events, the static placement of the camera reinforces its position of documenting rather than taking part in the action. People are often seen from the back and the view is repeatedly blocked. An hour into the film's running time the outcome of the civil protest remains open. Consequently, the sense of uncertainty of those who participated is mirrored in the pacing of the documentary. It also expresses Loznitsa's own experience of making the film:

> "Usually, when I start with a documentary, I build the entire structure of the film in my imagination. I know how that film begins, how the story will develop, and how it ends. The work on *Maidan* was completely different. I received new materials almost every day during January and February, while the tensions rose, the number of victims increased; and I edited the film, not knowing how it would end".[14]

Only some minimal framing for understanding in the direction in which the confrontation is developing is provided through the titles of the film's four parts – Prologue, Triumph, Armed Conflict and Postscript – and occasional written commentary.

The protracted tension span also sprouts anticipation; or, as one reviewer characterised the film's poetics:

> "Hewn from massive wide shots that reach for the panoramic qualities of a Bruegel painting, it's a grimly optimistic account of a popular revolution and the building of a national consciousness, *increment by increment*".[15]

This reviewer, evidently, was persuaded by the political conviction embedded in Loznitsa's narration of Euromaidan. Notwithstanding, one of the finesses of the film that greatly contributes to its persuasiveness is its soundtrack: consisting of more than 100 separate tracks, the final mix "'match[es]' the action on screen and direct[s] our gaze without overwhelming the image with a soundtrack".[16]

14 Sergei Loznitsa, "Chto takoe 'Maidan'? Vopros, otveta na kotoryi u menia eshche ne," interview by Svitlanda Shapoval, *Cultprostir*, July 2, 2014, http://cultprostir.ua/ru/post/sergey-loznica-chto-takoe-maidan-vopros-otveta-na-kotoriy-u-menya-esche-net.

15 Nick Bradshaw, "Different Drums," *Sight & Sound* 25, no. 3 (2015): 26–29; emphasis added.

16 Lilya Kaganovsky, "Maidan by Sergei Loznitsa," *Slavic Review* 74, no. 4 (2015): 895; Sergei Medvedev, "Getting the News on 'Vremia,'" interview by Bill Keller, in *Russia at the Barricades: Eyewitness Accounts of the August 1991 Coup*, ed. Victoria E. Bonnell, Ann Cooper, and Gregory Freidin (Armonk and London: M. E. Sharpe, 1994), 301–307.

The lack of narrative drive towards an inevitable climax sets Loznitsa's work apart from other Euromaidan documentaries, such as Netflix's *Winter on Fire: Ukraine's Fight for Freedom* (Evgeny Afineevsky, 2015), as does his restraint in showing graphic imagery and violence. For example, in Loznitsa's documentary there are two moments when a person appears to get (fatally) wounded. On the first occasion, a group of people is shown at a distance as they drag away a lifeless person whilst protecting themselves from sniper fire with shields. On the second occasion, a group of Berkut special police forces is shown on a roof. Moments later, one of them collapses. In both instances, details are difficult to make out; the exact nature and severity of the injuries is not visible. While there is little difference between how the casualty on the side of the protesters and the shot Berkut officer are shown, the fact that the camera is often positioned behind or on the side of the protesters (possibly informed by the accessibility of these spaces to the cameramen) imparts the film with implicit partiality.

The depiction of the events in the Netflix documentary *Winter on Fire* is the exact opposite in many respects. The poster of the film is highly suggestive: a young girl, dressed in Ukrainian national wear and seen from the back, confronts a solid rank of riot police carrying interlinked shields. The opposition is fortified by the black-and-white depiction of the armed forces in contrast to the girl's vividly coloured red-and-white dress and yellow-and-blue garland with flowy ribbons (the colours of the Ukrainian flag). The film's subtitle, "Ukraine's Fight for Freedom", reinforces the suggestion of innocence, excessive violence and national liberation. Edited for maximum emotional effect, *Winter on Fire* includes graphic depictions of wounded civilians; they are shown in close-up, the blood on their faces beaming in saturated red. This type of imagery is absent from Loznitsa's *Maidan*. Rather than displaying individual drama, the filmmaker is preoccupied with the concerted action of the masses – on the side of the protesters and on the side of their adversary. This focus on the collective rather than the individual is central to Loznitsa's interpretation of Maidan, and thereby his contribution to its memorialisation: the political crisis of Maidan is envisaged as the emancipation of the Ukrainian nation. It should be stressed, however, that Loznitsa's depiction of Maidan and Ukraine's "united nation" is, to a certain extent, idealised and artificially homogenous. For instance, Loznitsa's contribution to the formation of the memory of the Maidan crisis excludes some of the less appealing aspects of the protests, including the controversial involvement of far-right groups. The absence of graphic depictions of violence, then, may also be seen as presenting a 'cleaner' image of this supposed birth of a political nation than is corroborated by reality.

The second documentary, *The Event*, premiered the following year and is clearly intended to complement the Maidan documentary. It consists of a compilation of archival footage that was shot in Leningrad by local cameramen during the August 1991 Putsch. Loznitsa crafted his understanding of the Soviet era civil protest from three hours of raw materials. Similar to in *Maidan*, the documentary images act as an enabler in witnessing a historic moment in time and to a certain extent transfer onto the viewer the experience of "being there". While the images of the 1991 standoff in Moscow are engraved into the collective mind, the fact that half a million people also gathered on Leningrad's Palace Square in anti-governmental protest has largely been forgotten. It is an event that largely failed to develop into a mnemonic event. The documentary, therefore, remediates a well-established memory of imminent political collapse while at the same time adding a new chapter to it. Notwithstanding the significance of *The Event* in altering common perceptions of 1991, and drawing attention to events that occurred outside the capital city, my argument here is that the compilation film is as much about contemporary Kiev as it is a re-examination of the Soviet Union's demise.

Loznitsa adopts a similar approach in both films: there is no main hero, no narrator or voice-over, no interviews; all indications about what is going on derive from *in situ* sound recordings and a handful of title cards indicating the main events. While the films are certainly not devoid of a political message, to which I will return, the filmmaker refrains from applying an interpretative frame throughout. Instead, he invites the viewer to reach their own conclusions. To a certain extent, the documentaries thereby mimic the experience of the people shown on screen: you hear what they would have been able to hear and see what they would have been able to see. As already noted, the pacing of both films reproduces this sense of uncertain outcomes. In an interview, Loznitsa indicated that his goal was to "bring the viewer to Maidan and give him the opportunity to experience 90 days of revolution".[17] The same is perhaps even more true for *The Event*, where the camerawork enhances the feeling of being part of the action to an even greater extent. Whereas in *Maidan* the camera is typically placed at the same height as the crowd but located at a slight distance – placing the viewer in the position of an observer – in *The Event*, the camera predominantly weaves its way through the crowd. The persons who step aside to allow the cameraman to pass them by are visibly less accustomed to being filmed than we are today: they look straight at the camera, that is, they look the viewer straight in the eye. Such instances of "direct eye contact" are rare in

17 Loznitza, "Chto takoe 'Maidan'?"

Maidan where no one is surprised to see a cameraman or, for that matter, to be filmed. But apart from being an interesting observation about changed societal realities, the resulting cinematic suggestion of integration into the masses and first-person experience is crucial for the film's viewer experience and therefore potential to serve as a memory text.

The productions exemplify the two styles that define Loznitsa's work as a documentary filmmaker. On the one hand, he produces films that silently observe and document the present, such as the film *Portrait* (2002) that consists of long takes of residents of the Russian countryside looking towards the camera. On the other hand, Loznitsa re-examines the past and its representation through a montage of archival film, for example in *Blockade* (2005), which is about the siege of Leningrad, and *Revue* (2008), a compilation of 1950s and 1960s Soviet propaganda newsreels. While markedly different in method, subject material and aesthetics, in the case of Loznitsa both styles are equally motivated by a drive to bear witness, to document, revisit and relive both past and present. The long takes and strong visual emphasis should therefore not be mistaken for an absence of intention.[18] Instead, as Denise Youngblood has argued with respect to the compilation film *Blockade*, Loznitsa shows:

> "not the past 'as it was', but, like all histories, a carefully constructed version of that past. […] By relying on images to the virtual exclusion of words, Loznitsa seeks to maximize the viewers' engagement with the material and minimize directorial intent".[19]

In the context of (re)framing the two revolutions that have had major consequences for contemporary Ukraine, this emotional engagement is instrumental in communicating the filmmaker's take on their politics.

(Re)mediating Political Crisis

As has been argued by Astrid Erll and Ann Rigney:

> "[…] most memorial media [on the one hand] strive for ever greater 'immediacy'. The goal is to provide a seemingly transparent window on the past, to make us

18 Erin Alpert, "The Visual in Documentary: Sergei Loznitsa and the Importance of the Image," *Studies in Documentary Film* 7, no. 2 (2013): 139.

19 Denise J. Youngblood, "A Chronicle for Our Time: Sergei Loznitsa's 'The Blockade'," *Russian Review* 66, no. 4 (2007): 697.

> forget the presence of the medium and instead present us with an 'unmediated memory'. On the other hand, this effect is usually achieved by the recycling and multiplication of media".[20]

These opposing tensions are evidently at work in *The Event*. One aspect it seeks to obscure from the viewer is the fact that, as a remediation of archival footage, the film constitutes a double framing of the crisis: both in the process of filming (which events are recorded and in what way) and in the process of producing the montage from these recordings by Loznitsa (which scenes are selected, how are they combined and sequenced, and what elements are omitted or emphasised).

The fact that the images of the Leningrad protest are not well known endows the filmmaker with relative freedom in how he chooses to present them; he is bound to a lesser extent to their medialised image and common perceptions. Connecting the images shown to those parts of the cultural memory that are widely-known is, however, important in ensuring the viewer's comprehension of the narrative, as well as in inviting them to reflect on the political crisis on a more abstract level. The soundtrack is instrumental in establishing this connection: the music of the Swan Lake ballet returns on crucial turning points as the political crisis unfolds. During the Putsch, state TV was firmly in the hands of the coup-makers. As all regular programming was cancelled, it showed the ballet piece repeatedly, interspersed with official statements. Here, Swan Lake serves as a "memory cue"[21] that associates the unknown images showed to collective memories of the Putsch and, more broadly, the collapse of Soviet Union. For those who lived through the events, the soundtrack may also trigger individual memories of those eventful days. The observer perspective, suggested by the way the camera moves through the crowds (noted above), can, in the absence of established memorialisation of the protest, come to mimic or substitute vernacular memory; through the "eyes" of the camera, the individuals protesting in Leningrad are reinscribed into the greater (visual) narrative of the Putsch.

As (re)mediations of political crises, the films' focus on the role of the masses (self-organised or not), rather than of individuals, is significant for the political

20 Astrid Erll and Ann Rigney, "Introduction: Cultural Memory and its Dynamics," in *Mediation, Remediation, and the Dynamics of Cultural Memory*, ed. Astrid Erll and Ann Rigney (Berlin and New York: De Gruyter, 2009), 4.

21 Alin Coman, Adam D. Brown, Jonathan Koppel, and William Hirst, "Collective Memory from a Psychological Perspective," *International Journal of Politics, Culture and Society* 22, no. 2 (2009): 128.

interpretations they imply. The emphasis on the collective is, in fact, embedded in the Russian title of *The Event*: the word "sobytie" etymologically derives from "being together". To be able to claim that the events amount to a *popular* revolution there first must be a concerted mass. In *Maidan*, in particular, this results in a fascinating investigation of how individual life trajectories intersect and interlace with big history:

> "[...] what's emphasised [...] is the number of levels on which we live: as microscopic, anonymous elements of vast historical narratives; as members of symbolic constructs such as nations, resistance movements and 'sides' of a conflict; as private individuals moving through our own subjective and enclosed dramas; and as social creatures in continual physical and emotional negotiation with others. By depicting these various conditions of existence in parallel, Loznitsa's film is also able to inhabit several diverse functions simultaneously. It is a dispassionate, close-range journalistic account of a succession of events, but also a delicate, even whimsical portrait of small-scale human interactions; it's a document of specific incidents, but also a timeless evocation of human reactions, both large and small, to crisis conditions".[22]

The documentaries draw attention to a particular aspect of the crowds that bears direct connection to the role of media in cultural memory formation and, when juxtaposed, is particularly insightful in understanding the fundamental difference between the two civil protests. In one of the shots included in *Maidan*, people hold up their mobile phones in lieu of candles at the funeral procession in commemoration of those who died during the conflict. Each light, however, represents much more: it stands for direct access to information; moreover, from multiple sources. It stands for a direct means of communication and therefore a means of political mobilisation. Each light represents a recording device and a means for immediate sharing of images with the rest of the world. While we are now accustomed to this reality, the comparison with the archival images from 1991 serves as a potent reminder of the tremendous impact of immediate medialisation of political crisis that has been enabled by the revolution in communication technology. *The Event*, in fact, revolves around communication and information flows; the issue of obtaining and fighting to get hold of information about what is going on runs as a thread through the film. With the television showing the Swan Lake ballet on repeat, the archival footage shows how people took to the streets to gather information from other sources. They

---

22 Hannah McGill, "Maidan," *Sight & Sound* 25, no. 3 (2015): 83–84.

are shown standing around in groups listening to the radio, and reading pamphlets and other sparse documents that are being handed out.

During the Putsch, Soviet media faced severe difficulties in continuing their operations. As Iain Elliot, the Associate Director of Radio Liberty who was in Moscow at the time, recounted in September 1991:

> "[...] some newspapers that immediately decided to defy the junta's ban found that they lacked the means to publish a normal issue – and not, in most cases that I heard about, because there were tanks barring the way to the printing presses. More often it was simply that the responsible official for the formerly Party-controlled newspapers refused to provide the keys, and since access to copy machines was still severely restricted, it was not always a simple matter to run off several thousand leaflets or brief 'emergency' issues of a newspaper. Even obtaining supplies of Xerox paper required considerable initiative".[23]

Access to cameras to record the ongoing events was equally obstructed.[24] In Leningrad, in a similar vein, the leaflets that were produced on the few remaining copy machines that had not yet been seized or blocked by the authorities became one of the principle means in disseminating information during the "almost complete information blackout, with the radio and TV continuously spreading lies".[25] As Valerii Kuchner – the then editor of the weekly newspaper *Rossiiskie vesti* – recalls, the limited number of leaflets they could produce were eagerly devoured by the underinformed audiences:

> "I remember taking a stack with me to Kalinin Prospect, and people simply tore them out of my hands. I believe the reason few people got hold of these leaflets is that they would quite literally tear them apart, trying to yank them out of one another's hands".[26]

23 Iain Elliot, "Three Days in August: On-the-Spot Impressions," reprinted in *Russia at the Barricades: Eyewitness Accounts of the August 1991 Coup*, ed. Victoria E. Bonnell, Ann Cooper, and Gregory Freidin (Armonk and London: M. E. Sharpe, 1991), 292.

24 Medvedev, "Getting the News," 302.

25 Valerii Zavorotnyi, "Letter from St. Petersburg," in *Russia at the Barricades: Eyewitness Accounts of the August 1991 Coup*, ed. Victoria E. Bonnell, Ann Cooper, and Gregory Freidin (Armonk and London: M.E. Sharpe, 1994), 153.

26 Valerii Kucher, "A Russian Reporter Remembers the Coup," interview by Mikhaleva, in *Russia at the Barricades: Eyewitness Accounts of the August 1991 Coup*, ed. Victoria E. Bonnell, Ann Cooper, and Gregory Freidin (Armonk and London: M.E. Sharpe, 1992), 327.

The image that Loznitsa sketches through his selection of images and editing in *The Event* suggests that this search for information actually was a major driver behind the mobilisation; people amassed on the streets of Leningrad not (only) to protest the Putsch, but to be informed about what was happening and learn what to do next. Flash forward to Maidan, in the highly-medialised reality of contemporary Ukraine, it was not the lack of but the free flow of information that, quite to the contrary, facilitated mobilisation. The documentaries testify to this transition from a complete lack of information to an information overload and the accompanying difficulty of assessing the credibility of sources. Located on opposite sides of the spectrum, both conditions can equally result in uncertainty regarding what is going on.

Throughout his documentary works, as well as in the two films explored here, Loznitsa demonstrates acute awareness of the significance of making recordings – that is, what is documented can be remembered, revisited, re-examined. *The Event*, for instance, explicitly features shots of the few cameramen and photographers that were on the scene. In *Maidan*, the frame is at times buzzing with photographers, cameramen and journalists. Since our understanding of events tends to change over time, documenting them allows for post factum reflection on these traces to reassess these occurrences and their consequences. Such a reassessment is clearly one of the aims of *The Event*. Through subtle hints (for instance in the title cards), Loznitsa argues that, despite the mass protest and notwithstanding the Soviet Union's collapse, political reality remained effectively unchanged. As political changes unfold that supposedly radically altered political reality, the soundtrack plays the light-hearted Dance of the Little Swans – a subtle but unmistakable commentary that, in reality, was simply business as usual. What appeared to be the rupture of established power structures later turned out to be only a concealed continuation of these very structures – a position that can be challenged. As the director has remarked on several occasions, he believes the 1991 revolution was staged from above.[27] The people were given their freedom, and that gift has since been taken back. The reason why nothing changed, Loznitsa appears to suggest, is that the Soviet people did not fight for their freedom – a suggestion that resonates with the classic heroic narrative of popular revolution.

27 E. g., Loznitsa, "Q & A Session."

Framing the Revolution

Taken together, the documentaries can be seen as an attempt to understand the nature of civil protest: they explore the dynamics and driving forces determining when, why and how large masses of people choose to gather to defy the political structure and demand change. Several elements return in both films and support their visual correspondence: the large crowds and speakers addressing them, barricades, banners and slogans, and musicians playing songs connecting to the political situation of the moment. In *The Event*, the past at times feels particularly topical, for instance in the repeated invocations of fascism to denounce the coup-makers. The intensity of the protest, however, is rather different. As they are mobilised in protest, the Leningrad crowd is largely passively awaiting what will happen next. The apparent lack of agency is quite the opposite to the seemingly organically self-organised networks of protesters on Maidan – from those who stand at the front lines of the confrontation to those who are organising food supplies. If we accept my hypothesis that *The Event* is not simply about the protest in 1991 but rather about reaching a greater understanding of conditions in contemporary Ukraine, then the juxtapositioning of the two films is intended to attest to a fundamental change in mentality. The Leningrad crowd is uncertain, hesitant, and lacking experience of protesting. The inclusion of Viktor Tsoi's emblematic song "We are waiting for change" in the soundtrack is highly suggestive in this respect. The protesters on Maidan, to the contrary, are shown as dedicated and organised. Most of all, they are framed as a people united. I agree with Lilya Kaganovsky, who states:

> "Loznitsa is attempting to document a revolution not simply on the streets of Ukraine but in the Ukrainian people, a profound change taking place in Ukrainian society. This is simultaneously an anticolonial revolution,[28] a 'mental' revolution against Russian power, and an anti-Soviet revolution that attempts to finally dismantle the Soviet state inside every individual".[29]

According to Loznitsa, then, the two films represent history coming full circle: a historical process of liberation and national emancipation that began during the final days of the Soviet Union has only now come to full fruition on

28 The application of postcolonial theory in relation to post-Soviet states is not without its critics, and in the context of this chapter it may be more productive to depart from the opposing notions of imperialist/nationalist.

29 Kaganovsky, "Maidan by Sergei Loznitsa," 895.

the streets of Kiev.[30] A revisiting of the memory of collapse becomes a visually persuasive argument in support of the claim that the Maidan revolution was "the real deal"; that, contrary to the 1991 revolution, it was a bottom-up revolution driven by a united people. The allegation of top-down orchestration of protest during the 1991 attempted coup-d'état is not without foundation. In an interview conducted on the 26th of August 1991, the then mayor of Leningrad (and later first mayor of St. Petersburg), Anatolii Sobchak, describes his involvement in organising a mass rally with factory workers from the Putilov metal-working plant:

> "And at six o'clock in the morning, I went to the Putilov factory. I managed to arrive before the shift started. There, at the factory gate, a car with a megaphone was already waiting. We held a rally. [...] As I was leaving, a large group of the Putilov workers, three or four thousand, was already marching down Stachechnyi Prospect [literally the Avenue of Strikes]. [...] We decided that people should go back to their places of work by 1:00 PM. That was exactly what happened. There were no no-shows".[31]

As was already mentioned, the unity and bottom-up self-organisation of Ukrainians taking part in Euromaidan, as it is presented by Loznitsa, obscures inner divisions within this 'emergent nation', as well as the involvement of controversial groups.

Some critics have suggested that *The Event* should instead be read as a call for protest in Russia. In this reading, the revisiting of the "failed" revolution of 1991 has the aim of inspiring the Russian people to follow the Ukrainian example of Maidan. While it is difficult to deny that the film has a political message that (also) pertains to Russia, I propose a more nuanced reading. When approached in combination with the film *Maidan*, *The Event* argues that effective political change is only possible when freedom is demanded and fought for by the people, who are, moreover, willing to sacrifice what they have to achieve it. In an interview, Loznitsa has commented on this apparent need of sacrifice and commemoration of victims in consolidating fundamental change:

30 Loznitsa, "Q & A session."

31 Anatolii Sobchak, "The Breakthrough: The Coup in St. Petersburg," interview by *Moscow News*, August 26, 1991, reprinted in *Russia at the Barricades: Eyewitness Accounts of the August 1991 Coup*, ed. Victoria E. Bonnell, Ann Cooper, and Gregory Freidin (Armonk and London: M. E. Sharpe, 1994), 224.

> "I could have ended the film differently. For instance, there was a festival, where Yuriy Lutsenko rejoicingly declared: 'We have won'. But to me that constitutes neither an ending, nor an important event. The farewell to the fallen was an event. It was necessary to pay tribute to their memory. The farewell to each of the fallen at the confluence of an enormous number of people – that is very important, especially to stop the processes of destruction in culture".[32]

Loznitsa does not grant such a moment of closure to his representation of the events of 1991. In my opinion, *The Event,* therefore, rather confronts its audience with a fundamental dilemma: has the passive mentality that it uncovers changed sufficiently since 1991 for a direct confrontation with the powers that be (as happened on Maidan) to be possible? Has the awareness spread that one is responsible for one's own fate, or are the Russian people still waiting for change? Loznitsa's apparent support for (heroic) self-sacrifice as a means of political change leaves the possibility of gradual reform (which may involve less personal suffering and material losses) beyond consideration. With the benefit of hindsight, it is fair to argue that the expectations of the what can be achieved through conflict and violent confrontation should be tempered.

The failed August 1991 Putsch is not typically used as a frame of reference for interpreting Euromaidan. In this chapter, I have demonstrated how Loznitsa employs the reworking of the memory of this previous state of emergency in *The Event* to validate the Maidan revolution as a grassroots revolution, contrary to the top-down revolution of 1991. The experience of the revolution that culminated in the collapse of the Soviet state is reinterpreted in such a way that it assists in overcoming the situation of crisis in recent memory. My analysis of the dynamic resonance between *Maidan* and *The Event* illustrates how the experience and memory of a previous collapse of political order premediates interpretations of the causes and significance of a current political crisis. Drawing upon the framework provided by the memory, initial attempts to explain and memorialise the ongoing or recently concluded crisis take place. By reframing the mass protest in Leningrad on the eve of the disintegration of the Soviet Union, Loznitsa effectively frames the revolution of Maidan.

---

32 Andrii Portnov, "Sergei Loznitsa: 'Evropeiskaia tsivilizatsiia zabyla, chto takoe sushchestvovanie v khore'," *Histor!ans*, March 31, 2015, http://www.historians.in.ua/index.php/en/intervyu/1475-sergej-loznitsa-evropejskaya-tsivilizatsiya-zabyla-chto-takoe-sushchestvovanie-v-khore.alper.

Bibliography

Alpert, Erin. "The Visual in Documentary: Sergei Loznitsa and the Importance of the Image." *Studies in Documentary Film* 7, no. 2 (2013): 135–145.

Bonnell, Victoria E., T. L. Cooper and Gregory Freidin, eds. *Russia at the Barricades: Eyewitness Accounts of the August 1991 Coup*. Armonk and London: M. E. Sharpe, 1994.

Bradshaw, Nick. "Different Drums." *Sight & Sound* 25, no. 3 (2015): 26–29.

Coman, Alin, Adam D. Brown, Jonathan Koppel and William Hirs. "Collective Memory from a Psychological Perspective." *International Journal of Politics, Culture and Society* 22, no. 2 (2009): 125–141.

Elliot, Iain. "Three Days in August: On-the-Spot Impressions." In *Russia at the Barricades: Eyewitness Accounts of the August 1991 Coup*, edited by Victoria E. Bonnell, Ann Cooper, and Gregory Freidin, 289–300. Armonk and London: M.E. Sharpe, 1994.

Erll, Astrid and Ann Rigney. "Introduction: Cultural Memory and its Dynamics." In *Mediation, Remediation, and the Dynamics of Cultural Memory*, edited by Astrid Erll and Ann Rigney, 1–11. Berlin and New York: De Gruyter, 2009.

Erll, Astrid. "Literature, Film, and the Mediality of Cultural Memory." In *Cultural Memory Studies: An International and Interdisciplinary Handbook*, edited by Astrid Erll and Ansgar Nünning, 389–398. Berlin: De Gruyter, 2008.

Kaganovsky, Lilya. "Maidan by Sergei Loznitsa." *Slavic Review* 74, no. 4 (2015): 894–895.

Kucher, Valerii. "A Russian Reporter Remembers the Coup." Interview by Mikhaleva. In *Russia at the Barricades: Eyewitness Accounts of the August 1991 Coup*, edited by Victoria E. Bonnell, Ann Cooper, and Gregory Freidin, 322–336. Armonk and London: M. E. Sharpe, 1994.

Loznitsa, Sergei. "Chto takoe 'Maidan'? Vopros, otveta na kotoryi u menia eshche net." Interview by Svitlana Shapoval. *Cultprostir*, July 2, 2014. http://cultprostir.ua/ru/post/sergey-loznica-chto-takoe-maidan-vopros-otveta-na-kotoriy-u-menya-esche-net.

Loznitsa, Sergei. "Q & A session." Interview on Rotterdam Film Festival, January 30, 2016.

Marples, David R. and Frederik V. Mills. *Ukraine's Euromaidan: Analyses of a Civil Revolution*. Stuttgart: Ibidem Verlag, 2015.

McGill, Hannah. "Maidan." *Sight & Sound* 25, no. 3 (2015): 83–84.

Medvedev, Sergei. "Getting the News on 'Vremia.'" Interview by Bill Keller, September 25, 1991. In *Russia at the Barricades: Eyewitness Accounts of the August 1991 Coup*, edited by Victoria E. Bonnell, Ann Cooper, and Gregory Freidin, 301–307. Armonk and London: M.E. Sharpe, 1994.

Plokhy, Serhii. *The Gates of Europe: A History of Ukraine*. New York: Basic Books, 2015.

Portnov, Andrii. "Sergei Loznitsa: 'Evropeiskaia tsivilizatsiia zabyla, chto takoe sushchestvovanie v khore.'" *Histor!ans*, March 31, 2015. http://www.historians.in.ua/index.php/en/intervyu/1475-sergej-loznitsa-evropejskaya-tsivilizatsiya-zabyla-chto-takoe-sushchestvo vanie-v-khore.

Shevel, Oxana. "Memories of the Past and Visions of the Future: Remembering the Soviet Era and its End in Ukraine." In *Twenty Years After Communism: The Politics of Memory and Commemoration*, edited by Michael Bernhard and Jan Kubik, 146–167. Oxford and New York: Oxford University Press, 2014.

Smith, Kathleen E. *Mythmaking in the New Russia: Politics and Memory during the Yeltsin Era*. Ithaca: Cornell University Press, 2002.

Sobchak, Anatolii. "The Breakthrough: The Coup in St. Petersburg." Interview by *Moscow News*, August 26, 1991. Reprinted in *Russia at the Barricades: Eyewitness Accounts of the August 1991 Coup*, edited by Victoria E. Bonnell, Ann Cooper, and Gregory Freidin, 218–225. Armonk and London: M. E. Sharpe, 1994.

Youngblood, Denise J. "A Chronicle for Our Time: Sergei Loznitsa's 'The Blockade.'" *Russian Review* 66, no. 4 (2007): 693–698.

Zavorotnyi, Valerii. "Letter from St. Petersburg." In *Russia at the Barricades: Eyewitness Accounts of the August 1991 Coup*, edited by Victoria E. Bonnell, Ann Cooper, and Gregory Freidin, 147–157, Armonk and London: M. E. Sharpe, 1994.

Valur Ingimundarson

Narrating Iceland's Financial Crisis: Contested Memories of Blame, Justice and Reconstruction

In April 2016, less than a decade after the collapse of the Icelandic banking system, the prime minister of Iceland, Sigmundur Davíð Gunnlaugsson, became the first global politician brought down by the Panama Papers scandal. It was revealed that he had co-owned an offshore company with his heiress wife that held millions of dollars in claims on the three Icelandic banks that went bankrupt during the 2008 financial crisis. The leak did not only raise ethical questions about keeping large sums of money in an offshore account but also about potential conflicts of interest. The Prime Minister was heavily involved in policymaking on the relaxation of currency and capital controls, which had been put in place through an emergency legislation prior to the crash. After mounting a defiant attempt to cling to power, Gunnlaugsson was forced to resign as prime minister. In addition, it was revealed that the Minister of Finance, Bjarni Benediksson, and the Minister of the Interior, Ólöf Nordal, had also had business dealings with offshore companies, even if they had been severed. While similar ethical concerns were voiced, the two ministers managed to hold onto their positions.

The leaks in the Panama Papers scandal sparked one of the largest mass protests in Iceland's history. The immediate reference point of a spontaneous manifestation of public anger was in the present, but it was also embedded in a recent past. Indeed, it was in part a throwback to and a re-enactment of the popular revolt in 2008, when sustained public demonstrations – dubbed the "Pots and Pans Revolution" – led to the fall of the government.[1] What is more, it conjured up another instance of historical equivalence: Iceland had been the first country to charge a prime minister for crimes in connection with the global financial crisis. To prevent a renewed crisis of legitimacy, the government saw no other option than to call early elections in 2016. This dramatic episode was a reminder that despite having recovered fully in economic terms thanks to a tourist boom, Iceland was – and still is – haunted by the trauma of the financial

1 On the Icelandic protest, see Jón G. Bernburg, *Economic Crisis and Mass Protests: The Pots and Pans Revolution in Iceland* (Basingstoke: Palgrave Macmillan, 2016).

crash, which is the largest that any country has experienced when measured in terms of the size of the economy.

In this chapter, I examine the response to the Icelandic financial collapse[2] by focusing on the politics of memory and justice to come to terms with a tainted past. I argue that the Icelandic case has many similarities with transitional justice processes, such as trials, truth commissions/reports, lustration or apologies, in countries undergoing transitions after a societal break-down. True, it was not about a civil conflict or a transformation from an authoritarian to a democratic regime.[3] But the politics of justice and regret after political shocks can emerge without "regime change" or democratic consolidation. The crisis response in Iceland was about a societal reckoning, and the moralistic terms associated with the politics of memory and transitional justice – responsibility, culpability, and victimhood – were central to the Icelandic experience. As I will show, punitive justice took precedence over restorative justice. No public venues were created for open truth-seeking, such as a truth and reconciliation commission, designed to achieve national reconciliation or to contribute to political stability after a societal shock. It was feared that such measures would interfere with criminal prosecutions and possibly require amnesties that could risk a public backlash. Yet, to respond to popular demands for accountability and democratic renewal, decisions were made to appoint an independent com-

2 On the Icelandic crisis, see Valur Ingimundarson, Phillippe Urfalino, and Irma Erlingsdóttir, eds., *Iceland's Financial Crisis: The Politics of Blame, Protest, and Reconstruction* (New York and London: Routledge, 2016); Eirikur Bergmann, *Iceland and the International Financial Crisis: Boom, Bust and Recover* (New York: Palgrave Macmillan, 2014); Robert Z. Aliber and Gylfi Zoega, eds., *Preludes to the Icelandic Financial Crisis* (New York: Palgrave-Macmillan, 2011); Guðrún Johnsen, *Bringing Down the Banking System – Lessons from Iceland* (New York: Palgrave Macmillan, 2014); Ásgeir Jónsson, *Why Iceland? How One of the World's Smallest Countries became the Meltdown's Biggest Casualty* (New York: McGraw–Hill, 2009); E. Paul Durrenberger and Gisli Pálsson, eds., *Gambling Debt: Iceland's Struggle with the New World Order* (Boulder: University of Colorado Press, 2015); Guðni Jóhannesson, *Hrunið* (Reykjavík: JPV, 2009); Roger Boyes, *Meltdown Iceland: How the global financial crisis bankrupted an entire country* (London: Bloomsbury, 2009).

3 On transitional justice, see Ruti Teitel, *Transitional Justice* (Oxford: Oxford University Press, 2000); Jon Elster, *Closing the Books: Transitional Justice in Historical Perspective* (Cambridge: Cambridge University Press, 2004); Jon Elster, ed., *Retribution and Reparations in the Transition to Democracy* (Cambridge: Cambridge University Press, 2006); Alexandra Barahona De Brito, Carmen Gonzalez Enriquez, and Paloma Aguilar, eds., *The Politics of Memory: Transitional Justice in Democratizing Societies* (Oxford: Oxford University Press, 2001).

mission to write a "truth report" and to elect a new constitutional assembly by popular vote designed to review or rewrite the constitution.[4] Thus, Iceland's approach towards the economic disaster contained both backward-looking and forward-looking elements.

The memory politics in Iceland took, in a simplified, the form of a dialectic between two metanarratives. After the collapse, many on the Left put the blame on the neo-liberal policies pursued by the Right, whose privatisation agenda had been accompanied by an ideological fixation on deregulation with minimum oversight. In contrast, the Right defended itself by pointing to the global financial crisis as a key factor in the fall of the banks, even if it was also critical of selective bankers for their reckless behaviour. Such simple dichotomies, however, ignored instances of shared political complicity. While the conservative Right was the driving force, centrist forces and the Social Democratic Left colluded with it and business interests during the pre-crisis period. The only political entity not tainted by the banking collapse was the Left Green Movement, which had been critical of the neo-liberal turn in the early 2000s. In general, what political elites had in common during the period leading up to the crash was a desire to manage an economic boom in a technocratic fashion without much government interference and to reap the political benefits from it.

Following the banking collapse, the politics of transition created new divisions and raised questions of selective justice and failed political reform. Notwithstanding a highly critical "truth report" about the failures of the banks and heavy prison sentences of bankers, political and financial elites refused to accept any responsibility, pointing fingers at each other. Moreover, the inability to implement the constitutional project after setbacks and the staging of judicial proceedings against the former prime minister – which ended in a sentence with no punishment for a minor charge – underscored the conflict-ridden nature of the transitional process. To be sure, from the start there was widespread public support for the jail sentences of leading bankers. Over 30 have

4 On the constitutional project, see the following contributions in Ingimundarson, Urfalino, and Erlingsdóttir, *Iceland's Financial Crisis*: Thorvaldur Gylfason, "Constitution on Ice," 203–19; Jon Ólafsson, "The Constituent Assembly: A Study in Failure," 252–272; Bjorg Thorarensen, "The Constitutional Council. Objectives and Shortcomings of an Innovative Process," 239–251; Jon Elster, "Icelandic Constitution-Making in Comparative Perspective," 187–202; Salvör Nordal, "Constitutional Revision. A Weak Legislative Framework Compounded by Political Disputes," 220–229; Pasquale Pasquino, "Constituent Power and Authorization. Anatomy and Failure of a Constitution-Making Process," 230–238. See also Hélène Landemore, "Inclusive Constitution-Making: The Icelandic Experiment," *Journal of Political Philosophy* 23, no. 2 (2015): 166–191.

received a combined prison sentence of close to 90 years. This punitive aspect of the response to the crisis in Iceland differed markedly from the experience in Spain, Ireland, Greece, or Portugal. In these countries, criminal prosecutions were neither part of a "reckoning with the past" nor of a future-oriented "reconstruction" agenda in the aftermath of the crisis, even if a few bankers have been prosecuted in Ireland and Spain. Yet, while the Icelandic banking collapse was generally seen as a catastrophic event, affecting Icelandic society as a whole, the question of blame remained contested.

As I illustrate here, one important explanatory factor is that the boundaries between the memories of the pre-and post-crash period became quickly blurred. This meant that the political memory battle over accountability was not confined to the period leading up to the crisis but also to the response to it. In this way, a direct relationship between the "old guard" and the "new regime" was established, which influenced, in a substantial way, the "politics of reconstruction". Therefore, the undoing of the pre-existing ideological order, which – as Ruti Teitel has argued – is crucial in all political transitions, did not succeed.[5] Major actors from the past have been punished through stiff prison sentences. But some of the dominant elements of the previous political and business elites were also able to shape the transition by reinventing themselves either in new or old roles and as part of rehabilitation attempts.

The Making of a Tragedy: From Financial Euphoria to a Societal Disaster

The global expansion of the Icelandic banks from 2003 to 2007 stemmed from neo-liberal policies, which were adopted – in the late 1990s – by a centre-right government under the ideological guidance of Iceland's largest party, the conservative Independence Party. What followed was a deeply flawed, politicised privatisation process,[6] which not only freed the banks from state control but also led to a strong cross-ownership arrangement between them and the largest companies. This ill-fated fusion created the conditions for a spectacular growth of the banking system, which had few historical parallels.[7] The expan-

5 See Teitel, *Transitional Justice*, 116.

6 See Johnsen, *Bringing Down the Banking System;* Guðrun Johnsen, "The Rise and Fall of a Financial Empire," in *Iceland's Financial Crisis. The Politics of Blame, Protest, and Reconstruction,* ed. Valur Ingimundarson, Philippe Urfalino, and Irma Erlingsdóttir (Basingstoke: Palgrave Macmillan, 2016), 37–53.

7 See Aliber and Zoega, *Preludes to the Icelandic Financial Crisis*; see also Gylfi Zoega, "Iceland's Financial Crisis: An Economic Perspective," in *Iceland's Financial Crisis. The*

sion was driven by access to cheap credit in global capital markets, which the banks also used to finance a debt-induced domestic consumer spree and to create a housing bubble.[8]

By 2008, the banking system had become ten times the size of Iceland's GDP. During this transformative period, a group of approximately 30 businessmen accumulated enormous economic power, enabling them to stage what came close to a societal "take-over".[9] Representing competing financial and political groups, these "oligarchs" became the main donors to political candidates and parties, purchased private media companies, and provided financial support to public/private education and cultural institutions. Political elites not only became highly dependent on this new capitalist class; they relished their role in initiating the massive transfer of power from the public sphere to the private sector. As then Finance Minister and later Prime Minister, Geir Haarde, put it in 2005: "[...] few things are more rewarding in politics than to see when a good idea becomes embedded and wins in the ideological struggle [...] I am sure that no one wants to return to the time when the financial sector was subjected to political control".[10] As a result, the state was sharply weakened, with politicians and financial regulators – including the Central Bank – relegated to the role of passive spectators in a show run by private financial interests.

To be sure, the architect of the Independence Party's privatisation agenda, Davíð Oddsson – who was Iceland's prime minister from 1991 until 2005 and a governor of the Central Bank from 2005 to 2009 – sometimes attacked the excesses of the new bank owners.[11] But his criticism was selective: apart from attacking specific businessmen and bankers, whom he saw as his foes, he targeted the largest opposition party, the Social Democratic Alliance, for its ties with some of them, while remaining silent on similar connections between the

Politics of Blame, Protest, and Reconstruction, ed. Valur Ingimundarson, Philippe Urfalino, and Irma Erlingsdóttir (Basingstoke: Palgrave Macmillan, 2016), 21–36.

8 See Jon Daníelsson and Gylfi Zoega, "Collapse of a Country," *Institute of Economic Studies – Working Papers Series* 9, no. 3 (2009), http://www.ioes.hi.is/sites/hhi.hi.is/files/W-series/2009/WP0903.pdf.

9 See Valur Ingimundarson, "A 'Crisis of Affluence': The Politics of an Economic Breakdown in Iceland," *Irish Studies in International Affairs* 21 (2010): 57–63.

10 Geir Haarde, "Address on the occasion of the SBV Day," April 7, 2005, quoted in Vigdís Þóra Sigfúsdóttir, "Réttarstaða ráðherra sem sakborninga fyrir Landsómi í ljósi stjórnarskrár lýðveldisins Íslands og Mannréttindasáttmála Evrópu" (ML thesis in Law, University of Bifröst, 2011), 1.

11 See, for example, *Morgunblaðið*, March 4, 2003; November 23, 2003 and November 25, 2003.

Conservatives and other business groups. Indeed, as noted, apart from the Left Greens, all political parties colluded with the new economic "masters", celebrating what became dubbed as the Icelandic "outrush" – an aggressive territorial aggrandisement strategy in global markets. The president of Iceland, Ólafur Ragnar Grímsson, played a key role in legitimising the project abroad by promoting, in essentialist terms, the "special brand" of Icelandic entrepreneurship with references to heroic mediaeval Viking myths.[12]

Given this state of euphoria, it should not have come as a surprise that the reaction of politicians to the first signs of trouble facing the banks in late 2007 and early 2008 was that of complete denial. Having stayed out of government from 1995 until 2007, the Social Democratic Alliance had no influence over the economic policies during this period. However, after joining a coalition government with the Independence Party in 2007, it became as seduced by the power of finance capital as other political forces. Placing their trust in the financial elite, the conservative Prime Minister Geir Haarde, and the Social Democratic Foreign Minister Ingibjörg Sólrún Gísladóttir even embarked on a "road show" abroad, where they went out of their way to vouch for the health of the Icelandic banking system at a time when it was visibly buckling under the strain and coming under fire abroad for its unsustainable growth and size.[13] When the three largest banks eventually crumbled in the early stages of the 2008 global financial crisis, the government had practically no defenses at its disposal, except for one contingency plan – admittedly an extremely important one – that prevented a total financial collapse. As a result of the banking system's gigantic size, there was no way the Icelandic government could save it. But when facing a bank run at home and abroad, the Icelandic parliament passed an emergency law to ensure that deposit holders were given priority to bond holders and to pave the way for all domestic assets to be transferred to new banks. What this meant was that the banking system shrunk, in one fell swoop, to a fraction of what it had been before the disaster. But to avert a sovereign debt default, an IMF bailout and emergency loans from the Nordic

12 See Guðjón Friðriksson, *Saga af forseta. Forsetatíð Ólafs Ragnars Grímssonar. Útrás, athafnir og einkamál* (Reykjavik: Forlagið bókabúð, 2008). See also Kristin Loftsdóttir, "Vikings invade present day Iceland," in *Gambling Debt. Iceland's Rise and Fall in the Global Economy*, ed. E. Paul Durrenberger and Gisli Pálsson (Boulder: University of Colorado Press, 2015), 3–15.

13 Ingibjörg Gísladóttir, "Islands økonomi, stærk og flekisbel," Icelandic Foreign Ministry, accessed January 22, 2018, http://www.utanrikisraduneyti.is/frettaefni/raedurISG/nr/4151.

countries and Poland were needed after the government had failed to attract emergency loans from Western countries and Russia.

The Politics of Justice: From a "Truth Report" to Legal Proceedings

Apart from the economic responses, the government and parliament were under intense public pressure from the beginning to explain and confront the crisis through political means. Iceland's crisis management strategy, which was developed hurriedly during a state of extreme political volatility in 2008–2009, was characterised by an uneven mixture of punitive and restorative instruments, with the former trumping the latter. To assign blame and punishment, a Special Investigation Commission was appointed with the aim of writing a "truth report" about the collapse of the banking system,[14] and a Special Prosecutor's Office was established to look into potential criminal charges. Moreover, in an act of "lustration", the three governors of the Central Bank were dismissed. Impeachment charges were subsequently filed against the former prime minister, and many bank managers were prosecuted and later sentenced for fraud and market manipulation.

When the report of the Special Investigation Commission was published in 2010, it proved to be highly critical of domestic political and financial elites. It went so far as to argue that the collapse of the banking system had been inevitable by the end of 2006 and that the banks had committed fraud by inflating the value of their stocks and, thus, engaged in market manipulation. Three former ministers, Prime Minster Geir Haarde, Finance Minister Árni Mathiesen, and Commerce Minister Björgvin G. Sigurðsson, were singled out for having possibly violated Iceland's 1963 Law on Ministerial Responsibility. Five other former officials were accused of acting with negligence in failing to prevent Iceland's banking collapse in 2008: The three governors of the Central Bank, including Davíð Oddsson, and the former Director of the Financial Supervisory Authority. In addition, blame was also assigned to former Foreign Minister Ingibjörg Sólrún Gísladóttir, as the leader of the Social Democratic Alliance,

14 See Vilhjálmur Árnason, "Moral Analysis of an Economic Collapse – An Exercise in Practical Ethics," *Nordic Journal of Applied Ethics* 4, no. 1 (2010): 101–123; Vilhjálmur Árnason, "Democratic Practices, Governance, and the Financial Crash," in *Iceland's Financial Crisis. The Politics of Blame, Protest, and Reconstruction*, ed. Valur Ingimundarson, Philippe Urfalino, and Irma Erlingsdóttir (Basingstoke: Palgrave Macmillan, 2016), 121–139. See also Guðni Elísson, "Ísland, anno núll. Rannsóknarskýrslan, spuninn, ábyrgðin og staðleysustjórnmál," *Tímarit Máls og menningar* 71, no. 2 (2010): 24–40.

even if the 1963 law was not seen as being applicable in her case or in those of the Central Bank officials.[15]

While the Commission had a broad mandate, it did not operate through an open process or organise any public staging of truth-telling. Its findings were based on documented evidence and testimonies from politicians, officials, and bankers. A delay in completing the report proved to be frustrating for a public in need of explanations for the disaster. Yet, when the report finally came out it served, for a short time, a cathartic purpose and instantly became a foundational document – an accepted interpretation of the causes of the crisis. It managed to fulfil the main requirement expected from truth commissions by giving a collective identity to a divided society.[16] Yet, precisely because of this emphasis on unitary coherence,[17] where individual and collective processes were treated largely in equivalent terms,[18] it gave different groups a chance to interpret it in ways that fit their own interests.

The report satisfied the expectations of the Left by mentioning the culprits and by giving an account of a tainted privatisation and deregulation drive. The Right welcomed the exposure of insider trading practices, especially of those members of the banking and business elite against whom it had a political grudge. The report was not about societal reconciliation, which is normally rooted in long-term processes beyond the capacity of a short-term commission. It was, critical, however, of the ideology and policies that led to the excesses of

15 Rannsóknarnefnd Alþingis, *Aðdragandi og orsakir falls íslensku bankanna 2008 og tengdir atburðir* (Reykjavik: Icelandic Parliament, 2010), http://sic.althingi.is/.

16 Brandon Hamber and Richard A. Wilson, "Symbolic Closure through Memory, Reparation and Revenge in post-Conflict Societies," in *The Role of Memory in Ethnic Conflict,* ed. Ed Cairns and Michael D. Roe (Houndsmills, Basingstoke and New York: Palgrave Macmillan, 2003), 144.

17 On truth commissions, see Priscilla Hayner, *Unspeakable Truths: Confronting State Terror and Atrocity* (New York: Routledge, 2001); Beth Rushton, "Truth and reconciliation? The experience of Truth Commissions," *Australian Journal of International Affairs* 60, no. 1 (2006): 125–141; Charles Maier, "Doing History, Doing Justice: The Narrative of the Historian and of the Truth Commission," in *Truth vs. Justice. The Moral Efficacy of Truth Commissions: South Africa and beyond,* ed. Robert Rotberg and Dennis Thompson (Princeton: Princeton University Press, 2000), 261–278; David A. Crocker, "Truth Commissions, Transitional Justice, and Civil Society," in *Truth vs. Justice. The Moral Efficacy of Truth Commissions: South Africa and beyond,* ed. Robert Rotberg and Dennis Thompson (Princeton: Princeton University Press, 2000), 99–121; Nenad Dimitrijevic, "Justice beyond Blame: Moral Justification of (the Idea) of a Truth Commission," *Journal of Conflict Resolution* 50, no. 3 (2006): 368–382.

18 Hamber and Wilson, "Symbolic Closure," 144.

the boom period. It also showed how politicians had become dependent on financial elites. In this way, it contributed to the production of social knowledge indispensable to societal transitions[19] by offering a politically viable narrative. But the report had few long-term effects, even if some of its recommendations for institutional reform were acted upon. Most importantly, its subscription to punitive notions of political accountability was only partially accepted, not least because of the Icelandic parliament's controversial handling of the issue.

A cross-party Parliamentary Committee entrusted with evaluating the report of the Special Investigation Commission accepted its findings. Hence, the committee recommended, if not unanimously, that three ministers as well as the former Minister of Foreign Affairs Ingibjörg Sólrún Gísladóttir[20] be prosecuted for dereliction of duty in connection with the fall of the banks. Consistent with the conclusion of the Special Investigation Commission, the governors of the Central Bank and the heads of the Financial Supervisory Authority were not on the list of those selected for prosecution on the grounds that the law was not applicable to them. The ministers who privatised the banks were also excluded due to statute of limitations considerations.

If parliament wanted to be absolved of the burden of charging several of its own members for crimes, it could have adhered closely to the recommendations of the Special Investigation Commission. Yet, as it turned out, parliament was unable to avoid partisan rancour when it voted on the issue in 2010. The majority of MPs decided only to refer the case of former Prime Minister Geir Haarde to the Special Court, defeating proposals to indict the other three. This outcome was mostly due to the paradoxical situation in which the Social Democratic Alliance found itself. Having been briefly a part of the "old regime" – as the coalition partners of the Conservatives from 2007 to the beginning of 2009 – it now wanted to be identified with the "new regime", which sought to distance itself from the past through a commitment to a left-wing agenda and constitutional reform. Unable to solve this dilemma, some Social Democratic members of parliament decided to vote for Haarde's impeachment as part of efforts "to come to terms with the past", while shielding their own ministers from prosecution.

A case that had been put forward to meet public demands for accountability of the political elite turned, instead, into an ugly debate over whether one poli-

19 Dimitrijević, "Justice beyond Blame," 376–377.

20 "Icelandic Parliament (September 2010)," Skýrsla þingnefndar til að fjalla um skýrslu rannsóknarnefndar Alþingis, accessed December 4, 2015, http://www.althingi.is/altext/138/s/1501.html.

tician should bear sole responsibility for the banking collapse. Not many were willing to subscribe to such a reductionist view, including those who strongly favoured criminal prosecution. When Geir Haarde's case was submitted to the Special Court, he was indicted for displaying "serious malfeasance of his duties as prime minister in the face of major danger looming over Icelandic financial institutions and the state treasury, a danger that he knew of or should have known of".[21] Other charges included a serious neglect of his ministerial duties, a lack of efforts to assess the financial risks facing Iceland or to take action to reduce the size of its banking system, and a failure to ensure that one of the Icelandic bank's saving accounts in the United Kingdom and Netherlands were split off into subsidiary companies in those countries before the collapse of the banking system.[22]

What makes the Icelandic Special Court different from other domestic courts is not only its function as a venue for holding politicians and officials accountable but also its mandate and composition. It operates under highly politicised conditions because the separation of legislative and judicial powers does not apply to its proceedings. Thus, it has to act on criminal charges issued by parliament, not the public prosecutor.[23] Moreover, it is a hybrid court composed of professional judges (including those of the Supreme Court), legal specialists, and also political appointees. The only leeway the court has vis-à-vis parliament is to make decisions on the validity of individual charges. In 2011, it dropped the two charges against Geir Haarde, which dealt with gross negligence and failure to have the financial risks assessed, but it continued with the case based on the four remaining charges.

The Law as Public Spectacle: The Criminal Case against a Prime Minister

The trial over Geir Haarde took place in March, 2012. A highly symbolic venue, the Centre for Cultural Heritage in the centre of Reykjavik was temporarily turned into a criminal courthouse. Over 40 people offered testimonies, including the ministers who escaped impeachment; the former governors of the

21 "Icelandic Parliament (September 11, 2010)," Tillaga til þingsályktunar um málshöfðun gegn ráðherrum, accessed July 8, 2017, http://www.althingi.is/altext/138/s/1502.html.

22 "Icelandic Parliament (September 11, 2010)."

23 On the Special Court, see, for example, Sigurður Líndal, "Um ráðherraábyrgð og landsdóm," *Skírnir* 184, no. 2 (2010): 522–532; Svala I. Ólafsdóttir, "Rökstólar. Landsdómur og ráðherraábyrgð," *Úlfljótur* 64, no. 2 (2011): 290–294.

Central Bank; and the former directors of the failed Icelandic banks, several of whom had been charged with criminal conduct by the Special Prosecutor. This was the first time that all the major actors in the banking crisis testified publicly in a court of law, but they had earlier given private testimonies to the Special Investigation Commission. Yet, as a contribution to retributive justice, the testimonies proved to be of small value. Nothing new came to light – and no one was prepared to concede any mistakes or assume responsibility for the 2008 disaster.

In line with the standard Conservative narrative, Geir Haarde put the blame on the Icelandic banks – which had acted irresponsibly, taken unacceptable risks, and been involved in illegal conduct – as well the global financial crisis. His government had not been in a position to do anything to prevent the crash, such as reducing the gargantuan size of the banking system or pressuring the banks to relocate abroad.[24] In other words, "preventive action" was not possible because the crisis was beyond the control of the government. A government intervention would only have hastened the downfall of the banks by undermining their standing in global markets. Misleading public statements or silence on the part of high government officials, such as the Prime Minister and Foreign Minister,[25] over the real state of the banks during the "roadshow" were explained away as an attempt to prevent something worse. To him, there was no way for ministers to know that the entire banking system was at risk.[26] Given the prevailing structural constraints, it was not possible to act differently.

This line of argument was incomplete because the government had ignored strong warnings of an impending disaster from foreign government officials, economists, and journalists.[27] Such sceptics were usually branded as spoilers or jealous distractors in the media prior to the crash. The former ministers, who testified at the trial, stated that the banking collapse could only have been prevented if something had been done several years before the crisis.

---

24 "The testimony of Geir Haarde before the Icelandic Special Court (*Landsdómur*, 5 March 2012)," accessed July 6, 2017, http://www.landsdómur.is/adalmedferd/nr/9.

25 *Financial Times*, March 27, 2008; *Iceland Review*, March 12, 2008.

26 "The testimony of Geir Haarde."

27 See Carsten Valgren and Lars Christiansen, "Iceland. Geyser Crisis," *Research*, March 21, 2006, accessed July 6, 2017, http://www.mbl.is/media/98/398.pdf; lecture by Robert Z. Aliber, "Monetary turbulence and the Icelandic economy," University of Iceland, 2008; Anne C. Sibert and Willem Buiter, "The Icelandic banking crisis and what do to about it: The lender of last resort theory of optimal currency areas." *CEPR Policy Insight* 26 (2008), http://willembuiter.com/iceland.pdf; Robert Wade, "Iceland pays price for financial excess," *Financial Times*, July 1, 2008.

In this way, they made the admittedly a-historical conclusion of the Special Investigation about the "inevitability" of the banking collapse after 2006 their own. To respond to accusations that they reacted irresponsibly by not having formal government meetings on the rapidly deteriorating economic situation in 2008, they defended themselves by saying that the state of the banking system had been discussed in general terms. It would have been impossible to reduce its size in 2008, they argued, because there were no willing buyers at that time.[28] That may be true, but the government had not made any attempt to do so earlier because it wanted to continue to rely on the revenues generated by the banks.

The central bankers blamed the banks for recklessness and high-risk gambles.[29] Former Central Bank Governor, Davíð Oddsson, made the point that he had warned the government, in the strongest possible terms, that the Icelandic banks were facing serious difficulties re-capitalising themselves as the European banks no longer believed in their stability.[30] The head of the failed banks blamed the international financial crisis as well as the government and the Central Bank for the fall of the banks.[31] It was a repetition of arguments that had been made ad nauseam since the crash. Those who expected the first public staging of truth-telling to create a cathartic moment similar to that evoked by the "truth report" were wrong. There were no public confessions, apologies or admissions of responsibility. The testimonies amounted to a wholesale whitewash of the conduct of the political and economic elites.

28 "The testimony of Ingibjörg Sólrún Gísladóttir, former Foreign Minister, 12 March 2012," accessed July 7, 2017, http://www.landsdómur.is/adalmedferd/nr/41; "The testimony of Árni Mathiesen, former Minister of Finance, 13 March 2012," accessed July 7, 2017, http://www.landsdómur.is/adalmedferd/nr/29; "The testimony of Björgvin G. Sigurðsson, former Minister of Commerce, March 6, 2017," accessed July 7, 2017, http://www.landsdómur.is/adalmedferd/nr/34.

29 "The testimony of Davíð Oddsson, former Central Bank Governor, 19 March 2012," accessed July 7, 2017, http://www.landsdómur.is/adalmedferd/nr/36; "The testimony of Ingimundur Friðriksson, former Central Bank Governor, 7 March 2012," accessed July 7, 2017, http://www.landsdómur.is/adalmedferd/nr/42.

30 "The testimony of Davíð Oddsson."

31 See "The testimony of Hreiðar Már Sigurðsson, former CEO of Kaupthing Bank, 8 March 2012," accessed July 7, 2017, http://www.landsdómur.is/adalmedferd/nr/40; "The testimony of Sigurður Einarsson, former Chair of the Board of Kaupthing Bank, 19 March 2012," accessed July 7, 2017, http://www.landsdómur.is/adalmedferd/nr/57; "The testimony of Sigurjón Þ. Árnason, former Director of Landsbanki, 12 March 2012," accessed July 7, 2017, http://www.landsdómur.is/adalmedferd/nr/59; "The testimony of Lárus Welding, former Director of Glitnir Bank, 12 March 2012," accessed July 7, 2017, http://www.landsdómur.is/adalmedferd/nr/55.

The Special Court convicted Haarde of only one minor criminal charge without punishment – of failing to hold government meetings over the precarious state of the banking system ahead of its collapse – and cleared him on three others: of not doing anything to reduce the size of the banking system, of not making sure that the Icesave internet accounts of the Landsbanki in Britain and the Netherlands were transferred to a subsidiary, and of failing to produce better results from the government's 2006 report on financial stability. Yet, what amounted to a defensive victory did not satisfy Haarde. He blamed the court for meting out political justice, describing the verdict as "ludicrously laughable".[32] Earlier he had termed the affair a political trial and farce, bordering on persecution. He claimed to have nothing to hide because he had a "a clean slate" – using a language fitting to transitional justice proceedings.[33] Until the fall of the banks, he had defended the cosy relationship he had with selected owners of the banks, notably Björgólfur Thor Björgólfsson, who was listed among the world's richest men and whom the Prime Minister boasted of meeting regularly.[34] But on the question of responding to the crisis, Haarde claimed that his own actions had actually helped save Iceland from economic ruin and national bankruptcy by rushing the emergency law through parliament. What is more, in an attempt to clear his name, he appealed his conviction to the European Court of Human Rights. In 2017, the Court ruled that Geir's rights had not been violated by the 2012 verdict.

Geir Haarde's interpretation was questioned by those who agreed with the Special Investigation Commission that he should be held accountable for doing nothing to avert the economic disaster. However, the judicial proceedings divided public opinion on the question of whether they should have been held at all.[35] The pressure for prosecution proved far weaker than it was in the beginning because many saw it as being wrong and unfair to charge Haarde alone and not to include the other ministers. The call for retribution is usually the strongest in the immediate aftermath of a major societal rupture and sentences usually become far more lenient as time elapses. The outcome of the Special Court trial over the highest representative of the Icelandic political elite

---

32 *Eyjan*, April 24, 2012.

33 See "Former Iceland Prime Minister on Trial, *RTE News*, 5 September 2011," accessed July 8, 2017, http://www.rte.ie/news/2011/0905/iceland.html; see also *Vísir*, September 28, 2010, accessed July 8, 2017, http://www.visir.is/geir-segir-akaeruna-jadra-vid-politiskar-ofsoknir/article/2010133815 50.

34 *DV*, September 30, 2008.

35 *Eyjan*, February 13, 2012, http://eyjan.is/2012/02/13/thjodin-klofin-vegna-akaeru-a-hendur-geir-haarde-svipadur-fjoldi-vill-haetta-vid-og-malid-afram/.

tended to confirm this trend; however, importantly enough, it did not affect the sentencing of bankers who continued to receive severe prison terms eight years after the financial collapse.

It is true that Geir Haarde's prosecution was a form of political justice. After a majority of the MPs issued the charges against him along political lines, the Public Prosecutor stated that she was bound by law to prosecute the case on the premises spelled out by parliament.[36] The political nature of the trial was also underscored by the fact that eight out of 15 members of the Special Court were political appointees. Yet, this should not have come as a surprise when the case is approached from a criminal justice perspective; the use of such mechanism is bound to be a highly politicised and contested process. For one thing, it is often difficult to argue that political accountability or negligence should be equated with criminal acts. Whereas the bankers could be charged with financial crimes, such as market manipulation or illegal financial gain, the politicians were not directly involved in such wrongdoing. The fact that Geir Haarde was sentenced only for refraining from holding formal government meetings on the precarious state of the banking shows this dilemma. On the other hand, the weakness of the case against Haarde does not clear him or his ideological allies of political responsibility. The tainted privatisation and deregulation drive did much to create the conditions for the catastrophe, and the close links between political and financial elites ensured that there would be no attempt to supervise and regulate the business practices of the latter.

The "Old Regime" and the Politics of Transition

When societies come to terms with a troubled past, the "old regime" is often not only capable of influencing the transition but also of staging a comeback. Previous elites may not be in charge of the hegemonic political narrative anymore, but they can ensure that old practices survive, if in a different form.[37] Thus, the question is not about defending or re-legitimising the past, but rather about the degree to which these elites can sustain themselves by infiltrating the transition. After being forced out of the Central Bank, Davíð Oddsson became the editor-in-chief of the second largest newspaper in Iceland, the conservative *Morgunblaðið*, which he used to propagate his own interpretation of the economic collapse in an effort to rehabilitate himself. In addition, he played

36 See *Morgunblaðið*, January 27, 2012.

37 Dimitrijević, "Justice beyond Blame," 371.

an important role in fighting the left-wing government policies on the constitutional project and other issues.

Conversely, the media empire, which includes the largest newspaper, *Fréttablaðið*, and a private TV station is still controlled by the wife of Jón Ásgeir Jóhannesson, who was one of the leading businessmen in Iceland in the 2000s. As the former CEO of Baugur Group, Jóhannesson had extensive dealings with all the major Icelandic banks and a controlling stake in one of the largest Icelandic banks before its collapse. After the banking privatisation, he was engaged in a fierce power struggle with Oddsson and his political allies during the latter's tenure as Prime Minister and as a Governor of the Central Bank, which lasted until the financial collapse. Indeed, this fight to some degree was reenacted within a different political context and on another public stage during the post-crisis period.

It is true that the success of the comeback of political and financial actors has been mixed. While Davíð Oddsson has made the most of his powerful media position, he made a failed bid to become the President of Iceland in 2016, receiving less than 15 % of the vote. Three other major political players, all of whom were singled out by the Special Investigation Committee for bearing responsibility for the crash, have received high-level jobs abroad. In a symbolic political act designed to rehabilitate Haarde after his verdict, the Independence Party arranged for his appointment as Iceland's Ambassador to the United States in 2014. In 2012, former Foreign Minister Ingibjörg Sólrún Gísladóttir became the UN Representative for Women in Afghanistan and later its Regional Director for Europe and Central Asia, and in 2017 she was made Director of the Office for Democratic Institutions and Human Rights at the Organization for Security and Co-operation in Europe (OSCE). In 2010, Árni Mathiesen, the former Minister of Finance, became the Assistant Director-General in the Fisheries and Aquaculture Department of the UN Food and Agricultural Organisation (FAO) in Rome.

The President, Ólafur Ragnar Grímsson, whose popularity had reached an all-time low after the crash as a result of his role in celebrating the Icelandic banks and their global expansion, managed to reinvent himself politically in a spectacular fashion. He sided with nationalist grassroots activists by refusing twice to sign a law concerning solving the Icesave issue and by agreeing to a taxpayer-funded liability claim in connection with the failed Icelandic bank in Britain and Holland. By doing so, he automatically triggered two referenda on the bill, which was overwhelmingly rejected by voters. In 2012, he was reelected president by popular vote for a fifth consecutive term. He eventually refrained from running again in 2016 after briefly entering the contest after the Panama Papers scandal on the grounds that he could ensure stability in a period of political turmoil.

As for leading businessmen, Jón Ásgeir Jóhannesson's economic position is much weaker than it was in the 2000s. Unlike most of the bank directors, he has been spared a jail term, but he was sentenced in a tax fraud case and received a suspended sentence. And despite having won a case before the European Court of Human Rights on the grounds that his human rights had been violated by Icelandic courts for punishing him twice for the same act, he is still facing charges by the Special Prosecutor in connection with the financial crisis. On the other hand, Björgólfur Thor Guðmundsson, who experienced a steep fall in the world of business during the financial crisis, has largely reclaimed his former wealth status. Moreover, he has not been charged with financial crimes by the Special Prosecutor. Thus, two rival tycoons from the pre-2008 period and former stakeholders in the banks have been able to continue to exert their influence, even if their positions differ substantially. Interestingly, both called for the establishment of a Truth and Reconciliation Commission to deal with the aftermath of the crash.[38] Yet, the problem with such a course of action was evident from the start. To opt exclusively for restorative justice mechanisms in the name of societal reconciliation would not only have shielded potential perpetrators from retributive justice; as noted, such a commission could also have provided the heavily compromised state with implicit power to "wipe out the slate clean". For this reason, it is not surprising that the idea put forward by two leading figures in the financial crash received no backing; rather, it was treated like a self-serving vehicle for restorative truth-telling without legal accounting or retributive justice.

Conclusion

What shows the deep societal impact of the crisis is that Iceland's surprisingly speedy economic recovery – which has resulted in high growth rates, full employment, and far lower debt levels than before the banking collapse – has failed to transform, politically, into a "new normal". Instead, highly contested political narratives about the causes and nature of the crash or about the assignment of responsibility have emerged. As I have shown here, the response has been heavily influenced by judicial mechanisms. The pressure for punitive accountability has not been followed by calls for other forms of reconciliation

38 See *Eyjan*, March 23, 2012; *DV*, March 28, 2012.

or amnesties, except in the form of selective public debt relief designed to underscore "collective victimhood". And despite the praise heaped on it, the "truth report" has not served as a blueprint for "societal reconstruction", even if it has frequently been used as a reference point. Indeed, the politically enacted process of "coming to terms with the past" has been characterised by conflict.

The rituals associated with the politics of justice were initially based on the notion that political time should be divided into "before" and "after".[39] The judicial proceedings against Geir Haarde were backward-looking and based on a law dating back to the early 20th century, when Iceland had not been granted sovereignty from Denmark. Even if the law was archaic, it became part of the constitution of 1944 and the 1963 Law on Ministerial Responsibility, underscoring historical continuity. But when the law, which had never been used, was evoked in 2010, it led to political instrumentalisation. As a result, the Right interpreted the trial of Geir Haarde as part of the left-wing government's vendetta against the policies and ideology of the "old regime". This view partly contributed to the erasure of the distinction between the pre-crisis and post-crisis periods in the battle of political memory. This was by no means a foregone conclusion. Massive popular mobilisation had discredited the Right in 2008–2009 and forced the Social Democratic Alliance – through a leadership change – to leave the government with the Conservatives and distance itself from their neo-liberal agenda. Yet, during the tenure of the left-wing government from 2009 to 2013, the former managed to reinvent itself through collective action and stage a political comeback. What proved to be a pivotal factor was the Right's nationalistic attack on the government's handling of the Icesave dispute with Britain and Holland, especially its willingness to assume Icelandic sovereign legal liability for debts of the bankrupt Icelandic private bank in these countries. Moreover, it was successful in dismantling core aspects of the agenda of the left-wing government, such as the constitutional experiment.

This success, however, has not led to a new revisionist account of the crisis. The Right has not been able to overcome its compromised past or rehabilitate itself; the Left, having had to adopt unpopular measures to deal with a state of exception after the banking collapse, also failed to capitalise on its early victories and to reclaim its moral high ground. To be sure, as noted, there has been much support for bringing bankers and businessmen to justice, and the Special Prosecutor has been successful in getting a number of guilty verdicts. But when it comes to the political elites, things have been much murkier due to a failure to restore political trust. This shows the ambiguities of the politics of

39 See Teitel, *Transitional Justice*, 116.

transition: the inability to construct universally accepted master narratives, the refusal to accept responsibility, and the persistent lack of distinction between the "old regime" and the "new" one. No permanent political realignment of power relations has resulted from the crisis.

Thus, the politics of memory has not led to the rehabilitation of political elites, whose legitimacy is still being questioned. 10 years after the crash, Icelandic society is still grappling with a memory of a troubled past in a state of renewed economic euphoria, which bears more than a faint semblance to the period before the rain in 2008. Karl Marx's often-quoted remark about history repeating itself – first as tragedy, and second as farce – does not have to become a self-fulfilling prophecy. But, as a warning from history, it has an eerie resonance in the present.

Bibliography

Aliber, Robert Z. "Monetary turbulence and the Icelandic economy." Lecture at the University of Iceland, 2008.

Aliber, Robert Z. and Gylfi Zoega, eds. *Preludes to the Icelandic Financial Crisis.* New York: Palgrave-Macmillan, 2011.

Árnason, Vilhjálmur. "Democratic Practices, Governance, and the Financial Crash." In *Iceland's Financial Crisis: The Politics of Blame, Protest, and Reconstruction*, edited by Valur Ingimundarson, Phillippe Urfalino, and Irma Erlingsdóttir, 121–139. New York and London: Routledge, 2016.

Árnason, Vilhjálmur. "Moral Analysis of an Economic Collapse – An Exercise in Practical Ethics." *Nordic Journal of Applied Ethics* 4, no. 1 (2010): 101–123.

Bergmann, Eirikur. *Iceland and the International Financial Crisis: Boom, Bust and Recover.* New York: Palgrave Macmillan, 2014.

Bernburg, Jón G. *Economic Crisis and Mass Protests: The Pots and Pans Revolution in Iceland.* Basingstoke: Palgrave Macmillan, 2016.

Boyes, Roger. *Meltdown Iceland: How the global financial crisis bankrupted an entire country.* London: Bloomsbury, 2009.

Crocker, David A. "Truth Commissions, Transitional Justice, and Civil Society." In: *Truth vs. Justice. The Moral Efficacy of Truth Commissions: South Africa and beyond,* edited by Robert Rotberg and Dennis Thompson, 99–121. Princeton: Princeton University Press, 2000.

Daníelsson, Jon and Gylfi Zoega. "Collapse of a Country." *Institute of Economic Studies – Working Papers Series* 9, no. 3 (2009): 1–24. http://www.ioes.hi.is/sites/hhi.hi.is/files/W-series/2009/WP0903.pdf.

de Brito, Alexandra Barahona, Carmen G. Enríquez, and Paloma Aquilar, eds. *The Politics of Memory: Transitional Justice in Democratizing Societies.* Oxford: Oxford University Press, 2001.

Dimitrijevic, Nenad. "Justice beyond Blame: Moral Justification of (the Idea) of a Truth Commission." *Journal of Conflict Resolution* 50, no. 3 (2006): 368–382.

Durrenberger, E. Paul and Gisli Pálsson, eds. *Gambling Debt: Iceland's Struggle with the New World Order*. Boulder: University of Colorado Press, 2015.

DV, September 30, 2008; and March 28, 2012.

Elísson, Guðni. "Ísland, anno núll. Rannsóknarskýrslan, spuninn, ábyrgðin og staðleysustjórnmál." *Tímarit Máls og menningar* 71, no. 2 (2010): 24–40.

Elster, Jon, ed. *Retribution and Reparations in the Transition to Democracy*. Cambridge: Cambridge University Press, 2006.

Elster, Jon. "Icelandic Constitution-Making in Comparative Perspective." In *Iceland's Financial Crisis: The Politics of Blame, Protest, and Reconstruction*, edited by Valur, Ingimundarson, Phillippe Urfalino, and Irma Erlingsdóttir, 187–202. New York and London: Routledge, 2016.

Elster, Jon. *Closing the Books: Transitional Justice in Historical Perspective*. Cambridge: Cambridge University Press, 2004.

Eyjan, February 13, 2012; March 23, 2012; and April 24, 2012.

Financial Times, March 27, 2008.

Friðriksson, Guðjón. *Saga af forseta. Forsetatíð Ólafs Ragnars Grímssonar. Útrás, athafnir og einkamál*. Reykjavik: Forlagið bókabúð, 2008.

Gísladóttir, Ingibjörg. "Islands økonomi, stærk og flekisbel." Icelandic Foreign Ministry. Accessed January 22, 2018. http://www.utanrikisraduneyti.is/frettaefni/raedurISG/nr/4151.

Gylfason, Thorvaldur. "Constitution on Ice." In *Iceland's Financial Crisis: The Politics of Blame, Protest, and Reconstruction*, edited by Valur Ingimundarson, Phillippe Urfalino, and Irma Erlingsdóttir, 203–219. New York and London: Routledge, 2016.

Hamber, Brandon and Richard A. Wilson. "Symbolic Closure through Memory, Reparation and Revenge in post-Conflict Societies." In *The Role of Memory in Ethnic Conflict*, edited by Ed Cairns and Michael D. Roe, 144–168. Houndsmills, Basingstoke and New York: Palgrave Macmillan, 2003.

Hayner, Priscilla. *Unspeakable Truths: Confronting State Terror and Atrocity*. New York: Routledge, 2001.

Ingimundarson, Valur, Phillippe Urfalino, and Irma Erlingsdóttir, eds. *Iceland's Financial Crisis: The Politics of Blame, Protest, and Reconstruction*. New York and London: Routledge, 2016.

Ingimundarson, Valur. "A 'Crisis of Affluence': The Politics of an Economic Breakdown in Iceland." *Irish Studies in International Affairs* 21 (2010): 57–63.

Iceland Review, March 12, 2008.

Jóhannesson, Guðni. *Hrunið* . Reykjavík: JPV, 2009.

Johnsen, Guðrún. "The Rise and Fall of a Financial Empire: Looking at the Banking Collapse from the Inside Out." In *Iceland's Financial Crisis: The Politics of Blame, Protest, and Reconstruction*, edited by Valur Ingimundarson, Phillippe Urfalino, and Irma Erlingsdóttir, 37–53. New York and London: Routledge, 2016.

Johnsen, Guðrún. *Bringing Down the Banking System – Lessons from Iceland*. New York: Palgrave Macmillan, 2014.

Jónsson, Ásgeir. *Why Iceland? How One of the World's Smallest Countries Became the Meltdown's Biggest Casualty.* New York: McGraw-Hill, 2009.

Landemore, Hélène. "Inclusive Constitution-Making: The Icelandic Experiment," *Journal of Political Philosophy* 23, no. 2 (2015): 166–191.

Líndal, Sigurður. "Um ráðherraábyrgð og landsdóm." *Skírnir* 184, no. 2 (2010): 522–532.

Loftsdóttir, Kristin. "Vikings invade present day Iceland." In *Gambling Debt. Iceland's Rise and Fall in the Global Economy*, edited by E. Paul Durrenberger and Gisli Pálsson, 3–15. Boulder: University of Colorado Press, 2015.

Maier, Charles. "Doing History, Doing Justice: The Narrative of the Historian and of the Truth Commission." In *Truth vs. Justice. The Moral Efficacy of Truth Commissions: South Africa and beyond*, edited by Robert Rotberg and Dennis Thompson, 261–278. Princeton: Princeton University Press, 2000.

Morgunblaðið, March 4, 2003; November 23, 2003; November 25, 2003; and January 27, 2012.

Nordal, Salvör. "Constitutional Revision. A Weak Legislative Framework Compounded by Political Disputes." In *Iceland's Financial Crisis: The Politics of Blame, Protest, and Reconstruction*, edited by Valur Ingimundarson, Phillippe Urfalino, and Irma Erlingsdóttir, 220–229. New York and London: Routledge, 2016.

Ólafsdóttir, Svala I. "Rökstólar. Landsdómur og ráðherraábyrgð." *Úlfljótur* 64, no. 2 (2011): 290–294.

Ólafsson, Jon. "The Constituent Assembly: A Study in Failure." In *Iceland's Financial Crisis: The Politics of Blame, Protest, and Reconstruction*, edited by Valur Ingimundarson, Phillippe Urfalino, and Irma Erlingsdóttir, 252–272. New York and London: Routledge, 2016.

Pasquino, Pasquale. "Constituent Power and Authorization. Anatomy and Failure of a Constitution-Making Process." In *Iceland's Financial Crisis: The Politics of Blame, Protest, and Reconstruction*, edited by Valur Ingimundarson, Phillippe Urfalino, and Irma Erlingsdóttir, 230–238. New York and London: Routledge, 2016.

Rannsóknarnefnd Alþingis. *Aðdragandi og orsakir falls íslensku bankanna 2008 og tengdir atburðir*. Reykjavik: Icelandic Parliament, 2010. http://sic.althingi.is/.

Rushton, Beth. "Truth and reconciliation? The experience of Truth Commissions." *Australian Journal of International Affairs* 60, no. 1 (2006): 125–141.

Sibert, Anne C. and Willem Buiter. "The Icelandic banking crisis and what do to about it: The lender of last resort theory of optimal currency areas." *CEPR Policy Insight* 26 (2008): 1–23. https://cepr.org/sites/default/files/policy_insights/PolicyInsight26.pdf.

Sigfúsdóttir, Vigdís Þóra. "Réttarstaða ráðherra sem sakborninga fyrir Landsómi í ljósi stjórnarskrár lýðveldisins Íslands og Mannréttindasáttmála Evrópu." ML thesis in Law, University of Bifröst, 2011.

Teitel, Ruti. *Transitional Justice.* Oxford: Oxford University Press, 2000.

Thorarensen, Bjorg. "The Constitutional Council. Objectives and Shortcomings of an Innovative Process." In *Iceland's Financial Crisis: The Politics of Blame, Protest, and Reconstruction*, edited by Valur Ingimundarson, Phillippe Urfalino, and Irma Erlingsdóttir, 239–251. New York and London: Routledge, 2016.

Valgren, Carsten and Lars Christiansen. "Iceland. Geyser Crisis." *Research* 21 (2006): 1–12. http://www.mbl.is/media/98/398.pdf.

Vísir, September 28, 2010.
Wade, Robert. "Iceland pays price for financial excess." *Financial Times*, July 1, 2008.
Zoega, Gylfi. "Iceland's Financial Crisis: An Economic Perspective," In *Iceland's Financial Crisis: The Politics of Blame, Protest, and Reconstruction*, edited by Valur Ingimundarson, Phillippe Urfalino, and Irma Erlingsdóttir, 21–36. New York and London: Routledge, 2016.

Internet Sources

"Former Iceland Prime Minister on Trial." *RTE News*, 5 September 2011. Accessed July 8, 2017. http://www.rte.ie/news/2011/0905/iceland.html.
"Icelandic Parliament (September 2010)." Skýrsla þingnefndar til að fjalla um skýrslu rannsóknarnefndar Alþingis. Accessed December 4, 2015. http://www.althingi.is/altext/138/s/1501.html.
"Icelandic Parliament (September 11, 2010)." Skýrsla þingnefndar til að fjalla um skýrslu rannsóknarnefndar Alþingis. Accessed December 4, 2015. http://www.althingi.is/altext/138/s/1502.html.
"The testimony of Árni Mathiesen, former Minister of Finance, 13 March 2012." Accessed July 7, 2017. http://www.landsdómur.is/adalmedferd/nr/29.
"The testimony of Björgvin G. Sigurðsson, former Minister of Commerce, March 6, 2017." Accessed July 7, 2017. http://www.landsdómur.is/adalmedferd/nr/34.
"The testimony of Davíð Oddsson, former Central Bank Governor, 19 March 2012." Accessed July 7, 2017. http://www.landsdómur.is/adalmedferd/nr/36.
"The testimony of Hreiðar Már Sigurðsson, former CEO of Kaupthing Bank, 8 March 2012." Accessed July 7, 2017. http://www.landsdómur.is/adalmedferd/nr/40.
"The testimony of Ingibjörg Sólrún Gísladóttir, former Foreign Minister, 12 March 2012." Accessed July 7, 2017. http://www.landsdómur.is/adalmedferd/nr/41.
"The testimony of Ingimundur Friðriksson, former Central Bank Governor, 7 March 2012." Accessed July 7, 2017. http://www.landsdómur.is/adalmedferd/nr/42.
"The testimony of Lárus Welding, former Director of Glitnir Bank, 12 March 2012." Accessed July 7, 2017. http://www.landsdómur.is/adalmedferd/nr/55.
"The testimony of Sigurður Einarsson, former Chair of the Board of Kaupthing Bank, 19 March 2012." Accessed July 7, 2017. http://www.landsdómur.is/adalmedferd/nr/57.
"The testimony of Sigurjón Þ. Árnason, former Director of Landsbanki, 12 March 2012." Accessed July 7, 2017. http://www.landsdómur.is/adalmedferd/nr/59.

Gunnþórunn Guðmundsdóttir

The Black Cone: Memory and Memorialisation in Post-Recession Iceland

How societies remember and how nations memorialise seminal events in their history has been the focus of much attention in recent decades and been one of the prime subjects of analysis in the ever-growing field of memory studies. The attention is not, of course, limited to academics and scholars, as we have many examples in recent times of how memory politics not only reflect but can also impinge upon our current political realities. The evocation of memories of the Franco-era in the current crisis in Catalonia is one such example. Here, incomplete memory or silenced/repressed memory leading to a problematic transition to democracy is blamed in some circles for the political and democratic crisis, and the conservative government's forceful response to the independence movement in Catalonia. What this attention to memory – collective memory and cultural memory – clearly demonstrates is that such memory is under pressure from many different forces. In short, representations of memory in society have to answer to political expediency, economic considerations, calls for social cohesion, cultural traditions, current aesthetic values, and local memory practices. In her seminal study on memory politics entitled *Tangled Memories*, Marita Sturken states:

> "Public commemoration is a form of history-making, yet it can also be a contested form of remembrance in which cultural memories slide through and into each other, creating a narrative tangle".[1]

One such "narrative tangle" is very much in evidence in the narratives told of a seminal event in Icelandic history: the 2008 collapse of the Icelandic banks, and the series of ever intensifying protests in late 2008 and early 2009 in Reykjavík, which have been termed, due to the protesters' use of pots and pans, the "Kitchenware Revolution" or the "Pots and Pans Revolution". In his study of the protests, Jón Gunnar Bernburg explains how they "attracted widespread

1 Marita Sturken, *Tangled Memories. The Vietnam War, the AIDS Epidemic, and the Politics of Remembering* (Berkeley: University of California Press, 1997), 44.

participation and support among the public, and involved a serious threat to public order".[2] The protests came to a head in January 2009 with thousands of people protesting every day in front of parliament (Althing) in the centre of Reykjavík. Protesters were calling for the resignation of both the government and the head of the Central Bank, and for new elections to be held. For the most part, the protests stopped with the resignation of the government led by the right-wing Independence Party a few weeks later, but as has become very evident in the years since, a new protest culture developed.

The meaning of these events, the collapse of the banks, the devastating economic effects it had ("the biggest that any country has ever suffered relative to the size of its economy"),[3] the huge debt the country and individuals were plunged into, the following protests, and the changes in the political party structure that followed, are greatly contested, as is evident for instance in Icelandic political discourse. There is no consensus on how the story of the unprecedented economic and political crisis should be told. And although the country now in 2018 is well under way in its economic recovery, the political ramifications seem far from being resolved, as governments have toppled twice in just over a year due to political scandals, and the political landscape is greatly affected by uncertainty with commentators, politicians, and journalists regularly evoking contested memories in their discourse of the recent tumultuous past. As Valur Ingimundarson suggests:

> "[…] one can describe the Icelandic experience as a struggle – within the context of the politics of memory – between two metanarratives. On the one hand, the Left […] blamed the crash on the Right, arguing that its neoliberal policies and ideology had, over the period of 18 years, transformed Icelandic society, with catastrophic results. On the other, the Right pointed to the global financial crisis as a key factor in instigating the crash, together with Icelandic bankers who had acted with supreme recklessness. Both sides – and the population in general – agreed on interpreting the economic collapse as a national disaster, affecting Icelandic

2 Jon Gunnar Bernburg, *Economic Crisis and Mass Protest: The Pots and Pans Revolution in Iceland* (London: Routledge, 2016), 7. See also his book for a detailed description of the unfolding of the protests.

3 Valur Ingimundarson, Phillipe Urfalino, and Irma Erlingsdóttir, "Introduction," in *Iceland's Financial Crisis: The Politics of Blame, Protest, and Reconstruction*, ed. Valur Ingimundarson, Phillipe Urfalino, and Irma Erlingsdóttir (London: Routledge, 2016), 1–18, here 1.

> society as a whole. However, the political question of how to account and assign blame was contested from the start".[4]

At one extreme of the narrative spectrum we have the story of an Icelandic financial success story that hit hard times due to world events beyond the politicians' control, which culminated in riots where hooligans threw rocks at the parliament building, thereby impeding the lawful political process and deposing democratically elected officials. On the other end of the spectrum, the banking crisis is seen as a turning point, where a corrupt banking system in cahoots with the political elite was exposed, and in its wake the nation had to experience some sort of rebirth – a return to less materialistic values – and ordinary people took to the streets with their pots and pans to show that politicians cannot get away with bankrupting a nation without suffering the consequences. This is the version that has travelled well, being for instance one of the inspirations for the protest movement in Spain called "15-M" or "Los Indignados".[5] Iceland is often cited as a shining example of a society where corrupt bankers are jailed and a new constitution adopted.[6] Two cartoons capture the very different response to this image of Iceland succinctly: on the one hand, a Spanish cartoon showing the "Icelandic Solution" as the firm response

4 Valur Ingimundarson, "The Politics of Transitions, Memory, and Justice: Assigning Blame for the Crisis," in *Iceland's Financial Crisis. The Politics of Blame, Protest, and Reconstruction*, ed. Valur Ingimundarson, Phillippe Urfalino, and Irma Erlingsdóttir (London: Routledge, 2016), 140–155, 141.

5 See for instance articles on the movement's website: "Islandia. Revolucion Islandesa," WordPress, https://movimientoindignadosspanishrevolution.wordpress.com/1248-2/. Hörður Torfason, one of the leaders of the Pots and Pans Revolution, claims that for much of the so called 15-M protestors Iceland was the model: "'Estoy alucinado de lo organizados qué están los indignados españoles': Para muchos manifestantes del 15-M, Islandia y los islandeses son el modelo." Hörður Torfason, "Estoy alucinado de lo organizados qué están los indignados españoles," interview by Najara Galarraga Gortázar, *El País*, June 23, 2011, https://politica.elpais.com/politica/2011/06/22/actualidad/1308768044_418504.html.

6 Many court cases were indeed brought through the courts in Iceland and some bankers received prison sentences. With most of them out of prison by now and the sense in society that they still engage in the same practices, Icelanders tend to be more disillusioned by the process than people who look at this from the outside. The new constitution, which held much promise for many, was never adopted. For a comprehensive analysis on this see "Part III: The politics of Iceland's constitutional reform," in *Iceland's Financial Crisis: The Politics of Blame, Protest, and Reconstruction*, ed. Valur Ingimundarson, Phillipe Urfalino, and Irma Erlingsdóttir (London: Routledge, 2016), 185–272.

to the stealing bankers (image 1), and a recent cartoon by the cartoonist Elín Elísabet published in the English language newspaper *Reykjavík Grapevine* in September 2017 (image 2), which proved popular among Icelanders (if shares on social media can be relied upon) and captures the Icelandic left's frustration with the idealization of the country, where corruption is still rife and the old parties are back in power.[7]

Fig. 1 La revolución silenciada. ©Azagra.

7 This view of the aftermath of crisis can also be seen in Elvira Mendez' book, *La Revolucion de los vikingos* (Barcelona: Planeta, 2012). The Catalan journalist Eric Lluent is not nearly as positive in his version of events in *Islàndia 2013. Crònica d'una decepció* (Barcelona: Eric Lluent, 2014), Kindle.

Fig. 2 Elín Elísabet, Jailing the Bankers. © Elín Elísabet.

Somewhere between these two narratives we have more complicated stories of a systemic failure, of a thwarted revolution, and of a new government that eventually betrayed the protesters, by not following through on the sweeping changes promised. The gap between these narratives has not been bridged, and there is no national consensus on how this time of crisis and disruption should be remembered. Of course, this lack of consensus comes as no surprise, as we know that such times of national upheaval have a complex relationship with the national narrative and collective memory. In remembering the recent past, we are not so much burdened with the discourse of "recovering" a lost past, which is the model of memory Ann Rigney terms the "plenitude and loss" model; rather, the dissonance of the narratives told make it clear that it would be more helpful to pay attention to Rigney's suggestion that we move away from that model to:

> "A social-constructivist model that takes as its starting point the idea that memories of a shared past are collectively constructed and reconstructed in the present rather than resurrected from the past".[8]

In this paper, I examine one instance of an attempt at the memorialisation of recent events that highlights these problems and ask the question, what happens at the convergence of activism, art, memorialisation, and cultural memory in the wake of crisis?

One of the ways in which a nation remembers is through various cultural activities, for instance in literature, but perhaps in a more official capacity in the building of public memorials. Memorials in Iceland have a history in the 20th century that more or less follows the development elsewhere in Europe, even though the timing can be slightly different; and for a country without a military (but with a heavy reliance on its fishermen), it is perhaps understandable that the tomb of the unknown soldier, which spread throughout Europe in the wake of World War I, should transform into the tomb of the unknown sailor in the late 1930s in Iceland.[9] The overall development has been described as a move from monuments to memorials – that is, from heroic monuments of battles won to trauma memorials to grieve for lost lives.[10] The memory boom at the turn of the millennium with its many memorials, museums, and narratives of war and the holocaust raised many questions about the role of such memorials. These are memorials that bear witness to our need to remember, but perhaps also expose a longing to forget our inglorious past. James E. Young believes that:

---

8 Ann Rigney, "Plenitude, Scarcity and the Circulation of Cultural Memory," *Journal of European Studies* 35, no. 1 (2005): 11–28, here 14.

9 Ketill Kristinsson, "Eyrnamörk gleymskunnar. Nokkur orð um minnismerki," *Ritið* 13, no. 1 (2013): 165–182.

10 See for instance Jay Winter, *Sites of Memory, Sites of Mourning: The Great War in European Cultural History* (Cambridge: Cambridge University Press, 1998).

> "Once we assign monumental form to memory, we have to some degree divested ourselves of the obligation to remember. In shouldering the memory-work, monuments may relieve viewers of their memory burden".[11]

But the memory work enacted in public memorials is not the only activity that has been tied to forgetting. The undertakings that we engage in regularly in the belief that they will help us remember – writing, building memorials, archiving the past – all bear within them the threat of forgetting.[12] As Ian Sinclair in *Lights Out for the Territory* claims:

> "Memorials are a way of forgetting, reducing generational guilt to a grid of albino chess pieces, bloodless stalagmites. Shapes that are easy to ignore stand in for the trauma of remembrance".[13]

Memorials, therefore, are objects at the crux of complex memory politics – political circumstances, society's expectations – in their motivation, design, execution, building, location, and their function in their environment. Are they sites of memory, forgetting, or simply indifference? It has been theorised that for a memorial to encourage remembrance, some sort of regular activity, be it ceremonies, less formal public events, or social traditions, must be connected to it. This, as do other acts of memory, takes place in society. Matthew Allen and Steven Brown have pointed out that:

> "It is society that maintains memorials, both by protecting them from damage, but not least by orchestrating some type of activity around them. If there are no ceremonies connected to memorials, at more or less regular intervals, they simply disappear into their surroundings, be it a natural landscape or cityscape".[14]

One memorial of a contested past that has now joined the memorial flora in Iceland is called *The Black Cone: Memorial to Civil Disobedience* and is the work

---

11 James E. Young, *The Texture of Memory: Holocaust Memorials and Meaning* (New Haven, CT: Yale University Press, 1993), 181.

12 I discuss this in more detail in my book: Gunnþórunn Guðmundsdóttir, *Representations of Forgetting in Life Writing and Fiction* (Basingstoke: Palgrave, 2017).

13 Iain Sinclair, *Lights Out for the Territory* (London: Granta, 1997), 9.

14 Matthew J. Allen and Steven D. Brown, "Embodiment and Living Memorials: The Affective Labour of Remembering the 2005 London Bombings," *Memory Studies* 4, no. 3 (2011): 312–327, here 323.

of the Spanish artist Santiago Sierra (image 3). It sits in Austurvöllur Square where Althing or parliament sits and where the country's cathedral is located. The sculpture consists of a large piece of rock that a black cone has been driven into so as to create a fissure in the rock. A plaque on the rock states in both Icelandic and English:

> "The Black Cone: Monument to Civil Disobedience. When the government violates the rights of the people, insurrection is for the people and for each portion of the people the most sacred of rights and the most indispensable of duties. *Declaration of the Rights of Man and Citizen* (1793)".

Fig. 3 Santiago Sierra, The Black Cone, Reykjavik. Photographer: Dagur Gunnarsson.

The memorial was erected as part of a Sierra retrospective at the Reykjavik Art Museum in 2012, three years after the Pots and Pans Revolution. In the performance the rock was placed on the square directly in front of Althing and the artist drove the black cone into the rock, the cone apparently alluding to the cone-shaped hats condemned persons were forced to wear during the Inquisition in the 12th century, a fairly obscure reference that I think is safe to say most Icelanders would miss.[15] Given this, immediately the question arises of the success of the imagery employed in the work. This also makes clear that rather than being a memorial created by the authorities to remember an event, the impetus instead came from the artist supported by the museum.

In his study of war memorials, Jay Winter wishes to shift the attention to smaller acts of remembrance, to the periphery rather than the centre: "from first-order to second- or third-order actors".[16] As he claims, one of the reasons for this is that the "great national sites of remembrance are exceptional, and their histories provide a misleading impression for thousands of others. Another is that in contemporary cultural history, multivocality is the order of the day".[17]

As such, recent studies have moved away from the top-down approach:

> "[...] which emphasised the capacity of dominant groups to act in effect as puppeteers, pulling the strings of cultural activity. That elites have tried to do so is self-evident [...]; less convincing is the claim that they effectively controlled the space within which all forms of cultural expression in general and commemoration in particular have developed".[18]

When the work was unveiled it was placed provocatively on Austurvöllur Square in a direct line of sight between the main entrance of Althing and the monumental statue of Jón Sigurðsson, the 19th century national independence hero. Initially, it was only supposed to be a temporary installation as part of Sierra's Reykjavík exhibition, but the artist donated the work to the city of Reykjavík with the clever proviso that it should stay in that square. The Reykjavik Art Museum recommended the city should accept the gift, and the city's cultural committee supported the idea. It is important to note in this context, and at that time, Jón Gnarr, a comedian and writer who had founded a sort of anti-political party called the Best Party, was voted in during the municipal elections in 2010 and was therefore mayor of Reykjavík. The Best Party was a direct result of the demands for a new political culture after the crisis and its main aim was not to espouse traditional political practice and discourse. The city was there-

---

15 Information on Sierra's exhibition and events related to it can be found on the Reykjavík Art Museum website: "Santiago Sierra: Kvikmyndir og önnur verk," Reykjavík Art Museum, last modified April 15, 2012, http://listasafnreykjavikur.is/syningar/santiago-sierra-kvikmyndir-og-onnur-verk.

16 Jay Winter, *Remembering War. The Great War between Memory and History in the Twentieth Century* (New Haven, CT: Yale University Press, 2006), 135–136.

17 Ibid.

18 Ibid.

fore in the hands of people very sympathetic to the protests and all forms of activism. The city did, however, suggest that the Black Cone should be moved to the southwest corner of the square, but this was still only a few metres away from Althing. Althing declared itself opposed to the placement of the Black Cone on that square, where it was thought it would "spoil the overall image of the square". The minority in the city council agreed and the Independence Party councillor claimed the work was connected to the 2008–2009 riots; and, even though most people had protested peacefully, violence was used and police officers wounded. As Kjartan Magnússon stated, who says he hopes such events will never be repeated: "Even though the violence wasn't extensive and involved mostly threats, a lawfully elected government was pushed from power". And furthermore, "I don't think that there is any reason to remember such events with a memorial. It could at least have been placed elsewhere, not in this sacred national place".[19] What Sierra's memorial and the circumstances of its donation remind us of is how complex it is for a nation to remember a contested past in a cohesive fashion.

Austurvöllur is indeed one of Iceland's primary lieu de memoire. It is in the very heart of the city in the shadow of Althing – the city's cathedral – surrounded by hotels and restaurants; and its crowning glory in the very centre of it is the statue of Jón, the independence hero. It is the square where national celebrations take place but also the site of the major protests in the country's political history – for instance, the protests against Iceland signing the NATO treaty in 1949 and the "Pots and Pans Revolution" during 2008/2009. Where memorials are placed is a decisive component of their effectiveness. The location of trauma memorials in particular, can be especially sensitive; it affects their meaning and their place in the national consciousness. Should we hide them in cemeteries, as we do with Reykjavík war memorials, or should we place them in the heart of the city like the holocaust memorial in Berlin? The Black Cone was moved a few metres so it is no longer an obstacle on the way from the main entrance of Althing to the statue of Jón – a route taken by politicians and dignitaries every year on the 17th of June, Jón's birthday and Iceland's Independence Day. It is, however, still on this all-important square, although slightly marginalised and its proximity to the bushes behind it could result in it being mistaken for a slightly bulky landscaping feature. In 2015 it was overshadowed by a relatively traditional statue of Ingibjörg H. Bjarnason (the first female parliamentarian in Iceland) created by the sculptor Ragnhildur Stefánsdóttir.

19 GAR, "Svarta keilan tákn um ofbeldi á helgum stað," *Fréttablaðið*, October 4, 2012.

Fig. 4 Ragnhildur Stefánsdóttir, Ingibjörg H. Bjarnason, Reykjavik. Photographer: Dagur Gunnarsson.

The statue of a woman with her skirt flying behind her as if she is facing a storm is raised on a plinth (about half the size of Jón's plinth) right beside Althing, directly across the street from the Black Cone. It was unveiled on the 19th of June 2015 on the centenary of women's right to vote in a very successful ceremony. That day, Austurvöllur was filled with thousands of (mostly) women, and the crowds were addressed by Vigdís Finnbogadóttir, the first democratically elected woman president. The memorial has received nothing but praise, which is perhaps evidence that women's rights is a less contested issue in the country than during the 2008/2009 protests, and that its aesthetics are more pleasing to the general public.

Despite the Best Party's enthusiasm for Sierra's work, not all on the Left supported it. Sierra is a highly political artist, and some of his installations have been very provocative indeed. For instance, one involved paying homeless people for having a line tattooed on their backs.[20] Sóley Tómasdóttir, a coun-

20 This is a series of works Sierra has performed in several countries. The fundamental principle is the same: the homeless, prostitutes, and the destitute are paid to take part. Their backs turned toward the camera, the artist tatoos a line across their backs. See

cillor for the Left-Green Party, stated it was all well and good to memorialise civil disobedience, however:

> "The work that is now going to be placed on the square cannot be considered appropriate for this, as it thereby celebrates an artist who has used his strong economic and social position to undermine other people's dignity who are not in a position to protest or refuse his offer of paid denigration".[21]

Therefore, his mode of political statement does not invite consensus. When asked whether the Independence Party would remove the memorial if it came to power in the city in the future, the aforementioned city councillor, Kjartan Magnússon, explained in typical political speak: "We have a certain outcome now and then we will see how this will turn out".[22] There are of course famous instances where memorials become controversial because of the artist themselves, as when a 21-year-old unknown Chinese-American won the contest to build the Vietnam War memorial in Washington DC, with her design for a memorial which moved sharply away from the triumphant war memorials of the past. It is debatable whether the artist's background in the case of the Black Cone would have been highlighted in this way if the work had been placed in a museum or in a remoter part of Reykjavík.

The work also raises questions about the role of art in political activism. This is a complex question beyond the scope of this paper but one I would nevertheless like to quickly reference, as it is of great relevance here. As stated above, when the memorial was erected it was in conjunction with a large exhibition of Sierra's work in the Reykjavík Art Museum, one of the two main publicly funded galleries in town, and thus the work was implicitly endorsed by the city authorities in charge at the time. Along with the performance of the installation of the memorial, another work of Sierra's was driven through the streets of Reykjavík. A large sign with letters forming the word 'NO' was placed on the back of a truck and was camped outside institutions such as banks, parliament and other relevant places. Benedikt Hjartarson has pointed out that Sierra's art raises questions about the political potential of art, and not least the avant-garde, which in Peter Burger's famous terms has lost its political relevance. The possibilities of street art must therefore also be limited since it has been in part

more information on Sierra's works to date on his website. Santiago Sierra, "Santiago Sierra," http://www.santiago-sierra.com.

21 GAR, "Svarta keilan tákn um ofbeldi á helgum stað."

22 Ibid.

or in whole commercialised and/or institutionalised[23] – issues, for instance, raised forcefully in Banksy's documentary, *Exit through the Gift Shop* (2010).

Returning to Reykjavík's Austurvöllur and the traditional monument in its centre – the statue of Jón Sigurðsson – we can see that it is a symbol of unity, a symbol of independence and the idea of Icelandicness. Jón Sigurðsson stands on a tall plinth in the middle of the power hub of the city. He is brought flowers on his birthday, but people have also climbed on top of him with various purposes, from drunken teenagers to performance artists, confirming that his presence speaks to a certain understanding of Icelandic history. The Black Cone and what it stands for undeniably interrupts this narrative of national unity and coherence, as it reminds us of all the protests that have taken place in that square: how it is a contested space where protests and activism exist alongside the symbols of power and nationhood.

Memorials can preserve the memory of a nation or hide it; they can be a symbol of unity or disharmony. In some ways, the Black Cone is successful as it questions the politicians' notions of national unity and identity. When the politicians place flowers at the foot of Jón's plinth on the 17th of June these days, they have to walk past the Black Cone – the narrative of a peaceful nation in docile awe of its government has been interrupted. The memorial reminds us that the square is also a place of protest and disharmony, as was evidenced in the Spring of 2015 where 26,000 people demanded that the PM leave office after the scandal that was revealed in the so-called Panama Papers.

Adopting Winter's "pluralistic approach to cultural history" allows us to acknowledge that:

> "Sites of memory are created not just by nations but primarily by small groups of men and women who do the work of remembrance. *They* are the 'social agents' of remembrance; without their work, collective memory would not exist".[24]

Perhaps the major problem with the Black Cone is that no one has taken ownership of it. It is more or less ignored, even during protests in the square. This might suggest that despite the success of the protests, people do not seem to have a need to memorialise or celebrate the "Pots and Pans Revolution" for a

---

23 Benedikt Hjartarson, "Fagurfræði neikvæðisins: Um arfleifð framúrstefnunnar og möguleika skapandi andófs á öld sjónarspilsins." A paper given at the symposium NEI! Symposium in The Reykjavík Art Museum on the occasion of Sierra's retrospective 11 March 2012. Quoted with the permission of the speaker.

24 Winter, *Remembering War*, 136. Emphasis in original.

variety of reasons. Perhaps this is mainly as a result of the sense of disappointment with the limited reforms that have been accomplished since. The memorial has also almost disappeared from public discourse, as there is hardly anything to be found on it since its installation – it simply is not mentioned any more. It seems as if this artwork/memorial has almost disappeared into the cityscape. The only activities I have witnessed around it are walking tours for tourists that evidently stop by it on their tour of central Reykjavík, and that children like to climb on it. The question this raises and one that remains is whether we assimilate artistic memorialisation of civil disobedience into the political and public landscape if its aesthetics do not speak to the society and if none of the relevant memory agents take ownership of the memorial.

Bibliography

Allen, Matthew J. and Steven D. Brown. "Embodiment and Living Memorials: The Affective Labour of Remembering the 2005 London Bombings." *Memory Studies* 4, no. 3 (2011): 312–327.

Bernburg, Jon Gunnar. *Economic Crisis and Mass Protest: The Pots and Pans Revolution in Iceland*. London: Routledge, 2016.

GAR. "Svarta keilan tákn um ofbeldi á helgum stað." *Fréttablaðið*, October 4, 2012.

Guðmundsdóttir, Gunnþórunn. *Representations of Forgetting in Life Writing and Fiction*. Basingstoke: Palgrave, 2017.

Ingimundarson, Valur, Phillippe Urfalino, and Irma Erlingsdóttir, eds. *Iceland's Financial Crisis: The Politics of Blame, Protest, and Reconstruction*, London: Routledge, 2016.

Ingimundarson, Valur, Phillippe Urfalino, and Irma Erlingsdóttir, "Introduction." In *Iceland's Financial Crisis: The Politics of Blame, Protest, and Reconstruction*, edited by Valur Ingimundarson, Phillipe Urfalino, and Irma Erlingsdóttir, 1–18. London: Routledge, 2016.

Ingimundarson, Valur. "The Politics of Transitions, Memory, and Justice: Assigning Blame for the Crisis." In *Iceland's Financial Crisis. The Politics of Blame, Protest, and Reconstruction*, edited by Valur Ingimundarson, Phillippe Urfalino, and Irma Erlingsdóttir, 140–155. London: Routledge, 2016.

Kristinsson, Ketill. "Eyrnamörk gleymskunnar. Nokkur orð um minnismerki." *Ritið* 13, no. 1 (2013): 165–182.

Lluent, Èric. *Islàndia 2013. Crònica d'una decepció*. Barcelona, 2014. Kindle.

Mendez, Elvira. *La Revolucion de los vikingos*. Barcelona: Planeta, 2012.

Rigney, Ann. "Plenitude, Scarcity and the Circulation of Cultural Memory." *Journal of European Studies* 35, no. 1 (2005): 11–28.

Sinclair, Iain. *Lights Out for the Territory*. London: Granta, 1997.

Sturken, Marita. *Tangled Memories. The Vietnam War, the AIDS Epidemic, and the Politics of Remembering*. Berkeley: University of California Press, 1997.

Torfason, Hörður. “Estoy alucinado de lo organizados qué están los indignados españoles.” Interview by Najara Galarraga Gortázar. *El País*, June 23, 2011. https://politica.elpais.com/politica/2011/06/22/actualidad/1308768044_418504.html.
Winter, Jay. *Remembering War. The Great War between Memory and History in the Twentieth Century*. New Haven, CT: Yale University Press, 2006.
Winter, Jay. *Sites of Memory, Sites of Mourning: The Great War in European Cultural History*. Cambridge: Cambridge University Press, 1998.
Young, James E. *The Texture of Memory: Holocaust Memorials and Meaning*. New Haven, CT: Yale University Press, 1993.

Internet sources

Reykjavík Art Museum. “Santiago Sierra: Kvikmyndir og önnur verk.” Last modified April 15, 2012. http://listasafnreykjavikur.is/syningar/santiago-sierra-kvikmyndir-og-onnur-verk.
Sierra, Santiago. “Santiago Sierra.” http://www.santiago-sierra.com.
WordPress. “Islandia. Revolucion Islandesa.” https://movimientoindignadosspanishrevolution.wordpress.com/1248-2/.

Franziska Sajdak

"So I decide for you": *Generation and Identity* in Göran Rosenberg's *A Brief Stop on the Road from Auschwitz*

Although constituting a part of Scandinavian societies since the 18th and 19th centuries, Jewish culture and identity have scarcely been present in Scandinavian literature and literary studies. Interest in Jewish issues first increased noticeably after the publication of Cordelia Edvardson's *Bränt barn söker sig till elden* (1984), in which she recounts her experiences in the German concentration camps and as a Jewish survivor in Sweden. Still, even in the years following Edvardson's autobiographical novel, comparatively few new literary texts addressing Jewish life in Scandinavia have been published. Considerable development in literary approaches to Jewish history, culture, and identity in Scandinavia specifically, has only been detectable in recent years. Since about the year 2000 many Swedish, Danish and Norwegian texts (fiction and non-fiction) discuss life in the wake of the historic caesura caused by the Holocaust.

This paper discusses Göran Rosenberg's autobiographical novel *Ett kort uppehåll på vägen från Auschwitz* (2012) as a Swedish example of new approaches to history and Judaism in Scandinavian literature.[1] In his novel, Rosenberg – the son of Polish Holocaust survivors who emigrated to Sweden after the Second World War – intends to create a bigger picture of the past by collecting and combining information about the historical situation and his family history. In order to do so he actually retravels his father's journey from Poland, through Germany and the German concentration camps, and then onwards to Sweden. As is revealed towards the end of the narrative, Rosenberg's father eventually commits suicide because he cannot handle his traumatic memories. Having lost his father as a child, he mainly remained a mystery to his son. Thus, Rosenberg's desire to undertake this journey is to gain a deeper understanding of the past and especially of his father. By focusing the narrative of his own past on the history and character of his father in particular, Rosenberg clearly bases his text on a generational approach. In the following I discuss how the novel negotiates the concept of *generation*, such as the genealogical perspective on father and son, by juxtaposing past and present, and how in turn these conceptions

1 For the following discussion I refer to the English translation: Göran Rosenberg, *A Brief Stop on the Road from Auschwitz*, transl. by Sarah Death (London: Granta, 2015).

of *generation* constitute a vital part of identity formation.[2] First, I discuss the significance of transgenerational connections when dealing with Jewish identity in the wake of the Holocaust. I refer to the transgenerational concept of *telescoping* introduced by the psychoanalyst Haydée Faimberg and apply this concept to Rosenberg's text as suggested by the literary scholar Sigrid Weigel. Then I argue how the novel's transgenerational approach also opens up a reverse, contemporaneous approach concerning *generation*, which in turn offers new conceptions of identity.

Discussing the familial consequences of experiencing the Holocaust, *A Brief Stop on the Road from Auschwitz* can be counted in the diverse category of international literature on transgenerational Holocaust-trauma and questions of identity. Well-known examples are works such as the graphic novel *Maus* (1991) by American cartoonist Art Spiegelman, the novel *Everything is Illuminated* (2002) by American novelist Jonathan Safran Foer, and *Vielleicht Esther* (2014) by Ukrainian-German author Katja Petrowskaja, all of which reflect the contemporary relevance of trauma.[3] In research, especially in Marianne Hirsch's analyses of *postmemory* in photography, the continuous impact of past experiences of trauma are illustrated. Hirsch introduced the concept of *postmemory* to describe the ways descendants of the survivors of trauma can identify, to some degree, with the traumatic memories of the previous generation insofar as they appear to be their own personal memories, while still being aware that these memories are *not* first-hand experiences.[4] Similarly, research conducted by Cathy Caruth on transgenerational trauma and literature and by Jeffrey Alexander on cultural trauma for instance, has established trauma as a central concept in cultural studies.

Yet, while there is extensive analysis on predominantly anglophone Holocaust literature (and to a lesser extent on Holocaust literature in other languages) that deals with transgenerational trauma,[5] Scandinavian literature on Jewish iden-

2 Cf. Ohad Parnes, Ulrike Vedder, and Stefan Willer, *Das Konzept der Generation. Eine Wissenschafts- und Kulturgeschichte* (Frankfurt: Suhrkamp, 2008), 302–303.

3 For further examples cf. for instance the anthology edited by Melvin J. Bukiet, *Nothing Makes You Free: Writings by Descendants of Jewish Holocaust Survivors* (New York and London: W. W. Norton & Company, 2002).

4 Marianne Hirsch, *The Generation of Postmemory: Writing and Visual Culture after the Holocaust* (New York: Columbia University Press, 2012); see also Marianne Hirsch, *Family Frames: Photography, Narrative, and Postmemory* (Cambridge and London: Harvard University Press, 2012).

5 Cf. for instance Dominick LaCapra, *Writing History, Writing Trauma* (Baltimore and London: The Johns Hopkins University Press, 2001).

tity and trauma is barely represented in literary studies. One of the few studies dealing explicitly with Jewish trauma in Scandinavian literature is Anders Ohlsson's *Men ändå måste jag berätta: Studier i skandinavisk förintelselitteratur* (2002), in which he offers an overview of texts discussing identity and memory after the Holocaust. However, considering the amount of new Scandinavian texts on Jewish heritage and identity published since Ohlsson's study, it is worth taking a look at this recent development and one of its representatives in the literary landscape. For this, Weigel's transgenerational concept of *telescoping* offers an appropriate approach because it illustrates how the past and present are intricately linked and poses the question of the literary representation of trauma confronted with memory gaps and silence, as well as of its function. This proves beneficial in analysing the writing of Rosenberg as a member of the so-called *second generation* who – as described by Hirsch – experience the past through their parents, the actual witnesses of trauma. The different perspectives offered by the concept of *generation* and the role they play in identity formation, which is depicted in *A Brief Stop on the Road from Auschwitz*, delineate the multi-layered nature of identity confronted with experiences of trauma.

Exploring the Shadows of the Past

Göran Rosenberg's autobiographical novel *A Brief Stop* represents an attempt to give a complete account of his family's history as well as to deal with issues raised by such history. The need to collect information and question the past arose from the fact that, for the most part, the past as well as Jewish religion and culture were kept silent in the narrator's family. His memory only consists of a few fragments "firmly trampled into the darkness and silence".[6] As a result the history and person of his father, who died when the narrator was still a child, often seem elusive, foreign and distant in retrospect.[7] His own person, too, appears to contain mysterious and puzzling elements. The narrator wishes to rectify this condition. Concerning himself as a child, he writes:

> "I wish I could make contact with him and explain a few things. That the Place [Sweden] cannot become his if it doesn't also become [his parents']. That he cannot make the Place his own if he doesn't know where he comes from. That he has a certain responsibility, small though he is, for the success of the Project.

---

6 Rosenberg, *A Brief Stop on the Road from Auschwitz*, 253, 305.

7 Ibid., 305–306.

> I'd also like to ask him a few things. About language, for instance. About those early words in Polish. Where did he hide them? Are they perching like lost birds in his memory, waiting to be discovered? There's something about Polish that, much later, I don't understand. The body recognizes the language, but the head does not. [...] Maybe if I hadn't been in such a hurry to put their [the parents'] world behind me, or if I'd gone back to it sooner, I too would have been able to unearth a forgotten language, or at least a few coherent sentences, not just in Polish but also in Yiddish, and perhaps over time even to understand them.
> And not only the languages, but also the worlds that went with them".[8]

At the same time as the narrator expresses the impossibility of reconnecting with his former self and therefore the past in search for answers, he confirms the inextricable links between his parents' past and his own identity. As the passage points out, these links are important for two reasons: first, in having been prompted by their past to leave their Polish home, the narrator's parents rely on their son to fulfil "the Project" (as he calls it) of a new life in Sweden – that is, on his ability as the first family member born in Sweden to explore the new country and to form the necessary connections in order to tie himself and thereby even his parents to this foreign place; and second, before their migration to Sweden they unconsciously left parts of themselves and their lives within their son, which are now part of him but are mysterious and seemingly waiting to be (re)discovered. Although he declares the futility of any attempt to grasp these mystifying elements of his identity retrospectively, he acknowledges beyond doubt their essential role and locates his own identity within these secret parts of himself.

How powerful the past is in shaping one's present life and future, the narrator witnesses as a boy with regard to his father's situation in Sweden. Superficially, Sweden offered him infinite possibilities to create a new life for himself and his family. However, the trauma of the Holocaust and the loss of his Polish home, as well as a lack in his ability to speak the language and to communicate his experiences to those around him who had not witnessed anything similar, prevented him from putting down roots. Consequently, his father seemed to be separated from Swedish life by an "invisible wall".[9] Likewise, the narrator's relationship to his father is shaped to a large extent by this silent past – the unresolved trauma – in that it also established something of an invisible wall between the two of them. Thus, trauma as a commonality between the two

8 Ibid., 40–41.

9 Ibid., 13–14, 240–241.

generations – although one that causes detachment – acts as a form of intergenerational connection.

Trauma as an unconscious bond between the generations causes the narrator's perception of his own identity to fragment and remain unfamiliar. From an early age he experiences unexpected re-appearances of this seemingly vanished past, being pushed towards it without really understanding why:

> "Occasionally something happens to thrust him back towards [their world], and their shadows momentarily penetrate him, and a sensation of darkness and cold lingers on. [...] he goes ice-cold every time he hears the word "Jew" in one combination or another. He knows that Mom and Dad are Jews, and that he and his little sister are too, and the Klein family on the other side of the railroad bridge, and Auntie Ilonka at the other end of the rowanberry avenue. And even if he doesn't know what it means, he knows it has something to do with the shadows".[10]

Although these shadows of the past are never discussed and often seem incompatible with his father's otherwise cheerful and energetic character,[11] and are therefore left to guesswork and the imagination, the narrator recalls the feeling of something indeterminate being transferred from father to son, which in turn creates distance between them and connects them at the same time. The narrator exemplifies this feeling through his memory of holding his father's hand on their way to the harbour:

> "I try to say something, perhaps I'm scared, but I have a powerful sense of your being somewhere else. I can feel it through your hand as it holds mine, and the sensation penetrates my body and hides there, waiting to be summoned again by a closely written aerogram in Polish, by a letter in Swedish with bold, leftward-slanting capitals, by a medical report in German, by an annulled draft contract, or simply by the lively imagination of someone determined at any cost to unearth a memory fragment or two and piece together a narrative".[12]

Having been previously eager to leave everything ambiguous behind him in order to fit into a "Swedish" lifestyle, the only option to reconnect with this silenced, vanished history is for him to put together memory fragments, hoping

10 Ibid., 39–40.
11 Ibid., 275–276, 279–280.
12 Ibid., 295.

they will fall into place like in a giant jigsaw puzzle.[13] His chosen method to do this is to retravel his father's journey from Auschwitz, through several German work camps and onwards to Sweden 60 years later.[14] Thus, *A Brief Stop* is an autobiographical novel that simultaneously narrates the past *and* depicts the process by which the present narrative of the past comes into being.

Additionally, the incremental process of research and writing is reflected in the style of the novel. Primarily, the text is formulated as a narrative that addresses the narrator's father directly using the Swedish pronouns *du* (*you*, 2nd pers. sg.) or *ni* (*you*, 2nd pers. pl.). Thus, the text strongly conveys the impression of a conversation between two people in which the narrator recapitulates family history in order to confront his father with questions concerning this history. The narrative is constantly deferred to by the narrator's thought process and by questions directed towards his father concerning the material found, as for instance following the reading of an old newspaper article issuing a warning about Swedish society accepting too many foreigners after the war:

> "Does it surprise you that such things are written? Or does it merely confirm what you already know or suspect about the land of the vast forests? I'm trying to understand why, over time, so many of you want to leave again, not because you're forced to but because you want to, in fact long to, and reading lines like these helps me understand a little better".[15]

The narrator's childhood and his relationship to his parents are fundamentally characterised by the silence and denial concerning the aforementioned shadows.[16] Only when trying to retrospectively combine and recount his collection of seemingly contradictory memories as an adult can the narrator discern the complexity of issues obliterated by it: the survivor's feeling of guilt over murdered family members and friends, the longing for a new and successful future,

13 Ibid., 50: "So I piece fragments together."

14 Ibid., 100–101, 119–120.

15 Ibid., 195.

16 Ibid., 44. He writes concerning a former home: "Had there been such a place, they [the parents] would have talked about it, would have given me a sense of its smell, its taste, taken me there, told me about the people who once lived there. But they tell me nothing. Where there must once have been a place like this one, there is now only silence. Silence and shadows. Whatever fragments of such a place lie hidden somewhere – and no human being lives without such fragments – someone or something has crushed them all too carefully and buried them all too deeply, in too-wide expanses of darkness."

and the loneliness originating from the indifference concerning Jewish experiences within Swedish society.[17]

Both, the novel's general impetus that understanding one's family history will help rediscover one's own forgotten parts and understand one's own person by giving those shadows a concrete shape, as well as the novel's narrative style, i. e. retelling the past as a conversation between father and son on a journey replicating the past, emphasise the narrator's intention of linking different generations. Thus, in *A Brief Stop* generational borders are crossed by the narrator's memory process and identification with his father's person, not only following in his footsteps and learning about his life but, literally speaking, on behalf of his father as his father was not able to express himself during his lifetime.[18] In this way, the novel represents an attempt to actively create a familial link that surpasses the obscure bond between parent and child caused by trauma, which was never really disputed as the son lost his father so early. Uncovering the silent parts of his family history and imagining speaking to his father is an attempt to overcome the distance – "the invisible wall" – between the two generations.

The *Telescoping* of Generations

In discussing the bonds, relationships and complex memory processes of trauma between different generations, *A Brief Stop* addresses the process of *transgenerational transference* originally described by Sigmund Freud.[19] The psychoanalytical concept of transgenerational transference denotes the process of transferring traumatic, and therefore suppressed, memory unconsciously from generation to generation. As outlined by Freud, the process of transgenerational transference is characterised by two principles: first, *compulsive repetition* as traumatic memory not only keeps affecting the generation that experienced it initially but also continues to affect following generations; and second, the principle *afterwardsness*, which identifies that trauma and its potential consequences can only be identified retrospectively.[20]

17 Ibid., 279–282.

18 Ibid., 277.

19 Sigmund Freud, *Der Mann Moses und die monotheistische Religion. Schriften über die Religion* (Frankfurt: Fischer, 1994).

20 Ibid., 77–78, 81–88, 99–100, 102–104. See also Sigrid Weigel, *Genea-Logik. Generation, Tradition und Evolution zwischen Kultur- und Naturwissenschaften* (Munich: Wilhelm Fink Verlag, 2006), 140–141.

Based on Freud's work, the psychoanalyst Haydée Faimberg has studied the process of transference between two or three generations. She introduced the term 'telescoping' for the transfer of unconscious information and conflict between the parent generation and child generation, as the image of a telescope depicts the way family memory can be pushed together, comprising different generational layers but ultimately consisting of the same essential elements.[21]

According to Faimberg, transgenerational transference is based on the child's unconscious identification with their parents.[22] She describes the result of this identification process as the "internal parents" of a person.[23] These "internal parents" do not necessarily have to correspond to the parents' actual characters.[24] Yet, they are constantly present in the unconscious and thus influence their children's lives into adulthood. As Faimberg explains, "with the identification process the psyche is fixed in an "eternity" characteristic of the unconscious in its quality of timelessness".[25] People experiencing transgenerational transference are unable to process past events as being part of the past, and therefore they live, according to Faimberg, in "a circular, repetitive time", which always implies multiple generations at the same time.[26]

As the impact of traumatic experiences can only be identified after some time has elapsed, Faimberg's method of analysis aims at retroactively identifying the different layers and factors involved in constituting individual processes of transgenerational transference.[27] This means that every psychoanalytical interpretation is based on analysing our "internal parents". For this, Faimberg observes the "private language" the patient uses to communicate the internal parents.[28] This includes analysing the exact course of the patient-analyst interaction, and also the silences and gaps in the patient's narrative, for example.[29] Faimberg emphasises the need to acknowledge:

> "[The] presence of an 'other' who participates from the beginning with his own psyche, including his unconscious psyche, in the constitution of the subject's psychic

21 Haydee Faimberg, *The Telescoping of Generations* (London: Routledge, 2005), 38, 60; Weigel, *Genea-Logik*, 102.

22 Faimberg, *The Telescoping of Generations*, 7.

23 Ibid., 8–11, 21.

24 Ibid.

25 Ibid., 11.

26 Ibid., 12.

27 Ibid., 87.

28 Ibid., 54.

29 Ibid., 39, 45–47, 48, 77–78, where she describes this process as "listening to listening".

makeup. All this implies a process that permits the recognition (in the history of the transference) of the conflictual modalities that place a human being in relationship with the generations that preceded his or her birth".[30]

Faimberg's idea of unconscious meaning beyond that which is communicated on the surface and brought into discourse by transgenerational transference is taken up by literary scholar Sigrid Weigel as a cultural memory concept in the context of literary analysis. She adopts Faimberg's term "telescoping" because it emphasises the complex, intricate and overlapping nature of transgenerational memory that is held together by the unconscious.[31]

Weigel criticises the general tendency to discuss trauma most often as gaps within memory.[32] In order for this to make sense, these gaps would have to be filled with information, which often is impossible to achieve. Therefore, trauma is in general defined as an obstacle in the memory process. Weigel opposes the idea of trauma as a gap because the image of a gap declares nothing more than the mere fact of irretrievable loss. Instead, she is interested in signs and symbols used to mark or cover up these "gaps", meaning the signs and images that are used as replacements for something that otherwise could not be expressed.[33] Thus, the apparent gaps produced by trauma within the overall structure of transgenerational memory are by no means devoid of content. By virtually constituting an archive of the signs, symbols and distortions traumatic memory has turned into in the unconscious, literature can benefit from a psychoanalytical approach focusing on unconscious communication processes.[34] In the context of literature transgenerational transference can therefore be understood as a specific form of communication. Trauma in literature therefore does not just indicate "the unspeakable" but reveals through the diversity of modifications and alterations its complex narrative processes, which can express multiple things – the conscious and the unconscious – at once.[35]

Weigel's literary approach to trauma undermines the general assumption that information is completely lost in the transgenerational memory process, and that the only things transferred are memory gaps. Instead, she demands a

30 Ibid., 114.

31 Weigel, *Genea-Logik*, 102.

32 Sigrid Weigel, "Télescopage im Unbewußten. Zum Verhältnis von Trauma, Geschichtsbegriff und Literatur," in *Trauma. Zwischen Psychoanalyse und kulturellem Deutungsmuster*, ed. Elisabeth Bronfen, Birgit R. Erdle, and Sigrid Weigel (Cologne: Böhlau, 1999), 71.

33 Ibid., 62, 65, 68–70.

34 Ibid., 62

35 Ibid., 69.

shift in focus to the extensive transfer of information that is actually happening continually.[36] Weigel does not claim that the developing signs and symbols provide adequate representations of the past and the trauma itself; yet, they constitute the archive that we refer to when addressing trauma and therefore offer at least the possibility of deciphering meaning retroactively![37] Weigel's approach could be summarised with the following question: what are we actually talking about when addressing trauma? According to Weigel, literary analysis benefits from the transfer of the psychoanalytical concept of *telescoping* into the literary field, as it offers the chance to identify so-called gaps not only as vacancies hindering further insight, but as essential, complex elements of communication processes, thus allowing for further analysis of the signs and meanings developing in connection with trauma.[38]

Looking at processes of transgenerational transference and defining trauma as a memory concept that represents a continual link between the unconscious across generations emphasises the vital importance of communication itself.[39] In order to approach trauma via the variety of signs and symbols the unconscious offers it is essential to keep narrating and thus (re-)constructing this unconscious meaning.[40] As a memory concept, *telescoping* is thus based on the act of narration itself and not on the maintenance of certain static memories.[41]

The *telescoping* approach emphasises that continuity, an essential aspect of any memory concept in terms of identity, is not necessarily achieved through the transferred contents but rather through the process of communication itself and its interminable continuation in the unconscious. Thus, as proven by the constant need for discussion in public discourse, illustrated for instance by the amount of texts dealing with respective issues, as well as by the variety of images generated by trauma, trauma in itself does not have to be a break within the overall structure of transgenerational memory.[42] Instead, it creates its own form of ambiguous and interlaced connections, and transgenerational continuity.[43]

By focusing on the communication process of trauma, Weigel's literary approach to the concept of *telescoping* allows for further discussion on Rosenberg's narrative attempt at crossing generational borders and getting to know his

36 Ibid., 71.

37 Ibid., 71–72.

38 Ibid., 69–72.

39 Ibid., 68, 76; Weigel, *Genea-Logik*, 102.

40 Ibid.

41 Ibid.

42 Weigel, "Télescopage im Unbewußten," 76; Weigel, *Genea-Logik*, 102–103.

43 Ibid.

father *beyond* the mere statement of immense loss of information, even if the narrator naturally has to face this irrevocable fact at every turn in his research.

"A place perfectly chosen": Narrating Transgenerational Trauma

The narrator's project of researching his father's journey, which brought him as a Jewish prisoner from his Polish home to Germany during the Second World War and then as a Holocaust survivor to Sweden, is supposed to retrieve the past by replacing the vast number of gaps in his family's history with useful information. He is convinced that only complete knowledge of the past will enable him to understand his father's story and character well enough to attain a concrete connection between father and son that surpasses and thus replaces the indistinct image of his father with which he is left. Yet, even though he definitely gains new insight into his father's story by putting together memory fragments, there are still many gaps left that cannot be overcome. They are left to speculation and can only be approached by the imagination,[44] although he declares he would "rather not speculate".[45] Concerning the train stations and places his father passed on his way, the narrator writes for instance:

> "[W]here did you get on the train? So many stations no one remembers anymore. So many places that no longer exist. So many trains to choose from. So many trains that stop too soon and for good. So I decide for you".[46]

Yet, when it comes to his father's life in the ghetto of Łódź and inside the German concentration camps the imagination fails,[47] even after meticulously visiting the sites of camps in which his father was imprisoned. Although the narrator discusses his use of the imagination in the process of writing in order to depict his father's life inside the camps, these experiences seem to remain inconceivable. For instance, the narrator only notes: "I try to imagine the loneliness in the [train] car", without following this sentence up with further comment.[48]

---

44 Rosenberg, *A Brief Stop on the Road from Auschwitz*, 73. The narrator repeatedly points out: "This I don't know, of course. I only imagine it to be so. [...] Maybe I'm wrong."

45 Ibid., 7.

46 Ibid., 47.

47 Ibid., 74: The narrator mentions that he is forced to begin the journey onboard the train because "[b]eyond the ghetto looms a wall I can't get past. A wall of darkness and silence. Almost no fragments at all. Not now and not later."

48 Ibid., 95.

The passages that deal with these events are instead superimposed by the enumeration of historic facts and technicalities that therefore stand between the narrator and the actual experiences of prisoners like his father.[49]

Realising the impossibility of any "direct" approach to the past, the narrator has to rely on the abstract data he collects along his way in order to deal with his father's personal story, even though it hardly seems to belong to his father's person at all.[50] As his father left negligible personal information behind, the only way to discuss his father's trauma is to consider ulterior issues that could be associated with it. Therefore, the previous question concerning the literarisation of trauma can be reformulated as follows: what is Rosenberg talking about – wishing to get closer to his father – when narrating his father's trauma?

In particular, he reflects on places and things in Sweden that he associates with his father (having experienced them together with him) and that, in their repeated mention, constitute the novel's basic incentive. The two most important places are the bridge just outside their hometown, Södertälje, and the local beach, *Havsbadet*. The bridge features prominently in the narrator's memory because its structure reminds him of the journey his father had to take in order to begin a new life in Sweden.[51] On the other hand, the regular visits to *Havsbadet* represent a happy family life. The narrator especially recalls the peaceful walks to the beach with his father, and enjoying the heat and light at the beach with family and friends.[52] He embeds his personal impressions of these places into the wider context of Södertälje's and Sweden's history. Thus, he manages to give an overview of the *Folkhem*-zeitgeist – the powerful idea of the Swedish social welfare state – that prevails in his childhood.[53] Depicting his own childhood and the town in which he grew up, he demonstrates on a smaller scale what affected the nation as a whole.

49 Ibid., 120–124.

50 Ibid., 51–52, where he points out: "Assuming it's necessary to make all the fragments fit together. But that isn't necessary at all. In this context it makes absolutely no difference on precisely which day you reach Auschwitz. Your journey has no timetable and no direction. You have no exact dates behind you and no exact dates ahead of you. On your journey, exact dates have no function. It's me they have a function for. […] so I don't lose sight of you." He emphasises that even if he could manage to achieve a correct chronology and to get hold of all the details, the result would still be very different from his father's actual experience.

51 Ibid., 3–7.

52 Ibid., 216–219, 267.

53 Ibid., 25–27, 87–93.

In effect, this means that Sweden – despite the narrator's focus on the journey itself – features extensively in the revision of his father's trauma. He virtually precipitates the journey's outcome, and although he admits to probably overestimating the place by bestowing special meaning on it when in fact various random factors were involved in leading his father to Södertälje,[54] reflecting Swedish history can indicate the importance Sweden as a destination could have had for his father. It is as if Södertälje had its own fortuitous character and history:

> "[...] like a magnet, [it] had attracted the most fortuitous of human destinies, making the fact that he got off the train at this very Place to start his life anew perhaps the least arbitrary element in the story. A place perfectly chosen for doing exactly that, in fact, or so it sometimes, much later, seemed to me: no strong ties to the past, no fixed plans for the future, no readymade scenario to step into – or be ejected from".[55]

The latter being supposedly the most important aspect of Sweden and its collective project of creating the *Folkhem* for homeless people like his father after the war, it offered the chance to participate in creating something together with others, which would feel new to everyone irrespective of the past:

> "[T]he Place seems to offer a world in which every dream is feasible, since it's a world where no dreams have been shattered, including the dreams that were shattered in the world you come from, which is a world the Project will help put behind you. In that sense, the Place is an ideal one because so few people here remember what you have to put behind you. [...] The past doesn't have a very strong position in this place, and oblivion is the foundation of the Project. Oblivion and optimism. As far as optimism is concerned, the Place has a competitive edge against practically the whole world, since optimism has never been challenged here. While the outside world collapses, and with it most people's futures, here nothing's collapsing. Here the best of all worlds is in full swing [...]".[56]

Therefore, *A Brief Stop* represents a shift in topic in that it – despite its focus on Holocaust trauma – actually (mainly) discusses the history of the Swedish welfare state and the childhood memories of witnessing its development. Thus,

---

54 Ibid., 222, 225, 236.

55 Ibid., 27.

56 Ibid., 225–226.

by juxtaposing two entirely different experiences, the unspoilt optimism of the Swedes and the horrors witnessed by the Holocaust survivors, the novel offers the chance to deduce new insights about one different from the other. In examining the promises made by the futuristic *Folkhem* idea and the appeal they most certainly had on young immigrants like his father who desperately pinned all his hopes and dreams on these promises, the son gets a chance to at least suspect the severity of his father's previous experiences. Clearly, the novel does not represent a complete account of his father's Holocaust trauma. Yet, as part of the familiar Swedish history the narrator can identify with, even his father's story becomes more tangible.

At the same time, his father's story opens up an alternative narrative of the Swedish *Folkhem*. On the one hand, it shows the legal restrictions and social structure by which foreigners were kept from fully participating in all the promises made by the *Folkhem*.[57] On the other hand, the relentless focus on future prospects could induce an indifference towards divergent narratives, as represented by foreigners, as well as a disregard for the past (not to mention of difficult subjects like the Holocaust) in Swedish society, which could not meet the psychological needs of traumatised people with very different backgrounds.[58]

The narrator's writing process shows the difficulty or even impossibility of dealing with the family's Holocaust trauma. Thus, for the most part the novel neglects to mention the horrors of the Holocaust itself, but addresses the historic premises and the consequences of his father's life in Sweden. Nevertheless, the son benefits from analysing the history and characteristics of the *Folkhem* as the insight he gained enables him to create images through which he can formulate details about his father's specific situation. Furthermore, he is able to communicate the role trauma played in his family and to eradicate – at least partially – the uncertainty concerning his own history, which in turn offers the chance to perceive a feeling of closure.[59] One of the novel's recurring images, for example, is the image of a horizon that refuses to open itself up to his father

57 Ibid., 222, 226, where he mentions the restricted areas so-called displaced persons were allowed to settle down, as well as 247–248, where he mentions the "Swedish alien status" his parents were granted. Regarding alternative narratives of the *Folkhem* see Peter Stenberg, ed., *Contemporary Jewish Writing in Sweden: An Anthology* (Lincoln: University of Nebraska Press, 2004), xxxii.

58 Rosenberg, *A Brief Stop on the Road from Auschwitz*, 78–80, 241–242.

59 Anne Adelman, "Holocaust-Erzählungen. Beobachtungen transgenerationaler Entwicklung," *Mittelweg 36. Zeitschrift des Hamburger Instituts für Sozialforschung* 5, no. 3 (1996): 44–52.

who continues to run up against it but keeps bouncing back.[60] At the end of his own journey into the past the narrator concludes his father's journey and his life in Sweden:

> "You just happen to get off at the wrong station on your road from Auschwitz. Yes, I think, in the end, that the Place has a part to play in this. It's too small a place for someone like you, with too few people who appreciate where you come from and what you carry with you, with a factory too large and too dominant to free oneself from, with too few exits to a future other than the one already mapped out, and with a horizon that never really wants to open up. The place where I make the world into my own is also the place where the world turns its back on you. And the place where you finally turn your back on the world. It never becomes a home to you. Not the way it does to me".[61]

In this way, similar to Weigel's rejection of the impracticable aspiration of finding a textual equivalent to the actual experience, Rosenberg's novel represents the insight that understanding and thereby connecting with the past and his father is not necessarily achieved by the absorption of specific content. Rather than penetrating the exact events and experiences that were life-defining for his father in order to be able to "catch up" with his father and thus conceive a sense of genealogical belonging and identity, the bond between father and son is instead created through the act of researching and narrating itself. As a way of processing trauma, writing – even when it is about the limited amount of knowledge left for one's retrospective – is a way to find new angles and images for the experience of trauma and thus to figuratively continue his father's incomplete geographical and mental journey away from the trauma that came to a sudden halt in Sweden.

The familial trauma has changed its form across generations. It is not the memories of Holocaust experiences that constitute a source of conflict in the son's psychological make-up but the father's suicide as one of their consequences. Likewise, the goal of his writing process undergoes a change in character. Transgenerationally, a sense of identity is not achieved by identifying and identifying *with* some imaginary origin of family history or by assigning the same intensity of trauma to oneself. Rather, Rosenberg's novel can be read as the

60 Rosenberg, *A Brief Stop on the Road from Auschwitz*, 294: "What I realize, much later, is that time after time you make a run-up toward the horizon, and time after time you fall back to earth again," as well as ibid., 259, 264–265, 301.

61 Ibid., 308.

realisation that the so-called second generation offers a role for identification. Identity is therefore still based on a genealogical concept as indicated by the numerical designation, yet it acknowledges the inherent differences between generations. The genealogical structure's coherence arises from the challenging process of perpetuating and communicating memory as a contribution to coping with trauma and its consequences.[62]

The Narrative of the Second Generation

Understanding trauma as an unconscious communication process across generations (through symbols, motifs, et cetera developing in connection with trauma) and identifying with the task of the second generation to continue to retell the past, shows the chances of *reshaping* this narrative. Consequently, this approach also offers descendants of the Holocaust a chance to dissociate themselves from previous generations. Therefore, Rosenberg's text can not only be read as an attempt to transcend generational boundaries in search of genealogical identity, but can also be a way to define himself regarding contemporary concepts of generation, as described by the sociologist Karl Mannheim. In *The Problem of Generations* (1928), Mannheim introduced *generation* as a social category for collectives characterised by similar experiences and features in a given time period. Mannheim's main argument is that generational identity is not simply the result of listing various features; rather, it derives from social interaction in a specific time and place, and most importantly, from the consciousness of being part of a particular context.[63] Literature as a means of negotiating human experience is part of this process.

Read in this different light, the narrator's previously discussed project of researching and retravelling is not only an attempt to recreate the past and identify with his father but constantly demonstrates its own artificiality. The many pieces of information that are still missing prove that the journey is a pale copy of the real historic event. As the narrator admits, "I'm not even sure if the fragments are real, still less whether I've put them together correctly",[64]

62 Hirsch, *The Generation of Post-memory*, 33, where Hirsch stresses the important task of the following generations to "reactivate and re-embody" memory structure – e.g. by using their personal, familial approach.

63 Karl Mannheim, "The Problem of Generations," in *Theories of Ethnicity: A Classical Reader*, ed. Werner Sollors (Basingstoke and London: Macmillan Press, 1996), 129.

64 Rosenberg, *A Brief Stop on the Road from Auschwitz*, 28.

and this insecurity is present throughout the text. It shows how much the story relies on the narrator's personal choices. Freed of the presumption of being an accurate account of history, the narrative can be understood as a *conception* of the past that enables him to create his own story and identity that both relates to and is in contrast to this imaginary past.

Rosenberg's conversation-like style is thus not only an expression of his wish to connect with his father, but it can be read in a much more confrontational sense. The binary positions of "you" and "I" also explicitly denote that "I am *not* you" and "you are *not* me"! Owing to the fundamental difference in experiences and situations, they express the discernment of limits to the transgenerational identification process. Therefore, the discussion of Swedish history and depiction of the *Folkhem* in *A Brief Stop* is not merely a substitute born out of necessity in the absence of other information; rather, it creates the narrator's specific generational experience as one of the early beneficiaries of the Swedish welfare state. Whereas his father never really lost his feeling of homelessness, the narrator himself found a home in Sweden.[65] Consequently, contrary to his father, he experiences "horizon after horizon [...] opening up to [him] with no effort at all", causing his own and his father's world to drift apart.[66]

Addressing the past is an important part of the process of coping with familial trauma; yet, in order to create a prolific concept of identity, it is necessary for the narrator to leave the past and his father's trauma behind to a certain extent.[67] Realising during the writing process the significance of his own story as a child of the Swedish *Folkhem*, he is part of the identity negotiation of Jewish post-war descendants who now attempt to narrate stories of their own.

---

65 Rosenberg, *A Brief Stop on the Road from Auschwitz*, 308: "*The place where I make the world into my own* is also the place where the world turns its back on you. And the place where you finally turn your back on the world. It never becomes a home to you. *Not the way it does to me*." (Ital. by F. S.).

66 Ibid., 295. The novel even ends on that note: "For me, a place with all horizons open. For you, a place with all horizons closed. For you, a brief stop on the road from Auschwitz." Ibid., 321.

67 Using Faimberg's words: through his writing process, the narrator thus receives the chance to leave the "circular, repetitive time." Faimberg, *The Telescoping of Generations*, 12.

Conclusion

Contemporary Scandinavian literature addressing Jewish history is marked by a shift in authorship. Whereas past texts dealing with the Holocaust were primarily written by eyewitnesses such as Cordelia Edvardson, who thus constituted the so-called first generation, now the majority of texts are written by descendants of Jewish Holocaust survivors. The autobiographical novel *A Brief Stop on the Road from Auschwitz* by Swedish author Göran Rosenberg exemplifies the continual implications and consequences of this traumatic experience from the perspective of the second generation.

The purpose of this paper was to show the significance of *generation* in the processing of identity. In *A Brief Stop on the Road from Auschwitz* the narrator's incentive in writing about his father (a member of the first generation) is the longing to eradicate the silence and ignorance caused by trauma with regard to family history in order to be able to fully identify with this history and thus to locate his own person within his genealogy. However, his project confirms the impossibility of recreating and directly reconnecting with the past. In place of this, in accordance with the concept of *telescoping* proposed by Weigel, the narrator realises that the transgenerational bond essential for identity formation is based on the act of communication itself, which is enforced by trauma. Furthermore, accepting the role of narrator bestowed by this "genealogy of trauma" also offers the potential to shape this communication individually and thus to create his own conception of Scandinavian-Jewish identity.

In the context of so-called Holocaust literature Rosenberg's narrative approach in general is all too familiar.[68] What is new, however, is that he writes in a Scandinavian context. Being among the increased number of texts that have brought Jewish issues into public discourse in Scandinavia in recent years,[69]

68 Regarding German literature see Hartmut Steinecke, "Die Shoah in der Literatur der 'zweiten Generation'," in *Shoah in der deutschsprachigen Literatur*, ed. Norbert Eke and Hartmut Steinecke (Berlin: E. Schmidt Verlag, 2006), 135–153. Correspondingly, regarding the general development in the US see Arlene Stein, "Trauma Stories, Identity Work, and the Politics of Recognition," in *Sociology Confronts the Holocaust: Memories and Identities in Jewish Diasporas*, ed. Judith M. Gerson and Diane L. Wolf (Durham: Duke University Press, 2007), 84–91.

69 Other examples of this development in literature are Rose Lagercrantz, *Om man ännu finns* (Stockholm: Atlantis, 2012); Danny Wattin, *Herr Isakowitz skatt* (Stockholm: Piratförlaget, 2014); Birte Kont, *En by i Rusland* (Copenhagen: Gyldendal, 2011); Ricki Neuman, *Ni är inte så märkvärdiga som ni tror* (Stockholm: Weyler, 2012).

Rosenberg's text participates not only in connecting past and present generations but in formulating the post-war generation's current realisation of a unique identity.

Bibliography

Adelman, Anne. "Holocaust-Erzählungen. Beobachtungen transgenerationaler Entwicklung." *Mittelweg 36. Zeitschrift des Hamburger Instituts für Sozialforschung* 5, no. 3 (1996): 44–52.

Bukiet, Melvin J., ed. *Nothing Makes You Free: Writings by Descendants of Jewish Holocaust Survivors*. New York and London: W. W. Norton & Company, 2002.

Edvardson, Corderlia. *Bränt barn söker sig till elden*. Stockholm: Norstedts, 1984.

Faimberg, Haydee. *The Telescoping of Generations*. London: Routledge, 2005.

Foer, Jonathan S. *Everything is Illuminated*. Boston: Houghton Mifflin, 2002.

Freud, Siegmund. *Der Mann Moses und die monotheistische Religion. Schriften über die Religion*. First published 1939. Frankfurt: Fischer, 1994.

Hirsch, Marianne. *The Generation of Postmemory: Writing and Visual Culture after the Holocaust*. New York: Columbia University Press, 2012.

Hirsch, Marianne. *Family Frames: Photography, Narrative, and Postmemory*. 2nd edition. Cambridge: Harvard University Press, 2012.

Kont, Birte. *En by i Rusland*. Copenhagen: Gyldendal, 2011.

LaCapra, Dominick. *Writing History, Writing Trauma*. Baltimore: The Johns Hopkins University Press, 2001.

Lagercrantz, Rose. *Om man ännu finns*. Stockholm: Atlantis, 2012.

Mannheim, Karl. "The Problem of Generations." First published 1928. In *Theories of Ethnicity: A Classical Reader*, edited by Werner Sollors, 109–155. Basingstoke: Macmillan Press, 1996.

Neuman, Ricki. *Ni är inte så märkvärdiga som ni tror*. Stockholm: Weyler, 2012.

Parnes, Ohad, Ulrike Vedder, and Stefan Willer. *Das Konzept der Generation. Eine Wissenschafts- und Kulturgeschichte*. Frankfurt: Suhrkamp, 2008.

Petrowskaja, Katja. *Vielleicht Esther*. Berlin: Suhrkamp, 2014.

Rosenberg, Göran. *Ett kort uppehåll på vägen från Auschwitz*. Stockholm: Albert Bonniers Förlag, 2012.

Rosenberg, Göran. *A Brief Stop on the Road from Auschwitz*. Translated by Sarah Death. London: Granta, 2015.

Spiegelman, Art. *The Complete Maus: A Survivor's Tale*. New York: Pantheon, 1991.

Stein, Arlene. "Trauma Stories, Identity Work, and the Politics of Recognition the Politics of Recognition." In: *Sociology Confronts the Holocaust: Memories and Identities in Jewish Diasporas*, edited by Judith M. Gerson and Diana L. Wolf, 84–91. Durham: Duke University Press, 2007.

Steinecke, Hartmut. "Die Shoah in der Literatur 'zweiten Generation.'" In *Shoah in der deutschsprachigen Literatur*, edited by Norbert Eke and Hartmut Steinecke, 135–153. Berlin: E. Schmidt Verlag, 2006.

Stenberg, Peter, ed. *Contemporary Jewish Writing in Sweden: An Anthology*. Lincoln: University of Nebraska Press, 2004.
Wattin, Danny. *Herr Isakowitz skatt*. Stockholm: Piratförlaget, 2014.
Weigel, Sigrid. "Télescopage im Unbewußten. Zum Verhältnis von Trauma, Geschichtsbegriff und Literatur." In *Trauma. Zwischen Psychoanalyse und kulturellem Deutungsmuster*, edited by Elisabeth Bronfen, Birgit R. Erdle, and Sigrid Weigel, 51–76. Cologne: Böhlau, 1999.
Weigel, Sigrid. *Genea-Logik. Generation, Tradition und Evolution zwischen Kultur- und Naturwissenschaften*. Munich: Wilhelm Fink Verlag, 2006.

Index